W9-BNW-932

WITHDRAWN

THE EVOLUTION OF
US PEACEKEEPING POLICY
UNDER CLINTON

THE CASS SERIES ON PEACEKEEPING
ISSN 1367-9880
General Editor: Michael Pugh

This series examines all aspects of peacekeeping, from the political, operational and legal dimensions to the developmental and humanitarian issues that must be dealt with by all those involved with peacekeeping in the world today.

The Evolution of US Peacekeeping Policy Under Clinton

A Fairweather Friend?

MICHAEL G. MacKINNON

Graduate Institute of International Studies, Geneva

Introduction by Sir Brian Urquhart

FRANK CASS
LONDON • PORTLAND, OR

148342

First published in 2000 in Great Britain by
FRANK CASS PUBLISHERS
Newbury House, 900 Eastern Avenue
London, IG2 7HH

and in the United States of America by
FRANK CASS PUBLISHERS
c/o ISBS, 5804 N.E. Hassalo Street
Portland, Oregon, 97213-3644

Website: www.frankcass.com

Copyright © 2000 Michael G. MacKinnon

British Library Cataloguing in Publication Data

MacKinnon, Michael G.
 The evolution of US peacekeeping policy under Clinton: a fairweather
friend. – (Cass series on peacekeeping; no. 6)
 1. United Nations 2. United States – Politics and government
 – 1993– 3. United States – Foreign relations
 I. Title
 327.7'3

ISBN 0-7146-4937-6 (cloth)
ISBN 0-7146-4497-8 (paper)
ISSN 1367 9880

Library of Congress Cataloging-in-Publication Data

MacKinnon, Michael G., 1969–
 The evolution of US peacekeeping policy under Clinton: a fairweather friend? /
Michael G. MacKinnon.
  p.   cm. – (Cass series on peacekeeping, ISSN 1367-9880 ; 5)
 Includes bibliographical references.
 ISBN 0-7146-4937-6 (cloth). – ISBN 0-7146-4497-8 (pbk.)
 1. United Nations–Armed Forces. 2. United States–Armed Forces–
Foreign countries. 3. International police. 4. United States–
Politics and government–1993– I. Title. II. Series.
JZ6377.U6M33 1999
327.73'009'049–dc21   99-17425
                                                           CIP

*All rights reserved. No part of this publication may be reproduced, stored in or introduced into
a retrieval system, or transmitted, in any form or by any means, electronic, mechanical,
photocopying, recording or otherwise without the prior written permission of the publisher of
this book.*

Typeset by Vitaset, Paddock Wood, Kent
Printed in Great Britain by
MPG Books Ltd, Bodmin, Cornwall

Contents

Dedicated to the memory of

my Mother, Mary Alice E. MacKinnon
(1937–1987)

and her Mother
Loretta Mary McMackin
(1906–1994)

Foreword

The United States is an original founder of the United Nations, the UN's host country, a permanent member of the Security Council and the organization's largest financial contributor. The UN's relationship to its most powerful member is a vital key to its success and effectiveness. In recent years that relationship has become increasingly problematic and negative.

Michael MacKinnon analyses the nature and main elements of the US/UN relationship through the study of a particularly important aspect of UN activity, peacekeeping. He uses the corkscrew-like evolution of Presidential Decision Directive 25 on US participation in UN peacekeeping as an intensely revealing test of the true nature and the twisted roots of the US attitude to the UN. His basic theme is the interaction and relative weight in the evolution of PDD 25 of four main groups – the executive, the bureaucracies, the Congress and public opinion.

MacKinnon opens with a masterly account of the confusing and contradictory signals that emanated from the Bush and, especially, from the Clinton administrations. He concludes that at the present time a resurgent Congress dominates what might charitably be called a highly flexible administration in setting policy towards international organizations. MacKinnon performs an invaluable service in cutting through the veils and mists of rhetoric, spin, public relations and doubletalk that increasingly confuse and misrepresent the relationship of national governments and international organizations, especially in Washington. For those who believe that the effectiveness and strengthening of these organizations are important to the future, his findings are not encouraging.

In 1991 the end of the Cold War and the apparent success of Operation Desert Storm against Iraq gave rise to a shortlived revival of US enthusiasm for the UN. President Bush spoke of a 'New World Order' and President Clinton of 'assertive multilateralism'. The latter's campaign speeches proclaimed strong support for the world organization and even advocated a UN Rapid Deployment Force.

Once in office, however, the Clinton administration steadily backed away from such undertakings. In September 1993 the UN General Assembly, accustomed to recent US enthusiasm for setting up new UN peacekeeping operations, was stunned to hear Clinton lecturing the assembled foreign ministers on the need for the UN to 'learn to say no'. The debacle of the US Rangers in Mogadishu a few weeks later created in Washington a vast backlash against peacekeeping.

In the background, the drafting of PDD 25 crawled along in Washington. Portrayed at the outset as the promulgation of a new and positive American policy on peacekeeping, the final document signalled a complete reversal of Clinton's earlier declarations and returned US policy to the Republican, Weinberger–Powell doctrine of extreme caution and non-support for international peacekeeping operations. Its questions and criteria governing the setting up of future operations are in themselves a formula for non-action in any likely future crisis. Like so much else in the Clinton administration, PDD 25 was, as MacKinnon puts it, 'largely the result of a self-perpetuating cycle of confrontation and conciliation played out between the White House and the Congress'.

This turn-around had immediate and tragic practical consequences, of which the most serious was the complete failure of the US-led Security Council to act in time to counteract genocide in Rwanda. In the longer term PDD 25, and the state of mind it represents, constitute a major obstacle both to effective and timely future international action and to any chance of improving and strengthening the UN's operational capacity. Coming from the UN's most powerful member, such a document can only have a disastrous practical and psychological effect on the development of the international system. We may have bitter cause to remember this when the next great human emergency finds no adequate response from the so-called 'international community'.

This book is a striking study of the over-caution, inhibiting interactions and political negativism that are stunting – let us hope only temporarily – the effort to build a serious international system. It carries a vitally important message both for the United States and the members of the UN as a whole.

Brian Urquhart
Massachusetts, August 1998

Preface

As the United Nations approaches the twenty-first century, it finds itself under great demand and stress. Although the number of peacekeepers in the field has dropped substantially since the early 1990s, other programmes and activities continue to press the Organization's limited resources. From the other side, and at the same time, the UN is being squeezed by member states which have a hard time remembering to pay their dues on time and in full. While there are many guilty members, the United States stands out from the rest in terms of the amounts owed and its tendency to make unilateral reform requests upon the Secretariat. To be sure, the UN is a fair target for some reform initiatives but quite often the US position constrains the UN more than its own inherent deficiencies. With the twenty-first century upon us, the UN and US must come to some sort of understanding as to what the relationship should be, and how to get there. Unless the UN is able to better manage its association with its most powerful member, the new era in international relations might be marked with more missed opportunities in the world's hot spots and for the international community's drive to establish the rule of law. The potential consequences are indeed great.

This book was conceived as a way to better understand the dynamics which have, so far, produced the erratic relationship we have watched develop this decade between the United States and the UN Organization. From UN-cheering after the Gulf War in 1991, to misleadingly implying UN error in the deaths of 18 US soldiers in Mogadishu in 1993, the US government has not approached the UN with a steady hand over the past eight years. The broader question I hope to answer in the following pages is, 'why?' I believe this question is fundamental to any attempt to grasp the true nature of US policy towards the UN and, accordingly, what this means for the UN in a new century.

To get at possible answers, I examined the US policymaking process which led to the drafting of the US peacekeeping policy released in 1994 (PDD 25). The question I pose is simple, and the means I employ are equally simplistic. This project grew out of a Master's thesis I prepared for the

Graduate Institute of International Studies in Geneva in October 1996. As such, the theoretical demands were secondary to articulating the question and devising a workable research programme. Because of this, some readers may be underwhelmed by the theoretical framework because I have taken an 'off the shelf' model of decisionmaking by Roger Hilsman and made only a few minor alterations for this case. It was never my intent to make a significant new contribution to the body of decisionmaking theory, so I hope the reader does not judge this work on the basis of theoretical content. I adopted a simple yet useful model to help me organize the study and I found Hilsman most effective for these ends.

I began work on this in the summer of 1995, and over the next two and a half years, I was guided, advised, supported and encouraged by many individuals, without whom this would have been a failing thesis, much less a book. I would like to first express my gratitude to my academic advisors. My Director, Dr Victor-Yves Ghebali, made the original suggestion that I pursue this topic because of its importance to the overall state of UN effectiveness. At the time, I was not too keen to embark on a study of US foreign policy, but I must confess that I now agree with him completely and thank him for leading me to look at such a crucial issue. Dr Keith Krause, my second reader, assumed a range of duties well beyond the usual job description for that title and, along with Dr Jennifer Milliken, helped me to map out the theoretical framework. As a result of their efforts, this paper presents a far stronger argument than it would otherwise have done, and I thank them. Dr Michael Pugh, of the University of Plymouth, has been the very patient editor who saw promise in the thesis and encouraged me to expand and revise it for publication. Had he not taken the time and showed interest in the paper, Frank Cass Publishers would not have known it existed, and for that I am deeply indebted to him.

It is impossible to envision this paper coming to a conclusion without the help and support of many people outside of Geneva. By virtue of my location for the first draft and subsequent follow-on research, I was dependent on people in New York City, Washington DC and other cities, for information which was not available to me in Geneva. To the following individuals, I extend my gratitude for their generosity with both their time and their personal material: Michael E. Brown, Maria Bishirigian, Susannah L. Dyer, Trevor Findlay, Lela Hooper, Frank Jones, Steven Kull, Virginia Page Fortna, Michael Renner, Scott L. Silliman, Barbara Somogyiova, Dr Fred Tanner. In addition, I would like to thank those who took the time to field my questions in interview sessions: John R. Bolton, Professor Donald C.F. Daniel, Steven Dimoff, Col. Douglas Fraser (ret.), Victoria Holt, Richard J. Rinaldo, Dr Benjamin Rivlin, Dr John Gerard Ruggie, Professor George Sherry and Sir Brian Urquhart. Also, a thank-you must be expressed to all of the officials from various governments and the UN who took the time out of their busy days to grant me interviews. Their contributions have been critical to this research, so I am very grateful to all of the anonymous sources referred to throughout this book. Special thanks are also due to Elsa Garza who managed to track down every public document I asked for and get them to me in short order, despite her hectic work schedule. On my behalf, she put her State and Hill connections to work, and the result has been a collection of government documents which helped a larger picture to come into focus. Many thanks for her help. A word of thanks and appreciation must also be extended to my former understanding employer, Counsellor Kim Young So, who accommodated my work schedule so that I could have the time to work at home on the first draft.

As this paper slowly took shape, I was fortunate enough to have a number of well-informed people review the early outline and make excellent comments. To Dr Clement Adibe, Dr David Black, Dr Donald Daniel, Daniel Volman and Steven Dimoff I express my thanks for taking the time to help put this project on the right track. Many friends and classmates helped in a number of different ways to ensure the original thesis was submitted before final deadline; from providing last-minute references or editing chapters, to bringing my computer back to life in the final stages. This team of do-gooders included Lara Bernini, Danilo von Sperling, Jennifer Gray, Geoff Brown, Debbie Ebanks Schlums and Galen Fairchild and I say thanks to each of them. For the transition from thesis to book, I wish to acknowledge the professionalism of my editors at Frank Cass, Hilary Hewitt and Andrew Humphrys, as they guided this manuscript through the publishing process. Their patience and attention to detail made the preparation of the manuscript much easier than it would have been otherwise for this first-time author, and I appreciate this fact greatly. I want to stress, though, that I take full responsibility for the errors which remain.

The support of one's family is often taken for granted, but the past few years have proven to me that their encouragement is crucial. My father John's and my brother Paul's support for my three-year adventure in Geneva always provided an enormous source of strength when needed, and I thank them.

My final acknowledgment of gratitude is my largest and goes to Lisa Jones, who provided much more than just the moral support to see me through this project. Beyond the editorial assistance, Lisa lived with the stress of this thesis-cum-book for more than three years, and was not able to escape it even when in Canada because I brought it back with me. Her patience and understanding made it possible for me to finish the project with my sense of humour intact, no small feat. To Lisa, I express my thanks and love.

MGM
Halifax, Nova Scotia
January 1999

Acronyms and abbreviations

CIS	Commonwealth of Independent States
DoD	Department of Defense
DPKO	Department of Peacekeeping Operations
FY	Fiscal Year
GA	General Assembly
JCS	Joint Chiefs of Staff
MNF	Multi-National Force
NATO	North Atlantic Treaty Organization
NSC	National Security Council
OECD	Organization for Economic Cooperation and Development
ONUC	Operations des Nations Unies au Congo
OSD	Office of the Secretary of Defense
PIPA	Program on International Policy Attitudes
PRD	Presidential Review Directive
QRF	Quick Reaction Force
RPA	Rwandese Patriotic Army
RPF	Rwandese Patriotic Front
SNA	Somali National Alliance
SRSG	Special Representative of the Secretary-General
UNAMIR	UN Assistance Mission for Rwanda
UNCRO	UN Confidence Restoration Operation in Croatia
UNFICYP	UN Force in Cyprus
UNIFIL	UN Interim Force in Lebanon
UNITAF	Unified Task Force, Somalia
UNMIBH	UN Mission on Bosnia and Herzegovina
UNMOGIP	UN Observer Mission in Georgia
UNOSOM	UN Operation in Somalia
UNPREDEP	UN Preventive Deployment Force
UNPROFOR	UN Protection Force
UNSC	UN Security Council
UNSF	UN Security Force in West New Guinea (West Irian)
UNTAG	UN Transition Assistance Group (in Namibia)
UNTSO	UN Truse Supervision Organization

Introduction

In October 1995, the United Nations (UN) marked the 50th anniversary of its creation. As is usual for occasions of this sort, member governments, UN officials and interested observers had much to consider when it came to reflecting on the Organization's record to date, and what that record might be in the future. Over the preceding 50 years, the United Nations had broadened its range of activities and, in the process, established a record of action in areas ranging from health and children's welfare, human rights, the environment, economic development and peacekeeping.

Unlike previous birthdays of significance, however, the context for reflection and prediction had changed dramatically by 1995. During the Cold War, tense relations between the Soviet Union and the United States meant there was often little opportunity for the UN to play an active role in world events deemed important by the competing superpowers. But when heads of state and government gathered in New York for the anniversary ceremonies, the Cold War was over and the UN was five years into a new period of its history which was expected to be its most successful and dynamic. Despite the early optimistic forecasts of the UN finally assuming the position in international politics intended by its founders, the role of the UN in this new era was very uncertain.[1] Uncertainty stemmed from a number of issues facing the Organization and its member states, but none was more pressing than the UN's relationship with the world's sole superpower and its most important member, the United States.

THE SHORT HONEYMOON

The end of the Cold War had the initial effect of raising hope for a new, more active UN role in world affairs through increased cooperation among the more influential member states (in particular the five permanent representatives on the Security Council, or P5). No other world leader did more to spread the belief in this possibility than United States President George Bush, during and after the war to evict Iraq from Kuwait. Bush's theme throughout this period was that the world was witnessing the dawning of a 'new world order', and that the UN held a central position in this vision.[2] He reasoned that American–Soviet relations were improving to the point where real cooperation was now possible on peace and security issues, thereby drawing to a close virtually 40 years of deadlock in the Security Council. The 'new world order' would allow for the relations among states to be governed by the rule of law, as the framers of the United Nations Charter had intended.

This vision for the new era in international relations was welcomed by many at the UN, both in the Secretariat and by other member states, because it represented two important developments. The first was explicitly stated by Bush, and recognized by many others, namely, that the abrupt end to Cold War stalemate and confrontation had the potential to give the UN a 'fresh lease on life', particularly through the actions of the Security Council. Provided relations between the United States and the newly formed Commonwealth of Independent States (CIS) (especially Russia) continued to improve, or at least maintained the current status, many observers agreed that prospects for unprecedented cooperation were good.

The second development, apparent in American statements and speeches during this period, was that the United States was prepared to reincorporate the United Nations into its foreign policy in a serious manner. Relations between the US and the UN had been in a steep decline during the preceding two and a half decades: as the 1970s and the Carter administration gave way to the 1980s and the Reagan administration, the United Nations increasingly found itself on the very periphery of American foreign-policy thinking. Perhaps even more troublesome for the Organization, however, was the sharp criticism of the UN by members of both parties (and not just of the conservative, isolationist/unilateralist camps) in the US Congress. Representatives and Senators alike seemed to eye the Organization with a great deal of suspicion leading them to aim at the UN, its programmes, its bureaucracy and, above all, the US contribution to it virtually every time the topic arose during committee hearings or general debate. Despite pleas from the White House and State Department to honour the government's treaty obligations to pay its assessed contributions, Congress repeatedly refused to allocate the necessary funds without attaching strings. Usually the strings were in the shape of reform measures to be adopted by the UN Secretariat or a reorganization of the State Department. These conditions were illegal, yet the practice continued to be a regular feature of Congressional hearings and amendments to the State Department's annual budget. Moreover, as was quite often the case, the reluctance on the part of Congress to permit the full payment of the US contribution (with or without conditions) meant that the US government was chronically in arrears with the UN.

The post-Gulf War policy of the Bush administration was a departure which gave many observers the distinct impression that the deteriorating relationship between Washington and the UN Secretariat was on the mend. Indeed, the discernible new direction of US policy towards the United Nations led one author to argue that an 'about face' in American UN policy was under way.[3] This shift in policy even survived the 1992 Presidential election. The incoming Clinton administration was in agreement with the departing administration's policy regarding Somalia and stated its intention to support the decision to send US troops to that country. The Clinton team then appeared to go one step further in strengthening the US–UN relationship when it appointed a respected academic to the post of Permanent Representative to the United Nations, and restored that position to Cabinet level. The then nominee, Madeleine K. Albright, stated during her confirmation hearing that she expected a proactive and high-profile mandate from the new president:

> When the President announced my appointment last month, he said that, in his administration, the post of ambassador to the United Nations will be one of the most critical foreign policy positions. With the end of the Cold War, the United Nations is poised to play a central and positive role for peace.[4]

Soon after taking up her post, Ambassador Albright embarked on pursuing a policy which she referred to as 'assertive multilateralism'. This policy indicated to many that the renewed American interest in the UN might prove to be more than a short-term fad.[5]

'ABOUT FACE' NUMBER TWO

By the time the world's leaders gathered in New York not quite three years later, the optimism accompanying the improvement in US–UN relations after the Gulf War was replaced by new worry and concern that the earlier *rapprochement* was eroding. In a matter of ten months after taking office, the Clinton administration began sending very different signals to UN officials and other member governments concerning its commitment to the Organization, and America's role in the UN system. These indicators came from many key administration figures including Ambassador Albright, Secretary Christopher and the President himself, and they were manifested in new policy statements and actions taken in the Security Council and other venues. One indicator, however, was more significant than the others. In May 1994, President Clinton signed Presidential Decision Directive 25 (PDD 25) which outlined the American position on reforming UN peace operations, and the circumstances and degree to which the US would become involved in those operations.[6] The terms and tone of this document signalled to many that the United States was retreating from its earlier position of 'assertive multilateralism' and beginning to put some distance between itself and the world organization. The 'fad' of assertive multilateralism lasted less than one year.

The actions of the administration were not the only proceedings of the US government to have an unsettling effect on the UN Secretariat and other member states. Congress had been stepping up its own efforts since late 1993 to induce a number of reform measures from the UN Secretariat, by not approving the budget requests from the White House. This long-standing battle between Congress and the administration on the issues of reform and US debtor status only compounded the negative interpretations of what PDD 25 meant for the US–UN relationship in the coming years.

FULL CIRCLE

The above discussion of the state of US–UN relations (as they were perceived in October 1995) paints a picture of policies and decisions which seem to have the United States on a policy course very different from the one it was on in early 1993. One might venture to say that perhaps the course change was significant enough that a second 'about face' occurred, and as a result, the United States and United Nations had come full circle in a very short time. From the American perspective, the UN could not be considered a tool for serious foreign policy matters because of questionable leadership and managerial abilities, and an unruly membership. Meanwhile, the United Nations Secretariat (and other member states to varying degrees) considered the US to be an irresponsible and unreasonable member state which was in the habit of making illegal demands upon the Organization in exchange for its financial support. The US, therefore, could not be counted upon to assist the Organization in carrying out its mandate, let alone the reforms Washington was demanding of the Secretariat. These broad generalizations obviously oversimplify the relationship as it stood in 1995, but they highlight the key point: US policy had undergone another dramatic shift, which seemed to foreshadow a strained US–UN relationship in this new era.

How did this come about? How could US policy toward the world's largest and (arguably), most important international organization be so seemingly chaotic, volatile and schizophrenic? Such shifts in policy would not be surprising if they developed over the span of decades, or through some revolutionary upheaval in a political system. This occurred, however, over the space of less than five years, with a second 'about face' initiated by the Clinton administration, *after* it had endorsed the direction and substance of the original 'about face' under President Bush.[7]

THIS RESEARCH PROJECT

Given the importance of American support, both financial and moral, to the United Nations, it is in the interest of that Organization's leaders, other member governments and UN observers to try to lift the fog surrounding US policymaking toward the UN so that the current policy can be better understood, that future policy shifts might be better anticipated, and perhaps even influenced before they are finalized. With this general goal in mind, this book proposes to explore the decisionmaking process of the US foreign-policy apparatus which leads to policy decisions concerning the United Nations. In an effort to narrow the scope of research, though, this study has adopted a case-study approach, and chosen the political process, which resulted in PDD 25, as its subject.

A detailed examination of the process which led to PDD 25 will reveal a number of factors which are found in the American policy-formulation process. These factors are of primary interest to anyone attempting to understand why the United States approaches the UN in such a seemingly uncertain, tentative and non-committal fashion. Therefore, the central question guiding this examination of US decisionmaking is:

> *What factors influenced the shift in US policy toward the United Nations as represented by PDD 25? And of these factors, was there a clearly dominant influence or consideration?*

While this question has the appearance of being rather narrow and straightforward, the scope of possible avenues to approach it is broad. There is a multitude of different theoretical perspectives and tools at the disposal of any analyst to bring to bear on the given question or puzzle.[8] In this case, PDD 25 will be examined as a product of a process best described by the 'Political Process Model' as put forth by Roger Hilsman.[9] Why this model was used, and how it was applied to this case will be discussed in detail in

Chapter 1, but it might be helpful to mention briefly here the units of analysis at the core of this study. PDD 25 will be viewed as a product of a political process, in which four actors, or power centres, played the dominating roles. They are: 1) the executive; 2) the bureaucracies (Department of State and the Department of Defense); 3) Congress and 4) public opinion. Each of these had some influence on the final substance and tone of the Directive and, of course, to varying degrees, but it is expected that one actor, or a combination of actors, will prove to be the most influential variable in the process and thus determining, more than the others, the contents of PDD 25. It is identifying this actor, should it exist, that is the central objective of this study because it can provide the insight necessary to understanding how the United States arrives at its UN policy, or in this case, its policy concerning multilateral, UN-led peace operations.

As is often the case when researching a puzzle, one begins the study with one or more possible answers to the question. This study began with two hypotheses, and the political process model was chosen, in part, as a means to test both. The first hypothesis expects to find that US policy is driven from one position to the next according to public opinion, especially in the case of US policy towards peacekeeping, in a very *ad hoc* manner. Using this conventional approach, one could expect to find the events of 3 October 1993 in Somalia as the turning point for US policy. Up to this point, the US was without any explicit policy guidelines on peacekeeping missions. After the deaths of US military personnel in Somalia, the Clinton administration was forced to take a much more restrictive line on UN peace operations in general, and an even tougher position on US involvement in missions of that sort. This move by the administration was a reaction to quell the perceived public-opinion backlash against the use of American forces in UN missions, and resulted in the restrictive conditions found in PDD 25.

The second hypothesis takes a different angle. In this scenario, the policy position found in PDD 25 is less a reaction to negative public opinion than an attempt to deal with the issue before political rivals make it a damaging and politically costly issue. This hypothesis does not share the view of the more conventional explanation that public opinion demanded what amounts to a virtual withdrawal from UN (led, or sanctioned) peace operations. Instead, the policy was directed and formulated based on the self-interested, political calculations of what the Clinton administration believed was necessary to appease hostile Congressional positions. By employing the political process model, it is hoped that one of these hypotheses can be confirmed, and the other dismissed, so that the nature of the US policy-making process towards the UN will become clearer, and thus be much better understood.

STRUCTURE OF THE BOOK

The results of the research will be presented in seven chapters. The first, as already mentioned, will explain the methodology and theory incorporated in the study, and why these choices were made over other possibilities. Also included in Chapter 1 will be a section devoted to the definitions of the terms used in this study. Chapter 2 will be the first of four chapters examining the various actors, or power centres involved in this process, and deals with the executive, which in this case has been considered to mean the White House, the National Security Council staff and assorted advisors. Chapter 3 will delve into the roles of the two principal bureaucracies concerned with foreign-policy matters: the Department of State and the Department of Defense. Next, the role of both houses of the Congress will be explored in Chapter 4, with the aim of determining where its jurisdiction begins and ends on this issue, and how effectively it was able to influence the outcome of PDD 25 within that mandate. The last power centre, public opinion, will be addressed in Chapter 5.

In Chapter 6, some analysis will be brought to bear on the findings of the previous four sections, with the goal of drawing conclusions as to how these power centres interacted over the issue of US involvement in multinational peace operations. As was just stated, the main objective of this research is to determine whether one of the four actors played a dominating role in the process. It is in this chapter that this objective will be addressed by identifying the most important actor in the political process leading to PDD 25 (if possible). It is hoped that by going through this procedure, the 'nature' of the US policy-formulation process on peacekeeping issues will be brought into better focus, making it easier to place the seemingly volatile US–UN relationship into some sort of context. The final chapter will provide a brief review of the power centres' roles in the process, the analysis seeking to illuminate the most influential actor, and how all of these actors merge and interact in this issue area to create policy. The second part of the chapter will then try to explain current US policy toward peace operations as it is presented in PDD 25, and what the future of US–UN relations might be like if the nature of the process remains unchanged.

NOTES

1. For three perspectives of the mood and atmosphere of the 50th anniversary ceremonies in New York, see: 'Midlife Crisis', in *Newsweek*, 30 Oct. 1995, pp.14–21; 'The UN at 50: Who Needs It', *Time*, Vol.146, No.17, 23 Oct. 1995, pp.22–42 and 67–71; and 'Can It Keep the Peace: The United Nations at 50', and 'United Nations: To Bury or to Praise', in *The*

Economist, Vol.337, No.7937, 21 Oct. 1995, pp.18 and 25–9 respectively.

2. For an overview of the 'new world order' Bush had in mind, see: President Bush, 'The World After the Persian Gulf War', address before a joint session of Congress, 6 March 1991, reprinted in *US Department of State Dispatch*, 11 March 1991, pp.161–3; and President Bush, 'The United Nations in a New Era', address before the UN General Assembly, 23 Sept. 1991, reprinted in *US Department of State Dispatch*, 30 Sept. 1991, pp.718–21.

3. See Robert W. Gregg, *About Face? The United States and the United Nations*, Boulder CO: Lynne Rienner Publishers, 1993, for a detailed examination of US–UN relations up to early 1993. He presents a great deal of evidence to support his claim that the US was in the process of a nearly 180-degree change of direction in its UN policy.

4. Quote from Madeleine K. Albright, 'Statement at Confirmation Hearing of US Ambassador to the United Nations', 21 Jan. 1993, reprinted in *US Department of State Dispatch*, Vol.4, No.15, 12 April 1993, p.229.

5. For a detailed and elaborate statement on this policy stance, see Madeleine K. Albright, 'Myths of Peacekeeping', Statement before the Subcommittee on International Security, International Organizations and Human Rights of the House Committee on Foreign Affairs, 24 June 1993, reprinted in *US Department of State Dispatch*, Vol.4, No.26, 28 June 1993, pp.464–7. Reproduced in Annex Four.

6. See Annex One, White House, *The Clinton Administration's Policy on Reforming Multi-lateral Peace Operations (PDD 25)*, *USUN Press Release* 74-(94) for the unclassified, Executive Summary of the directive.

7. Although Gregg (n.3 above) argues that the 'first about face' began late in the second term of the Reagan administration, I refer to President Bush in this case because the most explicit statements were made by him or his staff so he is the more dramatic example of this shift.

8. An excellent, single-volume work giving the full scope of theoretical approaches to the study of American foreign policy is, G. John Ikenberry (ed.), *American Foreign Policy: Theoretical Essays*, New York: HarpersCollins Publishers, 1989.

9. The complete theory behind the 'Political Process Model' is found in Roger Hilsman, with Laura Gaughran and Patricia A. Weitsman, *The Politics of Policy Making in Defense and Foreign Affairs: Conceptual Models and Bureaucratic Politics*, Third Edition, Englewood Cliffs NJ: Prentice Hall, 1993.

---◀◦▶---

ONE

The Methodology of Applying the 'Political Process Model'

This study has been guided by the 'political process model' of foreign and defence policymaking as it has been developed and enunciated by Roger Hilsman. The purpose of this chapter is to explain what this has meant in practical terms, and to give a more detailed account of the methodology used in applying this model to the process leading up to the signing of PDD 25. To that end, this chapter has two specific goals. First, the model itself will be described. This includes, describing, among other things, what the key definitions and components are; the units of analysis at the heart of this study; and how the model was adapted to better 'fit' this particular case. Second, the use of the model in testing the two hypotheses will be explained. In other words, an effort will be made to outline how this model was used to make the necessary connections between the resulting policy and the actors to prove, or disprove, the two hypotheses. But before taking up these two tasks, it might be useful to discuss why this theoretical route was chosen over other alternatives in the first place.

WHY THE POLITICAL PROCESS MODEL?

After the release of Presidential Decision Directive 25, many analysts and writers concluded that the United States would involve itself in a peacekeeping operation (UN-led or otherwise) only if national interests were at stake, and that it was a cold calculation of national interests which led, not surprisingly, to this policy.[1] If this were the case, then any effort to explain how the Clinton administration arrived at this new policy would be grounded in one of the traditional schools of international relations scholarship, realism. Drawing on the works of Morgenthau, Carr, Kennan or Kissinger, the investigator would frame the explanation in terms of power and the state's prerogative in an anarchic system. Roger Hilsman and his political process model, however, do not fall within the bounds of this school of thought. This raises two questions: 1) why was a decisionmaking theory adopted over another approach, such as realism? and 2) of the many different decision-making models available, why was this particular methodology chosen?

It is one of the central canons of realism to treat states as the only actors on the world's stage and as unitary decisionmakers. Their actions are directed, planned and implemented according to the rational calculations of the rulers, be they democratic or non-democratic in nature. This approach to studying and explaining state behaviour is commonly referred to as the 'black box' method of analysis because it views the state as a box and examines only the output of state action and assumes that the inputs to the internal decisionmaking process are generally uniform from case to case. It never bothers to open up the box to study the inner workings. This lack of interest in the internal dynamics of decisionmaking is a reflection of the assumption that the goals of states are prioritized according to their impact on national security. The black box model then, assumes that rational decisionmakers craft foreign policy according to the security goals of the state. The decisionmaking process, in this model of analysis, is expected to follow the same general course, and reach the same conclusions, regardless of which individuals are in the key decisionmaking positions.[2]

The political process model, however, operates on the assumption that the internal decisionmaking procedures are very important in understanding the foreign policy of states, because states (especially democratically governed states) are not unitary actors but comprise many components which operate within the foreign policymaking process, and others which influence the process from without.[3] While the black box model has many obvious strengths in analysing state actions in time of crisis, or when a state's vital interests are at stake (because at such times the decisionmaking powers are usually concentrated in the hands of the executive), the classical model clearly cannot account for the many examples when actors other than the executive have displayed a certain degree of influence on a particular foreign-policy position. This argument asserts that these other actors take on an even greater role in the foreign-policymaking of a state when the policy under consideration is the product of lengthy deliberations rather than a series of decisions in a crisis situation. Keeping in mind that PDD 25 was on the drawing-board for over 14 months, and that the Clinton administration held numerous 'consultations' with other government bodies, the process which led to the signing of PDD 25 has the initial appearance of being a superb example of this kind of foreign-policy decisionmaking. Therefore, at an early stage in the study, it became apparent that the black box would have to be opened in order to examine as many of the cogs and wheels of the American foreign-policy apparatus as possible. Any attempt to understand the development of PDD 25 in terms of a unitary state actor would uncover only half of the story at best.

Under the rubric of 'decisionmaking models', the political process model was not the only model available to this study. At the outset, the research agenda for this project envisioned PDD 25 as a product of bureaucratic politics, and planned to tackle the subject by using the bureaucratic politics model as developed by Morton Halperin.[4] After some initial investigation, however, it was evident that this model would not be appropriate for two significant reasons. First, and most important, the assumption that PDD 25 could be the result of *just* bureaucratic politics was far too simplistic, and pursuing that argument would risk missing the inputs of key sources of influence, namely the Congress and public opinion. The political process model, on the other hand, allows for a range of actors, or 'power centres' to be considered, and this allows for a more comprehensive examination of the evolution of foreign policy. The bureaucracies are certainly taken into consideration in the political process perspective, but they are not viewed as the sole or dominant actors.

Second, it must be noted that even if the bureaucratic model were useful in this case, it would prove to be almost impossible to implement due to the nature of the evidence required. To follow through with an analysis based on the bureaucratic model, one must have access to enormous amounts of internal documents, reports and memos, and access to officials willing to talk freely and candidly about the internal events involving the policy under study. This was simply not possible for this author because most of the required documents remain classified. Therefore, any attempt to study the development of PDD 25 through the lens of the bureaucratic model would ultimately come to a halt due to a shortage of evidence. This problem is averted, or at least minimized in a sense, with the political process model, in that only the general positions and interests of the actors are needed to map out the influence they brought to bear on an issue and how they interacted over a particular issue. This kind of evidence can usually be found in public documents and through interviews with officials participating in the process. Although classified, internal documents would help in confirming or disproving other sources of information, strict reliance on them is avoided through this method. Of course, this usually means the analysis will not have the depth which might be possible with the bureaucratic model in terms of the degree of detail, but the chances of getting closer to the true overall picture are greater.

As one can see, while the bureaucratic model can be very useful in certain cases, and helps to illustrate the need to 'open up' the black box, it is not applicable in all circumstances, and is perhaps even misleading or distorting at times. This danger is all the more likely when the problem of scarce information is encountered. Given these two principal considerations, the bureaucratic model was abandoned in favour of the more flexible and comprehensive political process model.

THE POLITICAL PROCESS MODEL APPLIED

Once the underlying assumptions are clarified, Hilsman elaborates on the model by identifying the actors, or power centres, which he sees as constituting the elements of the process, and how they relate to one another in terms of relative power. In this section of the chapter, the model put forth by Hilsman will be tailored to better fit the special conditions of this case. Regarding the study of the process which led to PDD 25, this has meant two refinements in particular. First, and as mentioned in the Introduction, the power centres examined number only four, which is less than half of the total number of power centres cited by Hilsman as having a role in the foreign policymaking of the United States. This needs to be explained. Second, the influence each of the power centres has *vis-à-vis* the other power centres (the 'power line-up') has been conceived in a different manner from that discussed by Hilsman in his book, and this, again, is due to the specific circumstances of this subject which will be explored below.

The Units of Analysis

For Hilsman, in the broadest sense, there are nine actors, or power centres, involved in the American foreign-policymaking process: 1) the President; 2) the President's staff and advisors; 3) the political appointees; 4) the Congress; 5) the bureaucrats; 6) interest groups; 7) the media; 8) public opinion; and 9) the electorate.[5] This list is presented in the form of three concentric 'rings of power'. The inner ring of power is occupied by those directly involved in the policy process, namely the power centres numbered 1–5 which comprise government officials. The second ring holds the interest groups and the media and is indicative of the influence both groups can bring to bear on an issue simply through publicity. The elusive power of public opinion and the electorate is incorporated into this model by being perceived to have a limited impact on the foreign-policy process. Hence, in Hilsman's conception, they are found in the 'outer ring' of the power-and-influence structure.

The process leading to PDD 25, however, illustrates the fact that the above list is merely an attempt to identify the power centres usually found in foreign-policymaking. While some like the executive and the bureaucracies are almost always involved, others, such as interest groups and Congress, may not be engaged in every decision. In short, the list of power centres will be slightly different in each case. It has been stated above that only four power centres have been identified as having a role in the formulation of PDD 25. Why these alterations to Hilsman's original listing? For the purposes of this study, the executive is a power centre composed of the president and his White House staff, including the National Security Advisor and his staff. This is not a radical departure from the classification scheme envisioned by Hilsman, just a slight reworking for two reasons. First, Hilsman's separation of the president from his advisors and appointees is unworkable in this case because without long-term, inside access it would be almost impossible to differentiate between the positions of the president and his staff. And second, this definition of the executive eliminates confusing overlap. Hilsman considers the cabinet to be among the president's advisors.[6] This is true at the technical level, but the cabinet has no real power in the modern scheme of US politics. *Ergo*, for the purposes of this discussion, it will be argued that the secretaries of State and Defense exert more influence in their roles as heads of bureaucracies, and as such, they will be examined in those positions. Moreover, the Hilsman label, 'political appointees', overlaps with most, if not all, of those in advising roles. For example, all the department secretaries are appointed by the president, the National Security Advisor is appointed, and all those appointees in turn, make a multitude of further appointments to fill the upper-level positions within their departments. Rather than dealing with some individuals under two or more classifications, this study has endeavoured to sort the appointees according to their jobs, and not according to how they obtained those jobs.

The second power centre identified in this study consists of the two predominant bureaucracies in American foreign-policymaking: the State Department and the Defense Department (Pentagon or DoD). This label is consistent with Hilsman in name, but deals with only half the bureaucracies which Hilsman includes in his discussion. Some omissions have been made, while some distinctions not put forth by Hilsman are considered. For example, other federal agencies, such as the Treasury Department, the Department of Justice, the Office of Management and Budget (OMB) and the Central Intelligence Agency were not considered.[7] The two former bureaucracies were left out of the analysis because there is very little evidence, if any, on the public record to indicate that they had any role in the outcome of this particular policy directive. The latter two were involved in the process, but according to government officials and available documents, they were involved more as consultants than policy inputs, and as such, played only supporting roles.[8] The Departments of State and Defense, on the other hand, were clearly involved in the policy formulation, and hence deserve our attention as Hilsman calls for it, but with one further distinction. Within the Defense Department, two entities were represented at the committee level, and each made its own impact on the proceedings and final product. Representing the uniformed members of the Pentagon was the Joints Chiefs of Staff (JCS), while the Office of the Secretary of Defense (OSD) conveyed the views and concerns of the civilian side of DoD. In light of this, discussions concerning the Pentagon will often be presented in two parts, reflecting divergences which occasionally appeared within that department.[9] The role of Congress, however, is incorporated into this study as the political process model envisions.

The fourth power centre examined in this paper is public opinion, and like the executive, it is an overarching label encompassing elements of other power centres listed by Hilsman. The first distinction to be made is between public opinion and the electorate. Hilsman seems to deal with these two power centres in only vague terms, over long periods of time, and makes no direct link between them.[10] Based on the arguments he presents, and common sense, this study has concluded that public opinion is better used as the power centre for the following reason. The evolution of PDD 25 took place over 14 months, just following the coming to office of the Clinton administration. The contents of PDD 25 were not the subject of an election, nor were they at the centre of a nationwide debate engaging the voters directly. Rather, PDD 25 was composed largely by various government agencies in the shadow of continuing foreign operations. From this perspective, it is difficult to claim that the electorate held any influence over the process because the next chance for its views to be effectively expressed was late 1994 (mid-term congressional elections), or more importantly, late 1996 (presidential election). Given the lack of clear distinctions between these two power centres, and the lack of an explicit vote on the Directive, it seems most sensible to focus in the study on the role of public opinion.

Finally, a few words concerning the omission of interest groups or non-governmental organizations (NGOs) and the press and television from the list of power centres in this study. There are a number of interest groups which focus their attentions and agendas on the US–UN relationship in one or more ways, such as the United Nations Association of the USA, the World Federalist Association, the Stimson Centre and the Heritage Foundation to name a few. For the most part, however, groups which are interested in the United Nations (either for or against) do not possess the resources, nor the mandate, to function like an effective lobbying group such as the National Rifle Association, for instance, does on gun-control issues. The principal role of these organizations is to 'inform' the debate on UN-related issues. No doubt they would like to have their views reflected in government policy, but it must be assumed that their influence goes only as far as helping to set the parameters of the debate. Conversations with government officials involved with the PDD 25 process confirmed this suspicion, but it was added that NGOs were briefed by the State Department on a semi-regular basis.[11] It is clear though, that the NGOs did not exert a direct influence on the final version of PDD 25.

Along similar lines, the role of the media, for this study, has been taken as confined to informing the debate like the interest groups, but also, and more importantly, to placing the issue of US involvement in peace operations on the national political agenda in a far more effective manner than the various NGOs possibly could. This role, however, does not constitute the media being a power centre as Hilsman claims in his treatment on the press and television. There is no doubt that the images carried by the major US television networks of dead US soldiers being dragged through the streets of Mogadishu had an effect, but that effect was felt by the power centres of the executive, Congress and public opinion. The media were not a power centre in their own right. This study has concluded that the role of the media in the policy process leading to PDD 25 does not warrant their inclusion as a power centre, but rather as a variable in the process influencing the changing and evolving positions of the four acknowledged power centres.[12] For these reasons, interest groups and the media have been removed from the list of power centres deserving attention in this study, but have been considered as contributing variables which put the issue on the national agenda, and helped define the terms of the ensuing debate.[13]

The 'Power Line-up'

Once the actors, be they individuals or organizations, are identified as power centres in the political process, the next important step according to Hilsman is to ascertain the 'power line-up'. The power line-up is the term used to refer to the hierarchy of political power possessed by each of the centres. In other words, it is the ranking of the power centres from weakest to strongest in terms of how much influence they can bring to bear on the issue at hand. As Hilsman notes:

> The political process model sees … a number of individuals and organizations involved in the policymaking process. Each of these has power. Some have more than others, and the power of each varies with the subject matter. Each power centre shares a

commitment to state goals, such as power, prestige, and survival, but each may also have different views of the exact nature of the goals and even more frequently about how to achieve those goals. In addition, each power centre has goals of its own, ...[14]

While it would be impossible to assign actual values to the power possessed by each of the centres on given issues, it is clear that some wield more influence than others, and are therefore more likely to see their views reflected in the resulting policy.

The case of PDD 25 has proved to be an exception to this characteristic. Certainly the executive maintained its primacy in the foreign-policymaking process, but it was not necessarily exercised during the course of the policy review. It is the position of this study that the executive willingly allowed greater influence than usual to be exerted on the process by the other centres for two reasons. The first derives from the nature of the process itself in this case. As was noted earlier, PDD 25 is the policy result of a long, consultative review involving a number of government officials, agencies, departments and Congress. This was not a foreign-policy decision along the lines of the Cuban missile crisis or the invasion of Grenada where action was taken quickly and without Congressional or public consultation, much less approval. The implication of this for PDD 25 was that the White House made an effort to include many different perspectives from within government in the drafting of the Directive, and in a way which made it clear that it was willing to accommodate, as much as possible, the views of the bureaucracies and Congress. From this it is more difficult to label one of the centres as more powerful and influential than the others.

The second factor which makes it difficult to argue that there was a clear hierarchy of power and influence among the engaged centres was the widely recognized agenda of the Clinton administration which placed a premium on domestic issues.[15] Most foreign-policy issues which were not perceived to be affecting vital national-security concerns, like peacekeeping policy, were not high priority items for the White House. Consequently, the executive was not prepared to push a peacekeeping policy through the government which might cost dearly in terms of 'political currency' – currency which, in turn, would be required later to achieve items on the domestic agenda such as health care or federal-government reforms. With its priorities elsewhere, the White House granted a great deal more influence to other power centres than is usually the case, leaving the power line-up very much obscured.

The impact of these two circumstances on the research project is simple: the study was conducted on the assumption that it could not be taken for granted that the White House was the sole guiding force behind the policy direction set by the substance and spirit of PDD 25. In short, all four power centres had to be given due consideration because it could not be presumed that the executive branch was operating with a disregard for the views and opinions of the other power centres. The power line-up element of Hilsman's model, then, has not been applied in this study.

Measures and Connections

With regard to definitions of terms used in this study, only one merits a brief explanation: peace operations. The term peace operations is taken to mean the full range of multilateral military operations designed to provide humanitarian and peacekeeping services and peace enforcement as envisioned in Boutros-Ghali's *Agenda for Peace*.[16] A narrower definition would distinguish between UN-led missions and UN-sanctioned coalitions, but for the purposes of this book, the term peace operations will be used to refer to both types of command structures unless it is useful to make the distinction. Otherwise, the use of technical terms or jargon, has been kept to a minimum in this discussion.

As is often the challenge in social-science research, this study must prove or disprove the relationships at the heart of the hypotheses. To accomplish this goal, the study will present a research programme which examines the positions and views on peace operations of the four power centres, the units of analysis for this research, and attempt to 'plot' or highlight changes in those policy positions. Any changes in the units' positions will be deduced, or arrived at through a treatment which will be applied to each of the four units.[17] In this case, the treatment will be the American humanitarian intervention in Somalia which began in December 1992, and ended on 31 March 1994, after going through two operational phases. Keeping in mind that we wish to explain what, or whom, influenced the final substance of PDD 25, and that it has been widely reported that the contents and spirit of the Directive changed during the course of the drafting period, one might expect to find the answer connected to events which unfolded during the Somalia operation, and in its aftermath.[18] Changes or shifts will be discovered by a pre-test/post-test procedure, in which the positions of the units before the Somali intervention are carefully described and analysed, and these findings then contrasted with the positions and views held by the four power centres after Somalia. Conclusions will be deduced on the presumption that if a power centre's position did not change to any noticeable degree, then it is very unlikely that that power centre influenced the outcome of PDD 25 to any great extent. Conversely, if a significant position shift is detected in a power centre, signified by high level policy statements in the case of the

Executive or new legislation in Congress for example, then it will be determined that this power centre became a 'player' in influencing the new policy direction reflected in PDD 25. If more than one power centre is found to have undergone significant changes of views, then the Hilsman power line-up will be consulted in an effort to deduce where the final policy direction push came from, and why.

Somalia is selected for treatment in this exercise because US involvement there spans a period of almost 16 months, during which the review process was carried out. Its effect on the four power centres will be gauged more specifically around key developments: 1) the announcement of US forces being dispatched to Somalia in December 1992; 2) the deaths of Pakistani peacekeepers in June 1993; 3) the deaths of four US soldiers due to a land mine in August 1993; 4) the deaths of 18 US Rangers in October 1993; and 5) the complete pull-out in March 1994. While data might not be available for each of the units for each of the above incidents, it is believed that by paying particular attention to these developments, the range of the research might be made more manageable and the results more revealing.

To be sure, this methodology is not preordained to give flawless results. The methodologists have identified a number of possible pitfalls to this approach, but only one is of particular concern in this case.[19] Applying only one treatment to the actors leaves the conclusions deduced from the tests vulnerable to the claim that perhaps other developments or circumstances are responsible for the position changes revealed through the treatment. Certainly in the realm of international politics, it is impossible to declare, without reservation or qualification, that all factors were taken into account in any given investigation. Having said that, however, this study has been conducted on the assumption that only an event as dramatic as the intervention in Somalia could have produced the repercussions necessary to deflect the course of the Clinton administration as it allegedly did.

One might argue that other UN missions running at the same time might have had some influence on the US policymakers, not simply Somalia alone. Again, without access to classified internal documents it is impossible to be completely sure about this. But by working with the information available, it would seem that other UN missions were in fact having the opposite effect on the American position, with the exception of the UN Protection Force (UNPROFOR) in Bosnia. In late 1993, the UN was concluding an operation in Cambodia which was widely perceived as being a success, and UN efforts in Central America were acknowledged by all sides as being the key factor in implementing the Esquipulas peace agreements.

Events in Bosnia, on the other hand, did not place the UN's peacekeeping abilities in the kindest light, but it must be noted that the timing of the Somali adventure corresponded with the phase of detached, aloof involvement by the United States in Bosnia. As things took a turn for the worse in Somalia, US policymakers were still expecting their European counterparts to handle the war in the former Yugoslavia. Even the UN's role was understood to be very limited in nature, and conditions on the ground did not make it feasible to expand the mission's mandate. From just this brief recall of events, it seems very unlikely that the limited involvement of the UN and the US in Bosnia, in late 1993, could have matched in impact or exerted as much influence over American policymakers, legislators, bureaucratic 'experts' and public opinion as the events that were unfolding in Somalia. Bosnia was certainly in the back of many minds as a potential mission for US troops in the near future, but if there was any apprehension, it was being fuelled by events in Somalia. In sum, this paper will argue that Somalia is clearly the logical event to use as the treatment, and that based on the information available at the time of writing, no other event, or development could probably prove to be the source of any position shifts which might be detected in the course of this research.

NOTES

1. For a particularly cynical example of this view, see Phyllis Bennis, *Calling the Shots: How Washington Dominates Today's UN*, New York: Olive Branch Press, 1996, Ch.5.
2. This paragraph is a summation of the description of the 'black box' model presented in Hilsman et al., *The Politics of Policy Making in Defense and Foreign Affairs*, Englewood Cliffs NJ: Prentice Hall, 1993, Ch.3, pp.49–52.
3. The discussion contained in this section is putting forward an argument which is meant to be applied to only states with democratically elected governments, in the western, liberal sense of the term.
4. This model received its fullest elaboration in Morton H. Halperin, *Bureaucratic Politics and Foreign Policy*, Washington DC: Brookings, 1974.
5. Hilsman (n.2 above) intends his theory of the political process to be applicable to all democratic states in so far as the underlying assumptions apply, but his specific examples are drawn from a case study of the United States.
6. See Hilsman (n.2 above), Ch.10, p.146.
7. Hilsman's observations of the role played by these omitted departments can be found in ibid, Ch.13, pp.211–20.
8. Documents and reports in the public domain indicate that this was the situation, and they have been confirmed through interviews with government officials who were directly involved with the process. The individuals wished to remain anonymous.
9. Normally when discussing disputes within the Pentagon, one thinks of inter-service turf or budget battles. In this case, inter-service differences did not appear in the inter-agency meetings according to those involved. This might been explained in two different ways. First, only two of the services had any real interest in the peacekeeping issue, the marines and the army, yet their concerns and interests did not necessarily conflict. Second, if any

disputes did arise, they were addressed and resolved by the JCS, not by the inter-agency committee. My thanks to Professor Donald Daniel for drawing my attention to this issue.

10. See Chs.16 and 17 of Hilsman (n.2 above) for the full descriptions of his views on these two power centres.

11. Officials granted the interviews on the condition they remained anonymous.

12. One government veteran of the process illustrated this point by remarking how the review committee was forced to change its course in response to outcries from Congress over the tone the draft policy was taking. Congress, however, was not reacting to drafts submitted by the inter-agency committee, but rather to press reports which often contained erroneous information. Only in this indirect fashion did the media influence the final policy.

13. It is interesting to note that one author has argued that the media were more likely reacting to the government's policies than helping to shape them. See Jonathan Mermin, 'Television News and American Intervention in Somalia: The Myth of a Media-Driven Foreign Policy', *Political Science Quarterly*, Vol.112, No.3, pp.385–403.

14. Passage found in Hilsman (n.2 above), Ch.7, p.90.

15. To get an idea of just how concerned Clinton was with domestic issues, see Donald C.F. Daniel, 'The United States', in Trevor Findley (ed.), *Challenges for the New Peacekeepers*, SIPRI Research Report #12, Oxford: Oxford University Press, 1996, pp.85–98.

16. For the most widely accepted, comprehensive description of the possible range of peacekeeping roles and functions, see Secretary-General Boutros-Ghali, *An Agenda for Peace*, Second Edition, New York: United Nations DPI, 1995. Also refer to *General Guidelines for Peacekeeping Operations*, New York: United Nations DPKO, Oct. 1995, 95-38147.

17. This approach to research design is found in Thomas D. Cook and Donald T. Campbell, *Quasi-Experimentation: Design and Analysis Issues for Field Settings*, Chicago: Rand McNally Publishing Company, 1979, pp.98–103.

18. The policy shift during the drafting period was detected in a number of press articles. For example, see Barton Gellman, 'US Reconsiders Putting GIs Under UN: Concern over Somalia and Bosnia Prompts Backlash in Congress', *Washington Post*, 22 Sept. 1993, p.A1.

19. For a discussion of the dangers inherent in this 'pre test/post test' approach, see Cook and Campbell (n.17 above), pp.100–3.

——◄o►——

The White House View on Peace Operations

PRESIDENTS AND THE USE OF FORCE

American presidents are at the centre of any decision to deploy US forces abroad. Their position as commander-in-chief is enshrined in the United States Constitution and with that comes the ultimate authority over the dispatch of the armed forces. Although Congress has the exclusive right to declare war, many presidents have deployed troops without seeking this legal declaration. Since 1945, this practice became commonplace, as presidents, from Truman to Reagan, authorized military missions without consulting Congress or even obtaining its approval. These actions, however, were not in support of peacekeeping missions[1] because it was one of the unwritten rules during the Cold War that neither of the superpowers would participate in missions of this type.[2] Rather, US presidents tended to use the armed forces to conduct unilateral interventions.[3]

Vietnam, in many ways, proved to be a turning point with regards to the 'imperial' use of force by American presidents. For instance, it helped to redefine the relationship between the White House and Congress because it inspired the War Powers Resolution which attempted to clarify the decision-making relationship between the White House and Congress when the deployment of troops was under consideration. Another legacy of Vietnam with regard to the use of force by presidents was the so-called 'Vietnam syndrome' which cast military interventions in a negative, almost evil light. The Vietnam experience weighed heavily on the minds of decisionmakers – both political and military – during the 1970s. Throughout this period, the policy on interventions in general was simply to avoid them, the Golan Heights operation being one of a very limited number of small-scale exceptions.

The Reagan election victory of 1980 ushered in a new era in American politics, and foreign policy, not surprisingly, was altered significantly. Intervention was no longer a taboo, and action in Lebanon and Grenada sent that message clearly. But this new policy stance did not come without costs for the Reagan team, and the 1982 disaster at the Marines' barracks in Beirut was reason enough to pause and rethink this more proactive policy of intervention. The result of this reflective pause came to be know as the Weinberger Doctrine and it was presented to the public in a speech by the then Secretary of Defense, Casper Weinberger, in November 1984. He outlined six 'major tests' which should be applied when military force was being considered as a policy option.[4]Very briefly, these were: 1) vital interests must be at stake; 2) overwhelming force should be used so as to ensure victory (i.e. no half-hearted use of the military); 3) objectives, both political and military, must be clear; 4) proper resources must be made available, and if the situation on the ground changes, the force structure must be adapted; 5) before troops were deployed, there must be bipartisan support from Congress and from the American people; and 6) the use of armed force should be the last resort.

The Weinberger Doctrine became the guiding policy for matters which were not clearly concerned with central national interests (also known as 'less-than-vital' interests). The wish to avoid another Vietnam (or another Beirut) was very strong, and this doctrine was designed with that end in mind. The notion of contributing US ground troops to UN peacekeeping missions, however, was not part of the debate surrounding the use of the American military, nor did it register on the political radar in Washington as a subject for discussion. The perceived likelihood of the United States placing elements of its military under UN command for the duration of a peacekeeping mission were so remote that it was essentially a non-issue. Consequently, until the signing of PDD 25 in May 1994, there was no official, publicly released policy outlining how a US president could, or should, use the power of his office to order elements of the US military to operate under the UN flag, because there was no need for such a policy.[5] The need for a peacekeeping policy arose only recently, and largely as a result of the Cold War coming to an end. Therefore, two presidential administrations are of interest for this paper, those of George Bush and Bill Clinton. The purpose of this chapter is to review the positions and experiences influencing the Bush and Clinton views on peace operations and how these views evolved during the early 1990s.

BUSH AND PEACEKEEPING

George Bush's term in office coincided with two of the most dramatic transformations in international relations history: the end of the Cold War and the subsequent dissolution of the Soviet Union. It was noted in the introduction to this book that Bush's early vision of the potentialities for the new era on the near horizon was optimistic and that he was a champion of a stronger United Nations. Notwithstanding his post-Gulf War conversion, this was not always the case. When Bush assumed the presidency, he gave every indication of maintaining the same posture *vis-à-vis* military interventions as his predecessor, Ronald Reagan, namely, the Weinberger Doctrine – a posture which, implicitly, did not incorporate the direct use of US military personnel in peace operations. The continuity of Reagan's position on military intervention was assured in the Bush administration with the appointment of General Colin L. Powell as Chairman of the Joint Chiefs of Staff. When Weinberger drafted his six tests in 1984, Powell was his military advisor at the Pentagon and viewed by some as one of the Doctrine's authors.[6] Once given a chance to plan and conduct interventions himself, Powell stayed true to the perspective of his former boss. So much so in fact, that the Weinberger Doctrine soon became known as the Weinberger–Powell Doctrine.[7] The 1989, Bush-ordered invasion of Panama, which came early in his term in office, seemed to confirm this initial expectation to observers, specifically, that the traditional US policy of acting alone, or leading allies in military operations was to be carried on into the 1990s. Moreover, it provided an example of what the Weinberger–Powell Doctrine looked like in practice.

The Gulf War

The Iraqi invasion of Kuwait in August 1990 presented Bush with a rare opportunity to explore the effects of recent policy shifts in the Soviet Union by seeking approval from the Security Council to reverse Iraq's annexation of Kuwait.[8] The success of American initiatives in the Security Council, which required the passive cooperation of both China and the Soviet Union, coupled with the impressive display of US military capabilities in the theatre, led Bush to speak enthusiastically about an emerging new world order. One of the most memorable examples of his optimistic vision was presented before a joint session of Congress just as the Gulf War came to an end:

> Now, we can see a new world coming into view, a world in which there is a very real prospect of a new world order. In the words of Winston Churchill, a world order in which the principles of justice and fair play protect the weak against the strong ...; a world where the United Nations – freed from Cold War stalemate – is poised to fulfil the historic vision of its founders; a world in which freedom and respect for human rights find a home among all

nations. The Gulf War put this new world to its first test. And, my fellow Americans, we passed that test.[9]

It is apparent that the United Nations was to have a central role in the emerging new order, but that role was not clearly nor explicitly characterized. The principles guiding the new order were well publicized, but the practical means for its implementation were not offered by Bush. Six months later, he was given the perfect opportunity to expand and elaborate on this vision in a meaningful way with his annual address to the UN General Assembly.[10] This he did not do. Rather than outline the new measures that could be undertaken to enhance the UN's ability to help bring about his vision of a new world order, he spoke about history being held captive by communism for 45 years, repealing the GA resolution equating Zionism with racism and maintaining a firm posture against Iraq. No mention was made of reviewing UN peacekeeping operations with an aim of improving them or adapting them to the new international situation, nor was any statement made regarding a new US policy towards peacekeeping. Instead, UN peace operations were ignored by Bush, leaving the impression that he wished to stay the course with the existing position: no direct US involvement beyond logistics and financial support. Furthermore, it should be noted that Operation Desert Storm, just as Operation Just Cause in Panama, was a military action true to the criteria and spirit of the Weinberger–Powell Doctrine.

Somalia: Operation Restore Hope

In the aftermath of the Gulf War, Bush was confronted with two new and very serious challenges to his vision of a new world order. The first was the brutal civil war in the former Yugoslavia, which by early 1992 was spreading to almost all parts of that federation. The second was the staggering humanitarian disaster taking shape in Somalia at roughly the same time. The Bush administration had decided it was going to take a 'backseat' approach to the former and managed to maintain that position for two years. The latter crisis, obversely, was the target of a significant US intervention which became Bush's final grand gesture as he left the White House.[11]

A number of authors portray Bush as being very reluctant to become involved in Somalia.[12] This was an odd reaction for someone speaking so passionately about a new world order, but it reflected the lack of a practical framework for making the new order a reality. After months of idle statements, the influence of the media and a group of senators on public opinion finally forced Bush to act. His initial move, which came in mid-August, was to conduct a massive air- and sea-lift of food to particularly hard-hit areas of Somalia. It soon became apparent, though, that this was wholly insufficient. Over three months later, Bush ordered a large force comprising Marines and soldiers to enter Somalia with the mission of providing a safe and secure environment so that relief supplies could be distributed. This was the lead component of the multinational force known as the Unified Task Force (UNITAF) conducting Operation Restore Hope. At its peak in January 1993, the number of US troops amounted to 25,426 out of a total international force of 38,301.[13]

The operation, though unique in its humanitarian motives, was very much guided by the Weinberger–Powell Doctrine.[14] Bush and his advisors offered to UN Secretary-General Boutros-Ghali a US-led force only. While many reports claim the Secretary-General would have preferred the operation to be under UN command and control, that possibility was never on the table as far as the White House was concerned. The reason for this was that the dominance of the Weinberger–Powell Doctrine was so complete, no other method of deploying troops could be conceived.[15] Therefore, Bush authorized a mission which was limited to a few months, and involved a powerful force, whose goal was simply to protect the aid workers in their distribution of food and other relief supplies. He expressed this very clearly in his address to the nation as the operation was beginning:

> To the people of Somalia I promise this: We do not plan to dictate political outcomes. We respect your sovereignty and independence. Based on my conversations with other coalition leaders, I can state with confidence: We come to your country for one reason only, to enable the starving to be fed.[16]

Despite the apparently clear position of the US on the goal of the operation, some differences soon became apparent between the US government and the UN Secretariat in New York. Former Assistant Secretary of State, John Bolton, has reported that during the negotiations concerning the American proposal between the then Acting Secretary of State Eagleburger and Secretary-General Boutros-Ghali, no mention was made of any 'nation-building' tasks in Somalia. Their conversations were focused only on the finer details of Bush's proposal, the general terms for a 'hand-off' to a follow-on UN force, and what the potential consequences would be if the incoming administration did not support the operation.[17] After the Security Council had adopted Resolution 794, which authorized the US-led coalition, Bolton notes that Boutros-Ghali tried to incorporate other tasks and goals into the US mission such as a major disarming campaign, demining the country and the establishment of a civil administration and police force.[18] This version of events seems to be verified in a letter from Boutros-Ghali to Bush, dated 8 December 1992, just one day before US Marines landed in Somalia. In this correspondence, the Secretary-General asked Bush to undertake roles not apparently discussed with Eagleburger, foremost of which was the disarming of the militias.[19]

From this foregoing account, it appears that by the time Bush was preparing to leave office and the operation was underway, there were some serious misunderstandings between the US government and the UN Secretariat regarding the role and methods to be used by UNITAF in order to achieve its objective of a safe and secure environment for the distribution of relief supplies. It can be argued that this confusion in large part stemmed from a lack of congruence between the Weinberger–Powell Doctrine and traditional peacekeeping doctrine as practised by the United Nations. It would appear that Bush was resisting the Secretariat's request for disarming the factions because, in the prevailing perspective on interventions, this appeared to be too risky and carried the potential of dragging the US deeper into the civil war. The Secretary-General, on the other hand, considered the disarming of factions to be crucial to the creation of the 'secure environment' which was called for in Resolution 794.

Boutros-Ghali and his staff, however, did not fully recognize this aversion to serious involvement felt by Bush, hence their belief that the mission could be redefined, or further defined, after it had already begun, without causing any serious problems. The Secretariat's misunderstanding of the US position is a bit easier to account for in the light of Bush's speech to the General Assembly just two months before these negotiations started. During this address, Bush spoke of his instructions to the Secretary of Defense to 'place a new emphasis on peacekeeping' and implement a full range of peacekeeping curricula in the US military schools.[20] Though he did not pledge to contribute US troops directly to UN-led missions, he did stress the need for greatly increased cooperation and support for peacekeeping and humanitarian missions by the US military for a host of activities and roles. Washington was sending very positive signals at the rhetorical level, but as the Secretariat discovered during the negotiations over UNITAF's mission goals, these did not necessarily translate into a meeting of like-minded views at the implementation level.

Just two months later, however, the UN Secretariat was given further reason to believe that perhaps change was coming with regard to Washington's perspective and conceptualization of peacekeeping. In his farewell address, in January 1993, Bush offered his own doctrine of when, where and under what circumstances the United States should use military force.[21] His address marked a major departure from the Weinberger–Powell Doctrine in that he claimed it was impossible to apply 'rigid criteria' to deciding whether to use force in a situation. Each case, he stated, would have to be studied in its own right, and, more surprisingly, he added that it is impossible to decide ahead of time what interests should be defended by military means. In short, Bush was using his last major speech as President to signal a weakening of the military doctrine which had guided US intervention policy for over nine years. This, of course, did not represent a complete rejection of the earlier doctrine, but it certainly watered-down the strict set of considerations which had been used in determining whether the US military became involved in an intervention at all.[22] With this apparent rethinking about intervention taking place in the background, Bill Clinton arrived in Washington after a campaign in which he had staked out a very different position on the use of military force from that of the incumbent.[23]

BILL CLINTON AND ASSERTIVE MULTILATERALISM

During his campaign for the White House, Governor Bill Clinton made it very clear that domestic issues, such as bringing the economy out of recession and reforming the nation's health-care system, were at the top of his priority list.[24] If elected, he told voters repeatedly, the domestic agenda would be the focus for his administration. In April 1992, in a break from domestic issues, he made a foreign policy speech designed to set himself apart from the president, whom Clinton had been criticizing a great deal over US inaction towards Bosnia. In that speech, Clinton came out strongly in favour of a rapid reaction force for the UN, and other policy innovations which the Bush administration had not addressed.[25] His position was widely perceived as being more proactive and inclined to embrace a much more multilateral style of diplomacy than current Republican policies. This, of course, allowed him to launch effective criticisms of US policy in the Balkans.

His election victory was widely seen as a vindication of the Clinton/Gore campaign's message that the real issues concerning voters were domestic, mostly economic in nature, and that foreign policy was losing its political value as the Soviet threat was fast disappearing. The fact that the first three years of the post-Cold War era were marked by a serious recession did not help the Republican ticket either. Upon his arrival in Washington in January 1993, Clinton stated his intention to continue the mission in Somalia as it had been laid out by the departing administration.[26] This came as no surprise, given that his consistent criticisms of Bush's policies towards Somalia and Bosnia during the campaign year left him few alternatives. But more importantly, with regards to UNITAF, Bush had consulted with the president-elect, and Clinton had approved the plan.

In February 1993, Clinton made his first foreign policy moves. He instructed his National Security Council staff to begin a broad, inter-agency review process on peacekeeping issues, with the object of formulating the guiding policy for the new administration. Conventional wisdom at the time held that the policy review process would produce a document embracing the pro-multilateral positions of candidate Clinton, and that it would be completed and approved in time for the President's first address to the UN General Assembly seven months later.[27] Second, he presented his ideas for dealing with Bosnia in the form of a six-point plan, which in the eyes of one observer, 'represented a retreat from earlier promises' because it lacked any credible evidence that the US was serious about backing up the forceful rhetoric heard during the campaign.[28]

The UNOSOM II Mandate

With the review process underway, Clinton undertook his first initiative in Somalia as the mandate for the Bush-authorized UNITAF came to a close. As the original agreement stated, the US-led operation was to be replaced by a UN force known as the United Nations Operation in Somalia II (UNOSOM II). The timetable for the hand-over and the mandate for the UN operation were agreed upon and adopted by the Security Council in its Resolution 814, of 26 March 1993.[29] Regarding the timetable, the transfer of authority from UNITAF to UNOSOM II was scheduled for early May 1993, which was later than US officials had originally planned. The delay was due to many logistical factors but also because the increase of violence in the capital city led many in the US military and the State Department to believe that UNOSOM II would not be able to maintain the 'secure environment' established by UNITAF. This conclusion, coupled with the far-reaching mandate given to UNOSOM II by the Security Council Resolution 814 made it obvious that a sizeable American presence would be required in Somalia to assist the UN force. The number of US troops which remained with the UN operation was roughly 4,000, which included logistical personnel under UN command, and a quick reaction force (QRF) of 1,300 Marines stationed off-shore, which was under US command.[30]

The new ambitious mission given to UNOSOM II was a significant development in that it was fully endorsed by Clinton, thus representing his decision to venture much further than his predecessor into new and uncharted waters. While Bush had pledged to the Somali people only four months earlier that the United States had no intention of influencing the political outcome of the civil war, Clinton signalled his intent to do just that. With strong US support, the UN was instructed, through the Secretary-General, to 'seek, as appropriate, pledges and contributions from states and others to assist in financing the rehabilitation of the political institutions and economy of Somalia'.[31] In short, the UN was tasked with the reconstruction of a member state. This change of mission goals certainly had implications for the UN relationship with a number of Somali factions, in particular with General Aideed of the Somali National Alliance (SNA); but the implications for the internal policy process of the US government were equally profound. One author has characterized this resolution as transforming Somalia into a laboratory for Clinton's vision of 'assertive multilateralism'.[32] The UN officially took over responsibility for the operation on 4 May 1993, and a former American admiral, Jonathan Howe, was named the Secretary-General's Special Representative.

Clinton's policy of assertive multilateralism seemed to continue to dominate the administration's thinking throughout the spring and early summer of 1993. In fact, the policy took on an even more assertive posture in the wake of the ambush of UN peacekeepers in Mogadishu on 6 June 1993, which left 24 Pakistani soldiers dead. The Security Council acted quickly in passing Resolution 837 which called for the arrest and prosecution of those responsible for the killings.[33] This resolution, not surprisingly, led to more frequent confrontations between UN/US forces and militiamen under the control of General Aideed. Clinton sought to 'strengthen the organization's credibility' by ordering strikes on a number of targets in areas under Aideed's command.[34] Adding to the sense of escalation was the parallel increase in US forces, including a detachment of Army Rangers given the task of arresting the rogue General. These new forces, like the QRF, were not placed under UN command, but remained under the US Southern Command in Tampa, Florida. This reluctance to allow all US forces in Somalia to be placed under UN control reflected something short of a complete commitment to 'assertive multilateralism'. The command issue notwithstanding, Clinton maintained the 'nation-building' programme of Resolution 814 throughout the summer, even though opposing voices were making themselves heard in Congress.[35]

An article in the *Washington Post* on 5 August 1993, reported that the PRD 13 process was wrapping-up, and that the advisors drafting the Directive, led by Samuel Berger, were ready to present the document to their seniors for final comments and revisions.[36] It claimed that the provisions of the policy statement were approved by senior officials on 14 July, and that the President was expected to sign it by the end of August. Its terms and substance, while not as ambitious as many were expecting from Clinton's campaign speeches, certainly aimed to broaden the US role in peacekeeping missions. According to the article's author, the document committed the US to support peace operations 'politically, militarily and financially', and that Clinton would accept foreign commanders leading US troops in the field. Moreover, the draft offered a new and broader definition 'of what constitutes a "threat to international peace and security", setting the stage for forcible UN intervention when a country undergoes "sudden and unexpected interruption of established democracy or gross violations of human rights".'[37]

On the other hand, however, the article reported that this draft ruled out the possibility of the US earmarking specific units for peacekeeping duty, and allowed for US officers to disregard orders from UN commanders deemed to be beyond the operation's mandate, illegal or militarily imprudent. Furthermore, the proposed directive announced the administration's opposition to a rapid deployment force, one of the central foreign policy positions of candidate Clinton during his election campaign. In sum, the draft directive in early August signified a step forward on some points, but in many more ways signalled a reversal from the more substantial proposals previously championed by Clinton.

Meanwhile, on 8 August 1993, four US soldiers were killed by a remote-controlled mine. Their deaths took the toll of US casualties to 12, with four of those being non-combatants.[38] While condemning the attack, Clinton was quoted by reporters as saying that he still considered the UN mission 'was well-conceived and properly undertaken'.[39] The newspaper account went on, however, to note unnamed administration officials expressing concern that the increasing casualties would cause problems in persuading Congress to grant the funding necessary for the operation's extension when the current mandate expired in late October.

Clinton, for his part, did not express any worries along those lines. Another article, quoting a senior official, made it clear that the administration did not want to pull out its troops in the wake of this setback because of the consequences for the mission as a whole.[40] The official, David Shinn, confirmed that the US would remain 'unless there are a lot of setbacks', that the PRD 13 review process had been 'accelerated' in the aftermath of the attack and stated that the plan was to have the troops home sometime during 1994. Press reports hinted that while Clinton planned to maintain the course in Somalia, the review process was not proceeding smoothly. Apparently, and notwithstanding the warning of 'serious setbacks', the deaths of the four servicemen did not deter Clinton from his policy of 'nation-building' in Somalia. Indeed, two developments in late August and late September clearly indicated that the President remained on this course.

The first development was a speech given by the Secretary of Defense on

27 August in which he restated the administration's aim of helping the Somalis rebuild their country. Moreover, he said that the President himself had given the instructions to 'stay the course with other nations to help Somalia'.[41] Presumably, this speech was designed to dispel any speculation that the administration was divided or wavering over its Somalia policy, and to indicate that guidance and support was still emanating from the White House. The second significant policy development came on 22 September, when the Security Council adopted Resolution 865, which reaffirmed the 'nation-building' principles of Resolution 814. This resolution gave the impression that both Clinton and the UN Secretariat did not consider the standing policy in Somalia as problematic, and that it should remain in place during the run-up to elections in March 1995.[42]

SERIOUS SHIFTS APPEAR ON THE HORIZON

On the same day that the Security Council adopted Resolution 865, the *Washington Post* printed an article which portrayed the administration as confused and very unsure of itself.[43] The draft directive which was leaked on 5 August had apparently undergone two major rewrites during the intervening six weeks. The report claimed that the events in Somalia, coupled with the possible deployment to Bosnia, were causing a great deal of anxiety in Congress, which, in turn, was forcing senior officials to reconsider their earlier plans to allow US troops to be placed under UN command. Needless to say, the new draft was not presented to Clinton for his signature as originally scheduled, and no tentative date was offered in the light of the differences yet to be ironed out among the senior officials. One begins to suspect that Clinton was 'staying the course' in late September by endorsing Resolution 865 simply because he had no other course to pursue.

The day before this story was printed, National Security Advisor, Anthony Lake, addressed the School of Advanced International Studies at Johns Hopkins University, and presented the administration's foreign policy doctrine.[44] According to Lake, the US was devoted to 'enlarging' the community of democratic and free-market governments in the world, as the notion of 'containment' was no longer needed in its foreign-policy thinking. The issue of peacekeeping was raised under the heading 'The Humanitarian Agenda', and Lake made a considerable effort to play down the significance of peacekeeping in particular, and multilateralism in general, to US policy. He claimed that the US operation in Somalia and the proposed one in Bosnia were particular aspects of the larger doctrine which 'do not by themselves define our broader strategy in the world'.[45] From these remarks, one senses that Clinton, through his key security advisor, was trying to place some distance between himself and Somalia by creating the room needed, at the strategic level, to abruptly change course on peacekeeping.

Clinton then made his first speech to the United Nations General Assembly on 27 September 1993, and instead of unveiling the proactive policy anticipated in February, the President offered a taste of what was to come some months later.[46] Clinton did not present a complete set of policy guidelines during this speech but rather he introduced the Secretariat and the other member states to some of the new criteria the US would be applying in the future to decisions on whether to launch new peace operations. This set of 'hard questions' was designed by US officials so that the UN would know 'when to say no' to new, ambitious and vague missions during the planning stages and not after the mission had been launched. News reports at the time, however, noted the stark contrast between this address, and the one that had been planned some seven months earlier, and that the set of criteria seemed more like a set of conditions for US participation in future operations, most notably in Bosnia where Clinton had promised up to 25,000 troops to enforce a peace agreement.[47] With the mission in Somalia under fire, both literally and metaphorically, and many in Congress growing nervous about US troops being sent to the Balkans, President Clinton used this speech to make a significant break from his earlier notion of assertive multilateralism, and the press began to speak of a policy in 'retreat'. In the meantime, the peacekeeping directive was undergoing yet another round of revisions.

Less that one week after Clinton's appearance before the General Assembly, tragedy struck US forces in Mogadishu. On 3 October, 18 Rangers were killed and 75 wounded in a battle with the SNA. The effects were felt immediately in Washington. Four days later, Clinton addressed Congress, and subsequently the nation in a televised speech. This marked the complete reversal of US policy in Somalia.[48] He announced that the troops would all be home by 31 March 1994, but that additional troops would be needed for enhanced security until the departure date. Moreover, he made it clear that the United States government was disavowing any responsibility in seeing Somalia rejoin the international community by saying that 'it is not our job to rebuild Somalia, or even create a political process that can allow Somalia's clans to live and work in peace; the Somalis must do that for themselves'.[49]

In a report to Congress on 13 October, the President went even further by stating, 'the US military mission is not now, *nor was it ever one of "nation-building"'* (emphasis added).[50] There was no doubt at this point that the notion of 'nation-building' had been disowned, just as Somalia was being abandoned. With regard to peacekeeping policy in general, however, little was said directly.[51] In a rare interview with reporters at the end of October, Lake went on the defensive. He claimed, again, that the apparent crises in Somalia, and potentially Bosnia, did not reflect a 'crisis' in US foreign policy at the strategic level.[52] He claimed that on the 'big issues' like Russia, trade relations with Japan and missile proliferation from the former Soviet Union, the Clinton team had, mostly, got it right. But he also asked for patience, pointing out that the Clinton administration was the first since 1945 to have to formulate a foreign policy in the absence of a bipartisan consensus. In other words, Congress, the American people and the world-at-large could expect more policy shifts in the future as Clinton and his advisors tried to find their way in the post-Cold War world.

While the review process continued to grind along out of sight, Lake – by now recognized as the administration's unofficial spokesman on this sensitive topic – took the initiative on the peacekeeping issue with an opinion piece in the *New York Times*.[53] In retrospect, the article was a very accurate fore-shadowing of what was taking shape in the review process. In line with other statements made since mid-August 1993, Lake stressed that peacekeeping was not a central, nor defining, aspect of the Clinton foreign policy, but that it was, and remained, a useful tool when the administration was faced with the decision of acting alone or doing nothing when less-than-vital interests came under threat. He reiterated the policy of opposing a standing UN rapid reaction force, and the earmarking of US troops for UN service. He then went on to outline five elements of the emerging policy. The first three were familiar: 1) the asking of tough questions in the Security Council when new missions are being discussed, including 'what is the end-point?', 'is the mission clearly defined in terms of political and military objectives?' and 'are the resources available?'; 2) the need to reduce the US's share of peacekeeping assessments; and 3) the need to improve the management abilities of the Department of Peacekeeping Operations. Two aspects were new, however. The first was found in the fourth element of the policy: namely that a division of responsibility was to be created between the State Department and the Pentagon in that the latter would be responsible for planning and financing missions likely to involve combat, while traditional missions not including US troops would fall under State Department control. The second new development revealed that a two-tiered system was envisioned in terms of questions to be asked. All proposed missions would be subject to the above questions, but the US 'will ask even tougher ones before we involve US forces'.[54] In sum, to outside observers the review process seemed to be increasingly veering further away from the original direction. The official final document, however, had still not been presented for signature, so additional patience was required.

PDD 25 FINALLY SIGNED

For those concerned with the future US position on peacekeeping, the wait for an explicit policy lasted until 5 May 1994, when the unclassified version of the Presidential Decision Directive, which was the result of the long PRD process, was released to the public.[55] It was a remarkable document for many reasons, not least for its length and detail. The name had been changed to PDD 25 from PRD, or PDD 13, and this was possibly a symbolic acknowledgment of the many revisions the document had undergone during the previous 14 months. The publicly released version of the Directive is reproduced in Annex 1, but the principal sections and terms will be described here.

The introduction to the Directive has two objects: 1) to outline the strategic rationale behind peace operations within the broader context of US foreign policy; and 2) to explain the need for reforming the way peace operations are conceived and implemented. With regard to the first objective, the authors make it very clear that the armed forces of the United States have a primary mission: to fight and win wars. Yet, specific circumstances can arise when 'multilateral action best serves US interests in preserving and restoring peace'. The Directive goes on to note that while many of the conflicts witnessed in the post-Cold War era do not threaten US interests directly, the cumulative effect does. In this new situation then, multilateral peace operations can be a cost-effective tool in trying to contain or resolve these types of conflicts. Peace operations are not the central aspect of US foreign or defence policy, but they have the potential to be a valuable option to the US government. The second theme in the introduction, 'need to reform', briefly touches on two concerns of the administration. First, the US would like to see the *ad hoc* nature of planning at the UN replaced by a more coherent and standardized approach so that economies of scale are not lost each time a new mission is launched. Second, the issue of management and waste is raised, with the Directive suggesting the creation of an Inspector General to increase accountability. The document claimed that since peace operations were in the interests of the US, then the US should make an effort to see these sorts of reforms through.

With the reasoning for supporting and reforming UN peace operations laid out, the Directive goes on to discuss six specific areas, or issues, targeted for reform or clarification. Section one is entitled, 'Making disciplined and coherent choices about which peace operations to support – both when we vote in the Security Council and when we participate in such operations with US troops' (underlining in original). In this first section, the administration lists very clearly, the types of questions it will be asking in the future and which questions will be applied as the level of US involvement increases. To Lake's two different levels of questions mentioned in February, the Directive adds a third.[56] The questions are now classified according to the degree of US involvement, or more specifically: 1) if the US is considering voting in favour of an operation or a regionally sponsored operation (Chapter VI or VII); 2) if the US is considering a contribution of forces to an operation; and 3) if there is a possibility that significant US participation in a Chapter VII operation will result in combat.

At the first level of consideration, eight questions would be posed. For example, would UN involvement advance US interests and does the international community have an interest in dealing with the given problem through multilateral means? Does the crisis represent a threat to international peace and security in the form of international aggression or an urgent humanitarian disaster coupled with violence or gross violations of human rights? Is there a cease-fire in effect? Are the objectives clear and is there 'an understanding of where the mission fits on the spectrum between traditional peacekeeping and peace enforcement'? Are the means and political will necessary to complete the operation successfully available? Finally, is the estimated duration linked to the objectives and criteria for considering the mission completed?

For the US to contribute troops to the mission, six additional questions would be put to the organizers. At this level, the Directive calls for decision-makers to consider how US interests will be advanced by contributing American forces, especially in the light of possible risks. Are the resources (personnel, funds, etc) required available? Is American participation necessary for the mission's success? Is the American role 'tied to clear objectives' and can 'an endpoint for US participation' be identified? Does domestic and Congressional support exist for the proposed operation, or can it be generated? And, lastly, are the command and control arrangements acceptable?

Finally, if there is a chance US troops will be drawn into combat as a result of the operation's mandate, three last questions must be answered in the affirmative. Is there a determination to deploy sufficient forces to achieve the objectives? Is there a plan to achieve those objectives 'decisively'? And, is there a commitment to 'reassess and adjust, as necessary, the size, composition and disposition of our forces to achieve our objectives?'[57] Although the document notes that 'any recommendation to the President will be based on the cumulative weight of the above factors (answers to the questions), with no single factor necessarily being an absolute determinant', this scale of criteria certainly constitutes an intimidating list for any future mission to pass.

Section two is a short discussion regarding the role of regional organizations in peacekeeping. The Directive quickly states that the US government will consider the UN as the 'primary international body with the authority to conduct peacekeeping operations'. Having said that, the authors add that the US will support efforts to strengthen the capabilities of regional organizations to launch effective peace operations. Finally, on this subject, PDD 25 states that if regional organizations or groups of states approach the UN Security Council for its endorsement of a mission, US support will depend on the mission's 'adherence to the UN Charter and meeting established UNSC criteria [...]'. Curiously, the Directive additionally states that these conditions also apply to any proposed operation in the former Soviet Union.

The third section deals with the already public efforts to reduce both the US's share of peacekeeping costs and the overall costs of all peace operations. A deadline was set of 1 January 1996 to have the US share negotiated down from, the then, 31.7 per cent to 25 per cent. Included in this section is a reiteration of the US desire to increase 'management efficiencies' and ensure that the peacekeeping budget is cost effective. Accordingly, PDD 25 goes on to outline a number of objectives it claims the US government will strive to achieve. In addition to the Inspector General proposal mentioned in the earlier section, the Directive's plans include: the enlargement of the revolving peacekeeping fund to $500 million in voluntary funds; disallowing the standard practice of 'borrowing' from the peacekeeping fund to cover shortfalls in the regular UN budget; and a unified budget for all peace operations.

Sections four ('Strengthening the UN') and six ('Strengthening US Support for Multilateral Peace Operations') are concerned with actual reform issues. The former lists 11 proposals offered by the US to make UN operations more efficient and capable, while the latter contains a summary of initiatives to be implemented within the US government to improve the manner in which it funds operations. For instance, in section four, PDD 25 calls for the reorganization of the UN Department of Peacekeeping Operations (DPKO) so that it would have: a planning division, 24 hours operations room, a logistics division, etc. In order to have a mission up and running quickly after being authorized, the Directive called, among other proposals, for the creation of a 'rapidly deployable headquarters team', a database of forces which member states could contribute on short notice and a modest air transport capability. Section six, on the other hand, contains a number of provisions designed to enhance peacekeeping operation through changes within the US government, such as training its troops for peacekeeping duties and seeking to have Congress release the funds necessary to cover the government's growing peacekeeping arrears. The centrepiece of this section, however, is the new division of financing and control responsibilities between the State Department and the Pentagon, named 'Shared Responsibility'. Under this plan, the former would receive policy and financial responsibility for operations launched with a Chapter VI authorization (i.e. traditional mandates) while the Pentagon would pay the UN assessment for Chapter VI missions in which US troops are participating and take on full managerial and financial responsibilities for missions with Chapter VII mandates (i.e. peace enforcement mission with possibility of hostilities).

Section five repeated the position that the President would never relinquish overall command and responsibility of US troops. But – and after noting that for over 200 years the US has placed its troops under the operational control of foreign commanders – it recognized that, on a case-by-case basis, it might make sense to place troops under the 'operational' command of a 'competent UN commander'. To be very clear, the Directive provides a sketch of how much authority the President would consider allowing a UN commander to assume, and what authority would never be granted.

Finally, section seven sets out the task for the Executive to improve communications with Congress and the American public on peacekeeping matters with the aim of promoting a common understanding of what interests are being served through peace operations. Among the initiatives called for in this section are: regularized briefings for Congressional members; informing Congress of upcoming votes in the UN Security Council and of command and control arrangements; and support for efforts to amend the War Powers Resolution. The hope is that through greater consultation and communication, an increased level of cooperation can be achieved between the two branches of government, and that the new policy can enjoy popular support. As a conclusion, PDD 25 offered this final assessment:

> Properly constituted, peace operations can be one useful tool to advance American national interests and pursue our national security objectives. The US cannot be the world's policeman. Nor can we ignore the increase in armed ethnic conflicts, civil wars and the collapse of governmental authority in some states – crises that individually and cumulatively may affect US interests. This policy is designed to impose discipline on both the UN and the US to make peace operations a more effective instrument of collective security.[58]

In the speeches and presentations following the signing by key administration officials, much effort was made to portray the Directive as an honest attempt to improve UN conduct of peace operations. Lake, at a press conference introducing the Directive, tried to convince the audience that this policy is intended to reshape peace operations into 'a more effective collective security tool for American foreign policy'.[59] The press, however, noted the dramatic shift in policy from what Clinton had been proposing during his campaign for the White House. As one reporter commented, this directive marked 'a sharp departure from Bill Clinton's campaign vision of the United Nations as the global policeman'.[60] Although this same reporter conceded that while this position differs greatly with the one championed by the then candidate Clinton, 'officials have articulated this position for some time' within the Clinton administration. This fact was stressed by Lake during the unveiling press conference when he pointed out:

> The essence of the policy is what we have been following since approximately I say last fall, *late last summer* when we began to ask harder questions at the United Nations and to try to work more closely with the Congress, etc. [...] So many of these things we've been doing before. This pulls it all together, lays it out in more detail, and I think expresses also a philosophy of doing this that we have been talking about, but not in as coherent, I think, a fashion before [emphasis added].[61]

SUMMARY

As a conclusion to this chapter, we will quickly review the evolving positions of the two presidents, George Bush and Bill Clinton. President Bush presided over the end of the Cold War, and the collapse of the Soviet Union, which in turn, left him unsure on how to proceed. His quick and decisive military action in the Gulf War, and the newfound diplomatic flexibility in the Security Council led him to speak of the UN being a central actor in the emerging new world order. In this atmosphere, UN peacekeeping took on a higher profile, and the number of missions expanded. The US did not respond well as a participant to this new wave of peacekeeping for a number of reasons, but the foremost was the lack of US experience in such operations during the Cold War, and even more so, because US military intervention doctrine of the time (the Weinberger–Powell Doctrine) did not lend itself well to the passive tenets of traditional peacekeeping. As the Somalia crisis unfolded, and eventually developed into a humanitarian disaster, Bush offered the UN a large, US-led force with the objective of creating a safe and secure environment for the distribution of relief supplies. The mission was organized and conducted true to the Weinberger–Powell Doctrine, but Bush began to show signs of moving the US military in the direction of preparing for future participation in peace operations, though these statements were vague, and came at the very end of his term in office.

President Clinton, on the other hand, staked out a very proactive, multilateral agenda for foreign policy during the 1992 presidential campaign. This position included support for a UN rapid reaction force and much more support from the US for UN-led peace operations, in the political, military and financial senses of the term 'support'. After winning the White House, he instructed senior officials to begin an inter-agency review of peacekeeping and the potential US role. It was widely expected at that time that the resulting directive would reflect many of Clinton's campaign statements, and that it would be ready in time for his first speech to the General Assembly in September 1993, some seven months later.

During the spring of 1993, Clinton made his first substantial decision regarding Somalia as the mandate for the Bush-authorized operation came to an end. He signalled his desire to pursue 'assertive multilateralism' with the passage of Resolution 814 in the Security Council, which was hailed at the time as designed to rebuild the Somali state and economy. The UN took over from the United States in Somalia on 3 May 1994, but Clinton left a number of American logistic troops under UN command, and a large, US-controlled QRF. A month later, the UN was severely, and tragically, challenged in Mogadishu when a Pakistani patrol was ambushed, and 24 peacekeepers were killed. Clinton responded by supporting a resolution in the Security Council which expanded the operation for the UN, as it was charged with arresting those responsible for the attack. To enforce the resolution, Clinton reinforced the QRF.

On 8 August 1993, four US soldiers were killed by a mine in Mogadishu, the largest single loss of American life in Somalia to that date. Clinton publicly reaffirmed the goals of the UN operation and the role of the US military in that operation. His statements notwithstanding, reports began to quote administration officials to the effect that events in Somalia, and the looming prospects in Bosnia, were having an 'accelerating' effect on the review process. These individuals played down the significance of these developments, but Congress was mentioned as having captured the attention of those drafting the policy.

By late September, the tone and attitude of the Executive branch was noticeably less enthusiastic towards a proactive peacekeeping stance. In speeches by National Security Advisor Lake, and the President himself, the administration's earlier embrace of 'assertive multilateralism' was greatly watered down; it was stressed that this was a secondary tool in US foreign policy. The President's speech to the General Assembly did not present the new peacekeeping policy of the United States, but rather, will be remembered as the address which told the UN it must learn when to 'say no' to peace-keeping operations. An unmistakable shift in administration thinking was underway.

Less than a week after his appearance before the General Assembly, Clinton learned that 18 US Rangers had been killed in a vicious battle with General Aideed's forces. The President then went before the nation to claim the US was never attempting a 'nation-building' policy in Somalia, and that all US troops would be out of Somalia by 31 March 1994, thus indicating the end had been reached for what some had called an experiment of assertive multilateralism. In the months that followed, Lake presented the President's new vision of what the peacekeeping policy should be, and it began to take the form of restrictive criteria designed to make future US participation more difficult.

When the review committee finally submitted its policy guidelines, Clinton ultimately signed a document which signalled a complete reversal of what he had intended to sign 14 months earlier. The policy directive known as Presidential Decision Directive 25 represented Clinton's formal abandon-ing of 'assertive multilateralism', and his intention to seriously limit US participation in peace operations in the future. Moreover, the terms found in the Directive have been viewed as a more elaborate and rigorous set of conditions than any previous ones for deciding if force should be used. Intentionally or not, President Clinton had come full circle back to the traditional, Republican position on intervention, the Weinberger–Powell Doctrine, which he had implicitly criticized during the 1992 campaign.[62]

NOTES

1. To be sure, the US military was a supporter of the following UN peace operations: UNTSO, UNIFIL, UNMOGIP, ONUC, UNSF, UNFICYP and UNTAG. The extent of US involvement, however, was almost exclusively limited to providing airlifts or logistical support. US troops never entered a theatre under UN command, nor in any other sort of high profile role. The Korean operation of 1950–53, while a UN action in the legal sense, was commanded by the US military, which in turn received its instructions directly from President Truman and was authorized under Chapter VII of the UN Charter. Hence, this cannot be considered US participation in a traditional peacekeeping operation of the Chapter VI variety. See *The Blue Helmets: A Review of United Nations Peace-keeping*, Third Edition, New York: United Nations, DPI, 1996, for an overview of US participation in peace operations during the Cold War years.

2. For a brief review of superpower involvement in peace operations during the Cold War, see Augustus R. Norton and Thomas G. Weiss, 'Superpowers and Peace-keepers', *Survival*, Vol.32, No.3, May/June 1990, pp.196–205.

3. Richard N. Haass provides a good summary of recent US interventions in, *Intervention: The Use of American Military Force in the Post-Cold War World*, Washington DC: The Carnegie Endowment for International Peace, 1994, especially Chs.2 and 6.

4. See Secretary of Defense Weinberger, 'The Uses of Military Power', Address to the National Press Club, Washington DC, 28 Nov. 1994, reprinted in Annex Two.

5. It must be noted that President Bush signed a directive in 1992 (NSDD 74) dealing with peacekeeping and emergency humanitarian relief, but this directive was, and remains (to this author's knowledge), a classified document. For a reference to this directive see David J. Scheffer (Senior Advisor and Counsel to the US Permanent Representative to the United Nations), 'Introductory Note, United States: Administration Policy on Reforming Multilateral Peace Operations', in *International Legal Materials*, 33 I.L.M., 705, May 1994, p.795.

6. As an example of some writers giving Powell a role in the drafting of Weinberger's six points, see Ivo H. Daalder, 'Knowing When to Say No: The Development of US Policy for Peacekeeping', in William J. Durch (ed.), *UN Peacekeeping, American Policy and the Uncivil Wars of the 1990s*, New York: St Martin's Press, 1996. However, Powell has stated that the Doctrine was drafted by Weinberger himself as an almost emotional response to the Marine Barracks disaster in Beirut the year before. Moreover, Powell claims he had some reservations about presenting the doctrine in such explicit terms to the public. For Powell's recollection of how this doctrine came to be, see Colin L. Powell with Joseph E. Persico, *My American Journey*, New York: Random House, 1995, pp.302–3.

7. For example, see the reference and description of the doctrine in John L. Hirsch and Robert B. Oakley, *Somalia and Operation Restore Hope: Reflections on Peacemaking and Peacekeeping*, Washington DC: United States Institute of Peace Press, 1995, pp.46–7.

8. A criticism often directed at Bush was that he was slow to respond to the positive overtones from the Kremlin, and did not recognize quickly their meaning. See Terry L. Deibel, 'Bush's Foreign Policy: Mastery and Inaction', *Foreign Policy*, No.83, Summer 1991, pp.3–23, for an account of the Bush's decision to use the Security Council in his plan to evict Iraq. For the contrary interpretation of Bush's policy for dealing with the collapse of the Soviet Union, see Michael Mandelbaum, 'The Bush Foreign Policy' in, *Foreign Affairs*, Vol.70, No.1 (America and the World 1990/91), pp.5–22.

9. Passage found in President George Bush, 'The World After the Persian Gulf War', Address before a joint session of Congress, 6 March 1991, reprinted in *US Department of State Dispatch*, 11 March 1991, p.162.

10. For the complete text of this address, see President George Bush, 'The United Nations in a New Era', Address before the UN General Assembly, 23 Sept. 1991, reprinted in *US Department of State Dispatch*, 30 Sept. 1991, pp.718–21.

11. Bush's decision to intervene in Somalia, but not in the Former Yugoslavia is a telling indication of what priorities were taken into consideration during the decisionmaking process. Although the exact reasoning is somewhat obscure, surely the seemingly simple mission proposed for Somalia must have appealed to Bush. Former Acting Secretary of State Eagleburger has suggested that Bosnia was seen as a potential modern-day Vietnam, whereas Somalia could be done quickly and easily. See Lawrence S. Eagleburger, 'Making Foreign Policy: A View From the Executive Branch', an interview in *The Brown Journal of World Affairs*, Vol.3, No.1 (Winter/Spring 1996), pp.243–57.

12. For example see Theo Farrell, 'Sliding into War: The Somalia Imbroglio and US Army Peace Operations Doctrine', in *International Peacekeeping*, Vol.2, No.2 (Summer 1995), pp.194–6; and Hirsch and Oakley (n.7 above), pp.35–43.

13. These figures are quoted in Hirsch and Oakley, ibid, p.63, fn.7.
14. For descriptions of the force posture of UNITAF, see Hirsch and Oakley (n.7 above), pp.46–7; and John R. Bolton, 'Wrong Turn in Somalia', *Foreign Affairs*, Vol.73, No.1, Jan./Feb. 1994, pp.58–60.
15. This important observation is offered by Walter Clarke and Jeffery Herbst, in their 'Somalia and the Future of Humanitarian Intervention', *Foreign Affairs*, Vol.75, No.2, March/April 1996, p.75.
16. See President George Bush, 'Humanitarian Mission to Somalia', Address to the Nation, Washington DC, 4 March 1992, reprinted in *US Department of State Dispatch*, Vol.3, No.49, 7 Dec. 1992, p.866 for this passage.
17. Bolton (n.14 above) provides a very detailed chronology of events from the Bush administration's perspective, pp.56–66. He stresses repeatedly that Bush did not envision anything more than a powerful, short-term police action to restore order, then pass the operation over to the second UN attempt in Somalia, UNOSOM II, within a matter of two to four months. While Bolton is most likely correct about Bush's unambiguous position, one government official stated during an interview with the author that the differences between Washington and New York had their origins in Eagleburger's first meeting with Boutros-Ghali about a possible mission to Somalia. The nameless official claimed that Eagleburger gave UN officials the impression that the US would bring the militias under control and disarm the whole country. After that first meeting, according to this US official, Washington was forever backpedalling from the false impressions left by Eagleburger.
18. See Bolton (n.14 above), pp.60–1, for a good account of the initial 'disconnect' between the Bush administration and the UN Secretariat over the role and functions of the UNITAF.
19. See Document 36, letter dated 8 Dec. 1992 from Secretary-General Boutros-Ghali to President Bush, in *The United Nations and Somalia, 1992–1995*, Blue Book Series, Vol.VIII, New York, United Nations, DPI, 1996 pp.216–17. This letter was not released as a UN document. Also see this volume for the text of Security Council Resolution 794, under Document 35, pp.214–15.
20. Refer to President George Bush, 'Address by the President of the United States of America to the 47th Session of the United Nations General Assembly', 21 Sept. 1992, *USUN Press Release* 84–(92), for the text of this speech.
21. See President George Bush, 'America's Role in the World', Address to the West Point Military Academy, West Point, New York, 5 Jan. 1993, reprinted in *US Department of State Dispatch*: Vol.4, No.2, 11 Jan. 1993, pp.13–15, for the complete text of this speech.
22. One writer has pointed out, however, that Bush also warned against the urge to intervene in every conflict and that those with isolationist leanings could take this as a sign of Bush's reluctance to embrace a more aggressive multilateral policy. For this point see Stephen John Stedman, 'The New Interventionists', *Foreign Affairs*, Vol.72, No.1, Winter 1993/94, p.15.
23. For a brief, yet interesting, sketch of the candidates' competing foreign policy positions, see David C. Hindrickson, 'The Recovery of Internationalism', *Foreign Affairs*, Vol.73, No.5, Sept./Oct. 1994, pp.26–8. In this piece, the author likens the campaign rhetoric to a poker game in which the incumbent played a hand of UN-based internationalism, and the challenger went with essentially the same hand, only he raised him. For a good summary of the accusations levelled by Clinton during the campaign, see Mats R. Berdal, 'Fateful Encounter: The United States and UN Peacekeeping', *Survival*, Vol.36, No.1

(Spring 1994), p.35.

24. To get an idea of just how focused Clinton was on the his domestic agenda, see Donald C.F. Daniel, 'The United States', in Trevor Findley (ed.), *Challenges for the New Peace-keepers*, SIPRI Research Report #12, Oxford: Oxford University Press, 1996, pp.89–90.

25. Elements from this speech are quoted in Elaine Sciolino, 'US Narrows Terms for Its Peacekeepers', *New York Times*, 23 Sept. 1993, p.A8.

26. Hirsch and Oakley (n.7 above), on p.101, mention that during a speech to US troops in Mogadishu, outgoing President George Bush assured his audience that President-elect Clinton 'supported this approach' in Somalia.

27. For an example of what the expectations were for this policy review at the outset, see Mats R. Berdal (n.23 above), pp.30–5. During the drafting stage, the working document was known as Presidential Review Directive 13 (PRD 13).

28. See ibid, p.36, for a concise analysis of the Bosnian policy offered by Clinton in Feb. 1993, and how this could be viewed as setting the tone for Clinton's resolve to live up to his campaign positions on foreign policy issues, including, of course, peacekeeping policy in general.

29. The text of Resolution 814 can be found in, *The United Nations and Somalia, 1992–1995*, Document 52, pp.261–3.

30. These figures are provided by Hirsch and Oakley (n.7 above), p.112. John R. Bolton, however, claims that the Clinton administration 'contemplated' a force close to 8,000, plus the QRF, but he does not provide a citation for that assertion. See Bolton (n.14 above), p.62.

31. This particular passage is found in Security Council Resolution 814, 26 March 1993, Section C, para.17, but the theme of national reconstruction, or rehabilitation is woven into the entire resolution.

32. John R. Bolton, for one, argues that this resolution was not the result of 'mission creep', but a 'deliberate experiment in "assertive multilateralism"'. See Bolton (n.14 above), p.63.

33. See Security Council Resolution 837, adopted 6 June 1993, in, *The United Nations and Somalia, 1992–1995*, Document 55, pp.267–8.

34. Less than a week later, Clinton ordered a retaliatory strike by US forces. Using AC-130 gunships and various types of helicopters, the US and UNOSOM II units hit some of Aideed's weapon storage sites and Radio Mogadishu. See Michael R. Gordon, 'New Strength for UN Peacekeepers: US Might', *New York Times*, 13 June 1993, p.A2 for details of the attack, and Clinton's remarks afterwards.

35. For a description of the domestic context in which Clinton was pursuing his Somalia policy, see Mats R. Berdal (n.23 above), p.34; and Bolton (n.14 above), p.64. The characterizations referred to in this sentence come from this section in Bolton.

36. See Barton Gellman, 'Wider UN Police Role Supported', *Washington Post*, 5 Aug. 1993, p.A1.

37. See ibid, for this passage, and other examples of the forward, and backward policy directions in this draft document.

38. See Keith B. Richburg, '4 US Soldiers Killed in Somalia; UN Blames Land-mine on Warlord', *Washington Post*, 9 Aug. 1993, p.A1, for details on attack and casualty toll to date.

39. See ibid.

40. See Daniel Williams, 'US Troops To Remain in Somalia; Force Assisting UN in "Re-creating" Nation', *Washington Post*, 11 Aug. 1993, p.A1.

41. This speech is quoted in Bolton (n.14 above), p.64. Hirsch and Oakley, on the other hand,

present the speech in a slightly different light. They claim that Aspin called for a more narrow and realistic policy in Somalia, and for the UN and Organization of African Unity to bring the parties back to the negotiating table. For these authors, this signalled a rethink occurring in the administration due to the rise in violence which had transformed the operation into a running battle with Aideed's SNA. If this is the correct interpretation, Clinton still sent the Delta Force and Rangers to Somalia with orders to capture Aideed. See Hirsch and Oakley (n.7 above), p.125.

42. The text of this resolution, see *United Nations and Somalia, 1992–1995*, Resolution 865, Document 65, pp.302–4.

43. See Barton Gellman, 'US Reconsiders Putting GIs Under UN: Concern over Somalia and Bosnia Prompts Backlash in Congress', *Washington Post*, 22 Sept. 1993, p.A1. This article was followed by Elaine Sciolino, 'US Narrows Terms for Its Peacekeepers', *New York Times*, 23 Sept. 1993, p.A8, which presented a similar picture.

44. See Anthony Lake (Assistant to the President for National Security Affairs), 'From Containment to Enlargement', Address to the School of Advanced International Studies, Johns Hopkins University, Washington DC, 21 Sept. 1993, reprinted in *US Department of State Dispatch*, Vol.4, No.39, 27 Sept. 1993, pp.658–64, for the complete text of this address.

45. See ibid, p.663, for the complete passage.

46. See President William J. Clinton, 'Address by the President of the United States of America to the 48th Session of the United Nations General Assembly', 27 Sept. 1993, *USUN Press Release* 141-(93). Reproduced in Annex 6.

47. This analysis and speculation is found in Thomas L. Friedman, 'Clinton, at UN, Lists Stiff Terms For Sending US Forces to Bosnia', *New York Times*, 28 Sept. 1993, p.A1. Also see Thomas L. Friedman, 'Theory vs. Practice: Clinton's Stated Foreign Policy Turns Into More Modest "Self-Containment"', *New York Times*, 1 Oct. 1993, p.A3; and John M. Goshko, 'Clinton Seen Calming Hill on Peacekeeping; Caution in Committing US Forces Said to Defuse Confrontation on Presidential Prerogatives', *Washington Post*, 2 Oct. 1993, p.A16.

48. The change of course in Somalia is best summed up in Barton Gellman, and Daniel Williams, 'A Grand Bargain: Administration Would Rather Switch Than Fight', *Washington Post*, 20 Oct. 1993, p.A36. The authors describe the policy after the fire fight as '… accommodation above all, and withdrawal by April come what may'.

49. The text of this speech can be found in President Clinton, 'US Military Involvement in Somalia', Address to the Nation, 7 Oct. 1993, reprinted in *US Department of State Dispatch*, Vol.4, No.42, 18 Oct. 1993, pp.713–14. This quote is found on p.713.

50. See President Clinton, 'Report of Military Operations in Somalia Transmitted to Congress', 13 Oct. 1993, reprinted in *US Department of State Dispatch*, Vol.4, No.43, 25 Oct. 1993, p.747.

51. Peacekeeping became an even hotter topic in Washington that week for Clinton as the Navy landing ship USS *Harlan County* was turned away from attempting to land over 220 US and Canadian 'civic assistant' troops in Port-au-Prince because of a hostile mob at the pier. This humiliation came just a little over one week after the Mogadishu battle. See Douglas Farah and Michael Tarr, 'Haitians Block US Troop Arrival', *Washington Post*, 12 Oct. 1993, p.A1, for details.

52. For a detailed account of this interview session, see Thomas L. Friedman, 'Clinton's Foreign Policy: Top Adviser Speaks Up', *New York Times*, 31 Oct. 1993, p.A2.

53. See W. Anthony Lake (National Security Advisor), 'The Limits of Peacekeeping', *New*

York Times, 6 Feb. 1994, Opinion-Editorial Section.

54. See ibid.
55. The unclassified summary of the Directive was released as The White House, *The Clinton Administration's Policy on Reforming Multilateral Peace Operations (PDD 25)*, 6 May 1994, *USUN Press Release* 74–(94).
56. The reference here is to W. Anthony Lake (n.53 above), where he states that the US is already asking tough questions, 'and will ask even tougher ones before we involve US forces'.
57. According to officials who participated in the review process, this third tier was added during the final stages of the review in an effort to stem Congressional criticism of the policy. These individuals, from both DoD and State described the third tier as unnecessary, but included because of this political factor. One reason given for this attitude was that the drafters were considering peacekeeping operations only, not fullscale warfare. If war was engaged, then obviously these sorts of issues would be taken into consideration, but the policy did not have to speak so explicitly to these concerns.
58. See this passage in Annex 1, p.139.
59. This claim is found in W. Anthony Lake (National Security Advisor), 'Peacekeeping Directive Designed to Impose More Discipline', transcript of remarks by Mr Lake and Lt. General Weseley Clark, White House, EUR511, 6 May 1994, 5870, p.1.
60. This comment is found in Elaine Sciolino, 'New US Peacekeeping Policy De-emphasizes Role of the UN', *New York Times*, 6 May 1994, p.A 2.
61. See W. Anthony Lake (National Security Advisor) (n.59 above), pp.8–9.
62. This opinion is put forth in a candid fashion by, surprisingly, a Clinton administration official. See James P. Terry (US Department of the Interior), 'UN Peacekeeping and Military Reality', *The Brown Journal of World Affairs*, Vol.3, No.1 (Winter/Spring 1996), pp.135–43; in particular, the argument laid out on pp.137–40.

THREE

The Views and Interests of the State Department and the Pentagon

INTRODUCTION

Bureaucracies are often thought of as organizations which simply carry out the instructions of their superiors, be they in the public or private sectors. Hilsman argues that, while this is certainly the case much of the time, government bureaucracies also have the ability to influence the policy they are charged with implementing, through their roles as sources of information, legislation and innovation.[1] What persona did the bureaucracies exhibit in this case? Were they merely scribes putting the vision and ideas of their superiors into words, or were they sources of substantial input in their own right? Finding straight answers to these questions is all the more challenging when one considers the context. In the previous chapter, the limited US experience with peacekeeping during the Cold War was discussed, and it was noted that the United States, for a number of reasons, simply did not contribute combat units to UN-led missions. This lack of experience affected not only the views of both Presidents Bush and Clinton, but also the two major foreign-policy bureaucracies serving each administration, the State Department and the Defense Department (DoD or the Pentagon). Not only was there a general absence of a peacekeeping 'culture' within these two departments, but they were also each regrouping and in the process of developing new paradigms for the post-Cold War era. For the State Department that meant casting the UN in a more favourable light and working with it and in it accordingly. Meanwhile, the Pentagon was preparing itself for implementing the 'peace dividend' – reducing troop levels and shrinking budgets as a result of its principal adversary disappearing from the political map.

This chapter looks at the perspectives, positions and interests of the two principal bureaucracies involved in the PDD 25 policy review process, the State Department and the Pentagon. The analysis will place a special emphasis on statements made by their senior officials before and during the review process, but will also draw on interviews with bureaucrats involved in the policy review. Using this information, the discussion will then try to map those positions as the debate (if there was one) was engaged, and in relation to the policy which eventually took shape.

THE STATE DEPARTMENT

Before Iraq's invasion of Kuwait in August 1990, and before George Bush first pronounced his vision of a new world order, the US State Department was pursuing a new policy towards the United Nations. This was the first attempt to reframe US–UN relations in the new international circumstances that had apparently accompanied the fall of the Berlin Wall and the collapse of the Warsaw Pact. A concise presentation of this new US strategy was made by then Assistant Secretary of State, John Bolton, in March of 1991, when he laid out four basic goals his department had been pursuing during the previous year.[2] Two of the four objectives of this new policy were: 1) 'to strengthen the UN's efforts to promote international peace and security by strengthening its peacekeeping functions ...'; and 2) 'To re-establish America's image as a credible, reliable participant in international organizations. We must fully meet our financial obligations when they are due.'[3]

Bolton's goals clearly reveal the State Department's eagerness to approach the United Nations from a fresh angle, even before George Bush rediscovered the Organization during the Gulf War. As the crisis in Somalia grew worse in early 1993, however, and the fighting continued to spread in the Former Yugoslavia, the State Department cautioned against any ill-conceived notions of peacekeeping. The US Mission to the UN in New York reminded other Security Council members of the situations in which UN-led peacekeeping worked best. Months before the launching of the UNITAF mission by President Bush, a US diplomat argued against a UN intervention during the deliberations in the Security Council:

> Prior experience in peacekeeping operations throughout the world has shown us that the United Nations cannot perform effectively in a situation where the parties to the conflict are unwilling to create the conditions necessary to enable it to do so. [...] The United Nations cannot deliver humanitarian assistance where an active conflict is under way.[4]

The representative continued by stressing the importance of a stable cease-fire and that 'all parties must be willing to accept international supervision of it in order for United Nations monitors to operate with a modicum of safety. Without such agreements firmly in place, we would be placing the monitors in an excessively dangerous situation.'[5]

These remarks indicate that the US Mission to the United Nations was open to considering any possible peacekeeping operation to Somalia strictly in traditional terms (i.e. Chapter VI authorization where the consent of the parties is secured before the UN force is deployed) as the Security Council began to deal with the Somali famine and civil war.[6] This leads one to suspect that while the State Department was working for a more robust peacekeeping capability at the UN, they were thinking in terms of the 'traditional model' authorized under Chapter VI. State Department officials did not give the impression that they were inclined to push for the more intrusive and inherently more dangerous class of operations known as peace-enforcements, which require a Chapter VII mandate. Moreover, while it was quite apparent that the State Department's interest was to enhance UN performance in conducting Chapter VI mandated operations, the principle of excluding US combat troops in peace operations was not being seriously reconsidered in the early years of the post-Cold War period. This is to say that, while it was expected that the US military would continue its support of UN missions in the areas of logistics, communications etc., no one in the State Department, it appears, was arguing for a commitment by US ground forces to UN-led operations as part of the new stance towards the UN peace and security functions.[7]

Somalia and UNITAF

The situation in Somalia demanded more and more attention as the spring of 1992 arrived. Judging by the remarks of the US representative to the Security Council in March of that year, it appeared as though the State Department was content to maintain a cautious approach to the growing crisis. This may have been deceptive. Hirsch and Oakley reported that the State Department's two primary bureaus concerned with Somalia, the African desk, and the Human Rights desk, both argued behind the scenes for a more proactive policy.[8] According to these authors, a more active and involved position, however, was not supported by senior officials at the Cabinet level and therefore, it was not acted upon during the spring or summer of 1992. The various pressures on Bush began to reach a critical mass in late October and early November 1992. At this point, Acting Secretary of State Eagleburger became the contact person with the UN Secretariat, and presented Boutros-Ghali with the offer of a US-led operation to facilitate the delivery of relief supplies. Until the Clinton administration changed many of the people in key offices through new appointments, this cautious policy remained in place.

The Clinton Team

The 'changing of the guard' in the State Department in late January 1993 was marked by a different substance and style in foreign-policy prophesies. There is reason to believe that this new style of the Clinton appointees was more in line with the career officials at the State Department.[9] In contrast to Eagleburger's final address as Secretary of State – where he made only a passing reference to peacekeeping – the incoming Secretary indicated his belief that peacekeeping was capable of being a key foreign-policy tool for the United States.[10]

During his confirmation hearing, Warren Christopher acknowledged the 'paradox' facing the United States in the post-Cold War period; although the Soviet Union had disappeared as a likely threat, the physical demands on the US military were increasing.[11] These demands, often in the shape of numerous conflicts and crises around the world, caused an increase in global instability. While Christopher recognized the US as the main 'ballast' in the world, he stated his intention to follow a policy designed to share, as much as possible, this burden with other countries through collective arrangements. Central to his notion of 'burden sharing' was the United Nations and its role as the chief global collective security organization. He did not, however, reject the option of unilateral action and made this clear by saying that the foreign policy motto for the new administration was 'Together when we can; on our own where we must.'[12] Christopher's designated deputy at the New York Mission, Madeleine Albright, echoed this position during her confirmation hearings a few days later, leaving the impression that the United Nations was to be a key forum of activity for the United States.[13] In addition, Clinton's decision to return Albright's office to Cabinet standing only emphasized this impression.

The shape of the new administration's policy had begun to come into focus by February 1993, as State Department officials briefed Congress on the transition plans for the Somali mission as the UNITAF operation came to a close. Foreshadowing the Chapter VII mandate of the follow-on UN mission, State Department officer Robert Houdek outlined the various roles and functions of the proposed UNOSOM II, and declared that the US would support this operation by paying its peacekeeping assessment and with a sizeable number of logistical troops under the control of the UN commander.[14] More importantly, Houdek discussed the 'nation-building' objectives of the UN force. As he put it:

> We are moving to a new phase of our efforts in Somalia – from
> UNITAF to UNOSOM; from the job of re-establishing a secure
> environment to getting relief supplies to the most needy to the
> challenge of consolidating security gains and promoting political
> reconciliation and rehabilitation.[15]

This view was reiterated a number of times by Houdek's colleagues in the
days leading up to the adoption of Resolution 814 by the Security Council
on 23 March 1993.[16] During the Council's session after the adoption of this
resolution, the State Department's position was enthusiastically publicized
by Ambassador Albright herself, when she stated:

> By adopting this resolution, we will embark on an unprecedented
> enterprise aimed at nothing less than the restoration of an entire
> country as a proud, functioning and viable member of the com-
> munity of nations. This is an historic undertaking. We are excited
> to join it and we will vigorously support it.[17]

After being in office for only two months, the more proactive multilateral
policy of the State Department's chief officials seemed to be progressing as
planned.[18] The transition from UNITAF to UNOSOM II was completed by
4 May 1993 and as promised, the US did leave roughly 4,000 logistical troops
and their equipment under UN command. In addition, a 1,300-strong quick-
reaction force (QRF) was stationed off-shore as a security precaution for the
UN force, but under US command.

   The position and posture of the State Department's policy in Somalia
experienced a significant evolution during the early summer of 1993, largely
a result of increasingly bloody and defiant attacks on the UN force, like the
lethal ambush of a UN patrol on 5 June, which left 23 Pakistani soldiers dead.
These hostile actions were alleged to be the work of the SNA, under General
Aideed, and the UN responded with Resolution 837, which called for the
arrest of those responsible. The US firmly supported this more aggressive
course of action citing it as a 'necessary and appropriate' response. Some two
months later, the State Department was still strongly endorsing the Council's
actions on the grounds that UNOSOM II should not be undermined by the
actions of one group because it would send Somalia back into chaos and be
a humiliation for the UN and the US and their peace-enforcement efforts.[19]

   Perhaps not surprisingly, the policy shift in the Security Council was
accompanied by a new tone at the State Department. During congressional
testimony, two weeks after the ambush of the Pakistani patrol, Ambassador
Albright put forth the notion of 'assertive multilateralism'.[20] By this she

claimed that the United States had to enhance its foreign policy through multilateral forums, and that the State Department's intent was to ensure that those forums, particularly the UN, were sufficiently strengthened to carry out these policy goals. It can be argued that the actions carried out under Resolution 837 were an example of the US acting out 'assertive multi-lateralism' through the United Nations.

Second Thoughts

In mid-July, a draft of the peacekeeping review directive was leaked to the press, causing a political storm in Washington.[21] The complaints came largely from Congress over the intention of the drafters to permit US troops to serve under UN control, and the apparent acceptance of an increase in peace-keeping costs. As mentioned in Chapter 2, this draft was reworked at least twice between mid-July and early September. Despite the revisions ongoing with the policy review process, Albright continued to help craft ambitious resolutions regarding Somalia, especially Resolution 865, which reaffirmed the 'nation-building' objectives of UNOSOM II.

By mid-September, the press was reporting that the drafting committee had presented the latest revisions to the Cabinet-level officials, only to have some, like Secretary Christopher, become personally involved in the rewriting of especially sensitive sections. One writer has noted that Christopher wanted direct control over the criteria to determine whether US troops would be deployed in support of a peace operation.[22] Publicly, State Department officials made a series of speeches during which they gave careful observers a glimpse of the 'rethink' underway behind the scenes, and a taste of what President Clinton would present to the United Nations General Assembly at the end of the month. The most elaborate and revealing statement was provided by Ambassador Albright in her address to the National War College on 23 September 1993.[23] She used this opportunity to convey the views of the State Department on how, when and why the United States should use its military forces. Four goals were identified as elements of the overall objective of enlarging the community of democratic, free-market states. Within this strategic context, Albright claimed that peace-keeping, 'at its best ... can be very effective', but it was no substitute 'for fighting and winning our own wars'. She went on to outline a series of questions which she claimed must be asked if the efficiency and usefulness of peacekeeping was to improve. Moreover, the framework of the questions would be applied on a 'case-by-case basis'.[24] The questions were strict in tone and represented a sharp tangent from the Ambassador's earlier comments, leading many observers to conclude that the State Department was creating a great deal of distance between itself and the doctrine of assertive multilateralism.

The deaths of 18 Rangers in Mogadishu seemed to make the break with assertive multilateralism complete. Secretary Christopher, speaking to reporters after Clinton's address to the nation on 7 October, lamented UNOSOM II's drift away from the search for a political solution with Aideed in favour of a military approach.[25] He also made the point, explicitly, that the US strategy would now be a purely diplomatic one, and that the State Department was hoping to enlist a number of African leaders, to help find an African solution to an *African problem* [emphasis added].[26] Two weeks after this press conference, Albright appeared before a Congressional committee to defend her votes in the Security Council. She claimed that while the principles of the resolution authorizing the arrest of Aideed were correct, 'some serious problems did arise in the course of its implementation'.[27] Furthermore, she told the committee members that the government realized in late August that the Somali operation had become too dependent on military force for results, at the expense of the political track. She claimed that the administration's tactics were adjusting to a more political approach in September, 'but it took the shock of 3 October to turn the train completely around'.[28] After doing her best to disown these policies, she outlined the same guidelines and questions to be consulted when the government was contemplating the use of force as she had presented to the National War College in September. Following this, she stressed the importance of a consensus on peacekeeping between the Executive and Congress, and that it was essential 'to re-establish that consensus' so that a more 'politically sustainable policy' could be pursued.[29] In the wake of these speeches, peacekeeping fell from the top of the State Department agenda, as the bureaucracy continued its role in the policy-review process and waited for the 31 March 1994 withdrawal date from Somalia.[30]

The Release of PDD 25

For those keeping track of the State Department's peacekeeping position, which had been evolving over the previous 14 months, the tone, spirit and contents of PDD 25 came as no surprise. Ambassador Albright tried to put the best spin possible on the new policy, in her declaration that it '… is not intended to expand UN peacekeeping but to help fix it'.[31] With this in mind, she again listed the types of questions she would be asking of the Secretariat and other Security Council members when the launching of a peace operation was being considered. PDD 25, however, presented these questions in a hierarchical fashion.[32] The terms of the Directive were very restrictive in relation to the Ambassador's statements on peace operations in early 1993, and it gave the impression that the State Department was attempting to de-emphasize the importance of peacekeeping, in particular, but also perhaps, multilateralism in general, to US foreign policy. Albright went on to say that the UN's success would be judged not by the number of missions operating around the world, but rather by their quality.[33]

Later that month, the spirit of PDD 25 was evident in the Security Council when Albright's deputy, Ambassador Edward W. Gnehm, argued for the United Nations to be careful about wasting any more time in Somalia. The Council had just extended UNOSOM II's mandate by another four months, and Gnehm stated that the parties to the civil war must show the desire for a peaceful, political settlement, or be faced with a UN withdrawal.

> The restoration of normality in Somalia is primarily a job for the Somalis themselves. Outsiders, including the United States, remain willing to help Somalia, but it is up to the Somalis themselves to make the difficult decisions needed to bring about political reconciliation. ... Absent unambiguous indications to the contrary, the international community is not prepared to continue helping people who seem unwilling to help themselves.[34]

THE DEPARTMENT OF DEFENSE

Of all the factors influencing American views on military interventions during the 1970s and 1980s, few were as persuasive as the Pentagon. Their reluctance to be involved in any more open-ended, ambiguous missions, with little relevance to America's vital interests, was evident after coming out of the Vietnam War. The Weinberger Doctrine (later referred to as the Weinberger–Powell Doctrine) translated these reservations into a list of criteria that should be considered before deploying US troops abroad.[35] This list proved to contain the guiding principles for the use of US military interventions for a number of years, and was put into practice on at least two occasions: the invasion of Panama and Operation Desert Storm. As was discussed earlier, the substance of the Weinberger–Powell Doctrine was not terribly compatible with traditional UN peacekeeping doctrine.[36] Adding to this issue of very different approaches to military interventions, was the lack of peacekeeping experience stemming from the fact that the US had never contributed ground troops to UN missions; only observers, logistic and communication support and financing. This limited involvement in peace operations would eventually change with missions such as those to Macedonia and Somalia.

Operation Restore Hope

In the early stages of inter-agency discussions on the growing disaster in Somalia, most proposals were limited and cautious in nature. Hirsch and Oakley argue that this was largely the result of the Pentagon resisting the ambitious inclinations of the civilians at the State Department and the National Security Council (NSC). From the Pentagon's perspective, the idea of assisting a humanitarian relief mission was not problematic in itself, but the State Department and NSC's lack of a clear mission statement for the relief operation made the Joint Chiefs and senior defence officials very wary that they were being asked 'to fix the civil war'.[37]

The Defense Department began to take a leading role in the policy process on Somalia in the autumn of 1992 by drafting proposals instead of just receiving and reacting to them. This more active position came about after DoD recognized that the recently approved airlift (which the Pentagon was required to fund) would never make a dent in the famine, and that the small security force authorized by the Security Council could not possibly provide the level of security needed at the storage facilities, much less in the hardest hit rural areas. To be effective, a more forceful approach was needed. Apparently, the lead military official pushing this option was the Chairman of the Joint Chiefs, General Colin Powell himself, and he instructed Central Command in Florida to prepare a mission statement and plans for a large-scale US intervention in Somalia.[38] True to the form of the Weinberger–Powell doctrine of military interventions, Operation Restore Hope was a powerful armed force with a specific objective, and a reluctance to carry out any tasks which might drag the operation into the internal politics of the crisis. The one element missing was the motivation of national interests for the operation. This, however, was the responsibility of the political leadership to determine, and then explain to the country.

Near the end of the Bush administration, the issue of US participation in UN-controlled peace operations became a serious agenda item for the first time, because of the prospects of US troops remaining in Somalia after UNOSOM II assumed command of the operation. To the surprise of many observers, the DoD signalled a new direction in US peacekeeping policy during the press conference following President Bush's announcement that the US would lead UNITAF. At this briefing, Secretary of Defense Cheney and General Powell outlined the roles of US forces during the UNOSOM II phase, where some would remain under UN control. The implications of this briefing were very significant:

> Although it went largely unnoticed at the time, the briefing made explicit a major change in US policy toward UN peacekeeping.

... Cheney and Powell clearly stated their readiness for US forces
to serve as full members of the UN peacekeeping force that they
expected would follow the US-led coalition.[39]

With a change in government due just six weeks later, the Pentagon indicated
that a new flexibility, unthinkable just months earlier, might exist among the
military's leadership. It should be noted that this particular press conference
did not indicate the abandonment of the Weinberger–Powell Doctrine. As
they explained their plan, it was still obvious that the initial phase of the
operation (the most dangerous in their eyes) would be US-led, meaning US
troops under direct US control. Furthermore, the prospect of a large
contingent of US troops under UN command did not suggest an erosion of
Weinberger's views in DoD because the Doctrine did not address that specific
issue. Nevertheless, this willingness to show some flexibility and become a
potential contributor to UN missions, albeit a contributor of mostly support
troops, was very much in line with the publicly known views of the incoming
Secretary of Defense, Les Aspin, and other Clintonites.

IMPACT OF THE NEW ADMINISTRATION

Roughly six weeks before the presidential election in November 1992, Les
Aspin, Chairman of the Armed Services Committee, delivered a speech
expressing his difficulties in accepting the Weinberger–Powell Doctrine as
the sole determinant of when to use force in the post-Cold War period.[40]
Aspin did not present his own check-list on when or when not to use force
but rather argued that the 'all or nothing' approach of the Powell school of
thought was too rigid for the new international system. He claimed that
military leaders like Powell had feared escalation in a local conflict leading
to a confrontation with the Soviets. This fear was no longer justified, according to Aspin, because the Soviets no longer existed as a military rival to the
United States. In the light of this development, Aspin offered the 'limited
objective' school of thought, as championed by British Prime Minister,
Margaret Thatcher. In this case, Aspin told his audience that air-power-
derived compellence was at the 'heart' of the limited-school objectives, and
that recent technological advances, coupled with America's air superiority made
this sort of intervention even more possible for the United States. While his
address did not contain any reference to peacekeeping *per se*, Aspin clearly
came out in favour of redefining the Pentagon's doctrine on interventions. His
views were to carry a great deal of importance just weeks later, as it became
clear that he would be the new secretary of defence in the Clinton administration.

Taking a cue from his future boss, General Colin Powell published an article in *Foreign Affairs* just three months after the Aspin speech in which he discussed the future roles and challenges awaiting the US military.[41] He acknowledged the changes in the world, as pointed out by Aspin, and shared Aspin's conclusions that the new situation required some new thinking on how to use the military. Unlike Aspin, however, Powell dealt very directly with the peacekeeping issue: 'What sorts of missions can we envision? I believe peacekeeping and humanitarian operations are a given. Likewise our forward presence is a given – to signal our commitment to our allies and to give second thoughts to any disturber of peace.'[42] Even while keeping these remarks within the overall context of the US military's primary mission being to fight and win the country's wars (a point repeatedly made by General Powell), it appears that the change in thinking that Aspin proposed was already well underway before the new administration took office. With this article, Powell had gone on the record on two separate occasions in favour of an expanded peacekeeping role for the US armed forces, before the end of 1992.

As UNITAF evolved, the Pentagon assumed a very supportive position on leading peace operations, and was seriously considering the placement of its forces under UN command. This position remains the same today, some six years later. While the operation in Somalia unfolded, and experienced a number of setbacks, the Pentagon leadership did not balk at the peacekeeping role. Even as the number of causalities began to increase, Pentagon officials did not alter their policy.[43] This long-term commitment to peacekeeping is reflected in a number of DoD documents, which provide the practical guidelines for commanders in the field, and the strategic reasoning supporting US participation in such missions.[44]

From this brief review of DoD's perspective, it appears as though the leadership at the Pentagon, both military and civilian, has supported and adopted the Aspin argument that the doctrine of 'all or nothing' is liable to leave the United States in the position of having to choose between not acting, or acting alone. Both of these options, however, entail a number of possible problems and costs. By not responding to breaches of the peace or huge humanitarian disasters, the Pentagon risked allowing a sense of anarchy and chaos to arise and facilitate the possibility of small conflicts spreading and growing into larger regional crises. If the US must organize an *ad hoc* coalition or go it alone each time it wants to act, the costs in terms of lives, national treasure, and political capital may prove too high to conduct these operations on a regular basis. Recognizing this situation, it is not surprising that the DoD has been pursuing a pro-peacekeeping policy, relatively speaking, since 1992.

Although the top ranks in the Pentagon are behind the peacekeeping policy, it cannot be assumed that the lower ranks, or those outside the Pentagon's E-Ring, are necessarily falling in line. At the risk of over-simplifying, the US officer core can be divided into two general groups on this issue: 1) those who feel that most, if not all, peace operations threaten the military's readiness by diverting attention and resources from the primary *raison d'être* of the military – fighting and winning wars;[45] and 2) those who believe that peace operations are a good investment in the sense that they might prevent a crisis from growing into a more costly conflict, provided that the readiness of the forces is not adversely affected.[46] Readiness, it must be remembered, is not only conceived in terms of posture or attitude but also in terms of resources, or in this case, dwindling resources. Many officers who consider themselves to be in the former group point to the cost of conducting peace operations as a diversion of funds from other programmes. One senior officer, however, has countered this claim, by pointing out that many middle-level officers (who have a number of years left in the service) consider the peace operations as a future role which can be used by the Pentagon to slow or halt the steep, post-Cold War budget cuts.[47] The differences of opinion might never be settled but, for now, Colonel Seitz seems to represent the prevailing attitude when he writes:

> The United States military clearly understands that peacekeeping and peace operations are important missions for our nations. We have supported them in the past and we'll continue to support the growing commitment the United States is making to the United Nations to the extent that our national command authorities direct us. However, we must remember that you can use the word peace, and as a title it's very benign. It is easy to slip from being peacekeepers to entering an armed conflict without a conscious directive from the US executive or legislative branches, or the American people.[48]

PERENNIAL CONCERNS

Unlike their counterparts in the State Department, Pentagon officials have a particular set of concerns, or dilemmas, which they have identified as inherent in peace operations. These concerns are not to be confused with the other lists of criteria found in the various doctrines. These are issues which come into play after the decision to launch a mission has been approved, and will affect the outcome of the mission and the character of the forces involved after the force is withdrawn. Colonel Seitz alluded to one concern in the last sentence of the above passage, but Les Aspin provided a full explanation of these concerns in a speech delivered after he left the post of Defense Secretary.[49] First, the former Secretary said that the political leaders must understand that the mandate must match the conditions on the ground. People who are trained to be soldiers, are then told to be police officers and are retrained for that role. But if the circumstances on the ground change, without a parallel shift in the mandate, it is up to the individuals to determine when they are to react as police officers and when as soldiers. Aspin stresses that this is a terribly dangerous situation.

Second, this mandate issue leads to a need for training and retraining units detailed to a peace operation. Each unit sent on a peacekeeping mission must be trained for a number of months on how to perform police duties; it is then deployed, then retrained for an equal amount of time – after its tour of duty – on how to be a fighting unit once more. So, for every unit on a peace mission, two more are either preparing to replace that unit, or are in the process of being retrained to return to regular military duties. This strain on manpower is often overlooked in the media but it was the source of some tension between the two groups representing the Pentagon in the drafting review. According to officials present at these meetings, there was a difference of opinion evident between the Office of the Secretary of Defense (OSD) and the Joint Chiefs (JCS) on the matter of training.[50] OSD was in favour of specialized training for US personnel, beyond what was then under consideration. For its part, the JCS representative maintained that heavily armed, highly capable soldiers made the best peacekeepers, even for Chapter VI-mandated missions. As such, the JCS believed that the current levels of training were more than sufficient, further increases in peacekeeping curriculum would have an adverse effect on combat readiness, and this, as mentioned above, was already a sensitive issue for many in the officer corps.

Third, Aspin voiced the concern of the military that the political leadership is overly influenced and guided by the 'CNN factor'. Politicians, so the argument goes, rush troops into a crisis situation because of a public outcry, only to pull them out before the objective is secured because the public 'changes its mind' if the mission takes longer than expected or encounters some unforeseen problems which lead to causalities. This has the negative effect of sending wrong signals to allies and potential foes alike because American resolve is questioned each time the military is employed and then recalled as a result of reactionary policies driven by the media and short-term public opinion. Against the backdrop of operations in Somalia, this concern must have taken on a new urgency within the officer ranks. The message Aspin wanted to stress was that regardless of how tight, or loose, the policy is concerning peacekeeping, these concerns will always be found among military officers.

BUREAUCRACY INTERACTION

With pressure mounting to take decisive action in Somalia, the two bureaucracies proved their ability to work together to get a mission off the ground, and achieved the immediate goal of saving thousands from starvation. The next challenge was to devise a policy for conducting operations of this sort in a more organized manner and, much like the UN, the American government's approach to Somalia was very *ad hoc*. The State Department and the Pentagon both indicated in late 1992 their seriousness as participants about engaging in peacekeeping, above and beyond being the primary financial and logistical supporters. The actual terms of defining when and how the US would support or join such operations appears to have fallen to the State Department and the NSC. With the 'all-or-nothing' Powell school under reconsideration, the DoD left it largely up to the political officials at the State Department and the NSC to craft these guidelines. The positions staked out early in the drafting process were very progressive by American standards, and as such were viewed as examples of what a policy of 'assertive multi-lateralism' might look like in practice.[51] Many of these earlier proposals were concerned with the measures at the operational level, and in this area, the Pentagon had some significant reservations.

From the perspective of one DoD official, the Pentagon was not fully involved with the review process until July 1993 for a number of reasons, including the lack of knowledgeable staff and a general reluctance to get involved in what was considered to be largely a political exercise. The draft which was circulated in mid-1993 and was eventually leaked to the press in July caused this aloof posture to disappear. The reason was simple. The draft contained a number of provisions deemed 'radical' by both the OSD and the JCS. Foremost among these for the JCS was a call for the US military to earmark units for duty with UN forces. The JCS were prepared to provide information of potential resources for UN service to a UN database, but the specific designation of units was out of the question for training and readiness concerns. For the OSD, one of the most alarming aspects of this early draft was the total lack of any satisfactory funding arrangements. These issues, and others, caused an uproar in the Pentagon to the point that one officer speculated that the press came into possession of a copy of the draft courtesy of a DoD official hoping to draw Congressional attention to some of the proposals contained therein.[52]

If this was indeed the perpetrator's intention, it was successful. Congressional opposition to the terms of the draft was immediate and strong, thereby forcing the drafting committee to rewrite a number of key sections. By mid-July, State Department officials were continuing to voice support for assertive multilateralism, but significant revisions were going on behind the scenes. The public got its first hint of the internal revisions in speeches by Clinton, Christopher, Lake and Albright in late September. It was becoming apparent by this early date that assertive multilateralism was to be shortlived as official policy. The deaths of 18 Rangers in Mogadishu, which more than doubled the number of American combat fatalities thus far in Somalia, made the policy reversal complete. Peacekeeping virtually fell off the State Department agenda as a general policy question during the winter of 1993/94 (to the point that one official lamented the difficulty in keeping people's attention on the issue), and resurfaced in the form of the final PDD 25 in May 1994. By this point it was clear that the State Department did not consider peace-enforcement missions, or anything authorized under Chapter VII for that matter, a viable policy option if missions had to satisfy the ascending scale of questions and criteria.

The DoD, on the other hand, did not appear to go through such a dramatic policy shift as the State Department. One reason for this might be that Powell and Cheney did not send the Pentagon on such a far-reaching peacekeeping reform programme. In late 1992, they opened up the idea of a serious rethink concerning possible future US troops contribution to peace operations but nothing was explored in a very serious manner. Aspin, upon replacing Cheney, was given the chance to see his views expanded into government policy, but it was soon apparent that he had a different set of priorities than either the State Department or the NSC. As discussed above, the earlier draft of the Directive proved to be a wake-up call for DoD that it had 'to get smart' on peacekeeping issues before the State Department and NSC imposed their vision on the Pentagon. The first order of business was overcoming the Department's lack of an institutional memory. Due to the Pentagon's limited direct experience with UN peacekeeping, there was a very small number of people in DoD with any expertise in this area; in 1993 there were only seven people working on peacekeeping issues for the JCS. As the Department got up to speed on the issues being considered by the drafting committee, it identified four priority items. First was to ensure the Pentagon enjoyed total authority over the drafting of the command and control aspects of the Directive. Second, DoD wanted to squash any notions of earmarking units for UN use, as highlighted above. And third, the Pentagon became concerned that the contents of the earlier draft indicated a desire to deploy forces much too quickly and without enough thought to the full purpose of the mission.

Therefore, it was decided to make every effort to include as many, if not all, of the six Weinberger principles as possible. Finally, OSD was determined to secure a reasonable and workable funding arrangement. The current situation was the source of much friction between the State Department and DoD and definitely in need of a substantial overhaul.[53]

As DoD became more engaged in the process it was immediately given full sway over the command and control issues. The JCS was given the task of drafting these provisions and the responsibility never left the hands of its representatives. At the outset it took a very rigid position, in traditional peacekeeping terms, in that it called for a provision allowing US field commanders to disobey UN commands if the orders were deemed to be unsound or exposed the troops to undue risk. This demand ran into serious opposition from the NSC and the State Department because of the extremely dangerous precedent it would set. This provision was eventually struck out by Powell himself, because he was persuaded that it would deliver a fatal blow to the whole notion of UN command and control if other countries followed the US lead. The Chairman was no doubt aware, however, that US commanders would almost certainly have access to a parallel chain of command back to the Pentagon, outside of any UN arrangement.[54] Once this debate was settled, the command and control provisions remained virtually unchanged until the Directive was signed some eight months later.

The second concern for the Pentagon was mentioned briefly earlier, namely, the Pentagon's leadership was never keen on Clinton's interests in earmarking units for UN duty, a topic which was raised in one of the early drafts. In August, the Pentagon did manage to remove the provisions calling for the earmarking of units for UN service.[55] The JCS argued that it would be a permanent drain on resources if specific units were taken out of active duty for possible UN service, especially in the light of the stated military strategy to fight and win two nearly simultaneous regional conflicts which would require maximum air- and sea-lift capabilities. In addition, it made little military sense to advertise to possible opponents which units they might face in the case of an intervention (this type of argument certainly illustrates the lack of a peacekeeping culture). Finally, DoD officials pointed out that the US was not alone in its opposition to this practice as very few member states earmark units for potential use by the UN.

With regard to the third area of concern, the inclusion of the Weinberger Doctrine, the DoD team was equally successful. If one compares the six points of the Doctrine with the Directive, it becomes clear that those six points have been woven into the policy. The stress on determining political objectives and pursuing those objectives with sufficient force are just two examples of Weinberger's mark on PDD 25, almost ten years later. While it is perhaps natural to interpret this move as a sign of resistance on the part of the JCS to being involved in peace operations, this is apparently not the case. According to an officer who dealt with these issues, the JCS wanted some safety net built into the policy which would reduce the risk of overcommitting increasingly scarce resources. The uniformed members of DoD were not afraid to contribute to such missions, they just wanted to ensure they would not be asked to 'fix' every crisis which erupted around the globe with little forethought as to the objectives and how to conclude the mission.[56] Weinberger's six points were the most convenient means to that end. As soon as these three issues were addressed to the Pentagon's satisfaction, the committee members turned their attention to the major issue which caused most of the difficulties: who was to pay the bills.

According to at least one report, the policy directive was mostly in place by November 1993, after the serious revisions of that summer and in October. The principal reason why the document was not presented to President Clinton for another seven months involved a 'turf war' between the State Department and DoD.[57] This issue was certain to be central to any peacekeeping policy formulation because it had been a source of tension between the two departments for many years. Before the Directive was signed there was no clear policy on how to spread the costs within the federal budget. Usually, the State Department approved a mission in New York, and DoD would be asked to provide some sort of support at its own cost, but these charges were not usually reimbursed. During the operation on the Iraq–Iran border in the late 1980s, for instance, the State Department managed to get any charges for services provided by DoD credited towards the US-assessed peacekeeping bills, which is a State Department account, but State did not, in turn, reimburse the Pentagon.[58] Not surprisingly, DoD was not happy with this arrangement and used the policy review to formalize the funding procedures.

Apparently, these negotiations required a number of months as each side was reluctant to be seen as losing ground to a rival. Since money was at the heart of the issue, policy control was a related factor: the department which controls the money, controls the policy. Under the existing system, DoD was paying for operations which were voted for, then controlled by the State Department through its Mission to the UN in New York. From the viewpoint of State, conversely, if DoD was given control over peacekeeping policy it would become the *de facto* source for most UN policy, which would constitute a forfeiture of authority and jurisdiction by the State Department. Nevertheless, an agreement eventually took shape in the form of an NSC idea called 'Shared Responsibility'. This formula stipulated that operations authorized under Chapter VI would be the responsibility of the State Department and those with a Chapter VII mandate (potential for combat), or any mission in which US troops participated, would be placed under the authority of DoD in terms of funding and control. Ostensibly, the plan was designed to allow the two departments to take the lead planning and funding responsibilities for missions which could benefit from the particular expertise of each bureaucracy. In reality though, staff members claim that 'Shared Responsibility' was intended to permit funding for peacekeeping bills from the larger DoD budget and relieve some pressure on State's budget. The fact that the two principals involved in the funding debate had finally come to a mutually satisfactory conclusion, giving the appearance that a major 'turf battle' had been settled, would provide a false sense of achievement. The anticipated solution contained a fundamental flaw: the DoD budget contained no provisions for supporting UN operations, meaning that a new account would have to be added to the Pentagon's budget. Convincing Congress that this was the way to go was to be an uphill, if not impossible, battle. The role of Congress in killing this provision will be discussed further in the next chapter, but for now it is interesting to note that 'Shared Responsibility' remained in the draft when it was signed by President Clinton in May 1994, perhaps just for the sake of appearances. In presenting the new policy to the public, both departments expressed their satisfaction with the end product and appeared confident that the funding and management arrangements would function.[59] Whatever their statements at the time, it was clear that 'Shared Responsibility' was a stillborn solution to a problem which exists to this day for the Pentagon and the State Department.

There is little doubt that the final version was considerably more limited in scope than many of the officials had originally expected to craft. In spite of its earlier designs, the US government was now embarking on a much more restricted peacekeeping policy than was proposed in July 1993.

NOTES

1. A concise case for the different roles of bureaucracies is made in Roger Hilsman, with Laura Gaughran and Patricia A. Weitsman, in *The Politics of Policy Making in Defense and Foreign Affairs: Conceptual Models and Bureaucratic Politics*, Third Edition, Englewood Cliffs NJ: Prentice Hall, 1993, Ch.13, in particular, pp.208–11.
2. For the text of this testimony see John R. Bolton (Assistant Secretary for International Organization Affairs), 'FY 1992 Budget Requests For International Organizations', Statement before the Subcommittees on International Operations and on Human Rights and International Organizations of the House Foreign Affairs Committee, 5 March 1991, reprinted in *US Department of State Dispatch*, 11 March 1991, pp.172–4.
3. The other two goals of the strategy were, 1) to establish a new sense of responsibility at the UN and do away with 'the rhetorical excesses and politicization that had little to do

with developments in the real world'; and 2) to promote a new style of diplomatic activity through a 'Unitary UN'. This plan of action is interesting because it predates Bush's 'new world order' speeches by more than a year, and he could have pointed to these objectives as practical means to his envisioned end. See Bolton (n.2 above).

4. This passage is found in, United Nations Document Provisional Verbatim, S/PV.3060, United States Representative Watson's statement to the Security Council, 17 March 1992, pp.49–50.

5. See ibid, p.50.

6. The Charter of the United Nations contains two chapters dealing with the types of actions the Organization is able to take. Chapter VI deals with the 'Pacific Settlement of Disputes', and the measures laid out for the UN in this chapter require the consent of the parties involved. Chapter VII, 'Actions With Respect to Threats to the Peace, Breaches of the Peace, and Acts of Aggression', on the other hand, contains provisions enabling the Organization to implement the decisions of the Security Council, by force if necessary, to restore the peace. Refer to the Charter of the United Nations for the specific terms of the Articles of each Chapter.

7. This view was implied during the testimony of Asst Secretary Bolton, when he commented in March 1992, that UN missions 'have saved countless lives, and cost much less than direct US involvement'. See John R. Bolton, 'UN Peace-keeping Efforts to Promote Security and Stability', Excerpts from a statement before the Subcommittee on International Operations, Human Rights and International Organizations of the House Foreign Affairs Committee, 25 March 1992, reprinted in *US Department of State Dispatch*, 30 March 1992, p.244 for these remarks.

8. For their account of State's early positions see John L. Hirsch and Robert B. Oakley, *Somalia and Operation Restore Hope: Reflections on Peacemaking and Peacekeeping*, Washington DC: United States Institute of Peace Press, 1995, pp.36–9.

9. In his account of the decisionmaking process leading up to UNITAF's deployment, former Bush Administration official John Bolton refers to the more proactive arguments put forth by 'State Department careerists' implying a difference in perspectives between the careerists and the political appointees. See John R. Bolton, 'Wrong Turn in Somalia', *Foreign Affairs*, Vol.73, No.1, Jan./Feb. 1994, p.58.

10. See Acting Secretary of State Lawrence Eagleburger, 'Charting the Course: US Foreign Policy in a Time of Transition', Address before the Council on Foreign Relations, Washington DC, 7 Jan. 1993, reprinted in *US Department of State Dispatch*, Vol.4, No.2, 11 Jan. 1993, pp.16–19 for the text of this speech. He referred to peacekeeping only once in a lengthy, keynote speech, and that it was simply an issue the incoming administration was going to have to develop.

11. The text of the speech is found in, Secretary-Designate Warren Christopher, 'Statement at Senate Confirmation Hearing', Statement before the Senate Foreign Relations Committee, 13 Jan. 1993, reprinted in *US Department of State Dispatch*, Vol.4, No.4, 25 Jan. 1993, pp.45–9.

12. This motto and his remarks dealing with collective action through the UN and other organizations are found in ibid, p.47.

13. See Ambassador Madeleine K. Albright (United States Permanent Representative to the United Nations-Designate), Confirmation Hearing Statement before the Senate Foreign Relations Committee, 21 Jan. 1993, reprinted in the *US Department of State Dispatch*, Vol.4, No.15, 12 April 1993, pp.229–31, for the text of this speech.

14. See Robert Houdek (Deputy Assistant Secretary of African Affairs), 'Update on Progress

in Somalia', Statement before the Subcommittee on Africa of the House Foreign Affairs Committee, 17 Feb. 1993, reprinted in *US Department of State Dispatch*, Vol.4, No.8, 22 Feb. 1993, pp.99–101.

15. See ibid, p.100.

16. For example see Ambassador Madeleine K. Albright (US Permanent Representative to the UN), 'Current Status of US Policy on Bosnia, Somalia, and UN Reform', Statement before the Subcommittee on Foreign Operations, Export Financing, and Related Programs of the House Appropriations Committee, 12 March 1993, reprinted in *US Department of State Dispatch*, Vol.4, No.4, 5 April 1993, pp.207–11, and in particular, pp.209–10. In this testimony, Albright describes the proposed size, objectives and structure of UNOSOM II, and notes, that as of 12 March seven US soldiers had been killed during the UNITAF operation. She also draws the Committee's attention to the report of the Secretary-General of 3 March which contains the transition plan from UNITAF to UNOSOM, and that the plan's 'thrust is consistent with what we have been planning ... since Operation Restore Hope was launched last December'. In other words, the policy of shifting to a Chapter VII, 'nation-building' mandate had been part of the State Department's thinking before Clinton took office. See Houdek (n.14 above), p.209.

17. See United Nations Document, Provisional Verbatim, S/PV.3188, United States Ambassador Albright's statement to the Security Council, 26 March 1993, pp.18–19, for the text of this statement.

18. While the policy was being implemented, one senior State Department official gave an interview to a group of reporters in which he offered a reason for the new proactive multilateral policy, one not previously suggested by his superiors. Under-Secretary Peter Tarnoff, in May 1993, claimed that the US no longer had the resources to effectively influence events around the world, and would increasingly save its capabilities for vital interests only, leaving most other issues to allies, regional powers, or the UN. While this may have been, in fact, one of the motivations for the new multilaterally inclined policy of the State Department, Tarnoff's views were quickly dismissed by Secretary Christopher and Albright during the following weeks, as they tried to assure the international community that the US was committed to remaining actively engaged in its leadership role. This incident, however, hints at a divergence within State: the staff all considered multilateralism a worthy objective, but for some it was a more economical method to lead, while for others, it was a way to shrug off the burden of leadership. For further accounts of the 'Tarnoff Doctrine', see Mark M. Lowenthal, *Peacekeeping in Future US Foreign Policy*, CRS 94-260 S, Washington DC: Congressional Research Service, Update 10 May 1994, pp.5–6; William Lewis, 'The UN System and the United States: A Background Study', in Thomas J. Ward, Frederick A. Swarts and Alan Thibideau (eds), *The 104th Congress & The United Nations: Understanding the Issues*, New York: American Leadership Conference, Washington Times Foundation and the World Leadership Conference, 1996, pp.7–8; and Charles William Maynes, 'A Workable Clinton Doctrine', *Foreign Policy*, No.93, Winter 93/94, p.4.

19. For the characterizations 'necessary and appropriate', and other reasons for the more aggressive UN stance in Somalia, see Peter Tarnoff (Under-Secretary of State for Political Affairs), 'US Policy in Somalia', Statement before the Senate Foreign Relations Committee, 29 July 1993, reprinted in *US Department of State Dispatch*, Vol.4, No.32, 9 Aug. 1993, pp.567–8.

20. The text of this testimony can be found under Ambassador Madeleine K. Albright, 'Myths of Peacekeeping', Statement before the Subcommittee on International Security,

International Organizations, and Human Rights of the House Committee on Foreign Affairs, 24 June 1993, reprinted in *US Department of State Dispatch*, Vol.4, No.26, 28 June 1993, pp.464–7. Also reproduced in Annex 4.

21. See Mark M. Lowenthal, *Peacekeeping in Future US Foreign Policy*, CRS 94-260 S, Washington DC: Congressional Research Service, Update 10 May 1994, p.6.

22. See ibid.

23. For the text of this address, see Ambassador Madeleine K. Albright, 'Use of Force in a Post-Cold War World', Address at the National War College, National Defense University, Fort McNair, Washington DC, 23 Sept. 1993, reprinted in *US Department of State Dispatch*, Vol.4, No.39, 27 Sept. 1993, pp.665–8. Reproduced in Annex 5.

24. See ibid, pp.667–8.

25. For the text of the prepared statement presented during this press conference, see Secretary of State Christopher, Defense Secretary Aspin and Admiral Jeremiah, 'Remarks at White House press briefing', 7 Oct. 1993, reprinted in *US Department of State Dispatch*, Vol.4, No.42, 18 Oct. 1993, pp.715–16. These particular remarks are found on p.715.

26. See ibid. In particular, Christopher singled out Ethiopian President Meles as a central mediator for the State Department.

27. See Ambassador Madeleine K. Albright, 'Building a Consensus on International Peacekeeping', Statement before the Senate Foreign Relations Committee, 20 Oct. 1993, Federal Document Clearing House, Inc. 1993, Lexis/Nexis; also reprinted in *US Department of State Dispatch*, Vol.4, No.46, 15 Nov. 1993, pp.789–92. These comments are found on p.2 of the Lexis/Nexis version.

28. See ibid. Two weeks after Albright's testimony, Christopher spoke before the Senate Foreign Relations Committee, and expressed the same confidence regarding his department's corrected focus on the political track. See also Secretary Warren Christopher, 'Foreign Policy Review', Testimony before the Senate Foreign Relations Committee, 4 Nov. 1993, Federal Document Clearing House, Inc. 1993, Lexis/Nexis; also reprinted in *US Department of State Dispatch*, Vol.4, No.47, 23 Nov. 1993, pp.797–802.

29. See Albright (n.27 above), p.3 of Lexis/Nexis version.

30. This point was driven home by the fact that Secretary Christopher made no significant policy statements on peacekeeping until late Feb. 1994, during testimony before the Senate's Foreign Relations Committee. His comments were limited to the same basic thrust that had been repeated the previous September, October and early November. Moreover, his statement was concerned with the six strategic priorities for the State Department, and in sharp contrast to the 1993 priorities, peacekeeping was now portrayed as a secondary instrument of US foreign policy. Interestingly though, he did announce that the policy review had been completed, but it was not signed by Clinton for another two months. See Secretary of State Christopher, 'Foreign Policy Overview', Testimony before the Senate Foreign Relations Committee, 23 Feb. 1994, Federal Document Clearing House, Inc. 1994, Lexis/Nexis.

31. Albright's comments were made during testimony before a Congressional committee. See Ambassador Madeleine K. Albright, Testimony before the House Subcommittee on Appropriations for Foreign Operations, Export Financing and Related Programs, 5 May 1994, Federal Document Clearing House, Inc. 1994, Lexis/Nexis, p.1.

32. See Chapter 2 for a summary of the question and criteria scale, or PDD 25 in Annex 1. This organization of the criteria into an hierarchy of questions was first reported the previous September in Barton Gellman, 'US Reconsiders Putting GIs Under UN: Concern over Somalia and Bosnia Prompts Backlash in Congress', *Washington Post*, 22

Sept. 1993, p.A1, but instead of two tiers, was now expanded to three tiers.

33. Albright was quoted by a reporter as claiming PDD 25 was a success because of the number of missions which were blocked using the questions listed in the Directive. See Elaine Sciolino, 'New US Peacekeeping Policy De-emphasizes Role of the UN', *New York Times*, 6 May 1994, p.A2.

34. See United Nations Document, Provisional Verbatim, S/PV.3385, United States Representative Gnehm's statement to the Security Council, 31 May 1994, pp.9–10 for this passage.

35. See the discussion of the Weinberger Doctrine in Chapter 2 (along with the citations for the original speech of Nov. 1984) Or, see Annex 2.

36. See Chapter 2; and Theo Farrell, 'Sliding into War: The Somalia Imbroglio and US Army Peace Operations Doctrine', *International Peacekeeping*, Vol.2, No.2 (Summer 1995), particularly the account of the planning stages found on pp.198–9, and the impact of army doctrine in Somalia described on pp.203–8.

37. For this account of Pentagon thinking see Hirsch and Oakley (n.8 above), p.37.

38. This borrows from the Hirsch and Oakley record of events, found in ibid, pp.41–3. As the authors note, this represented 'a complete turnaround in Defense Department thinking from the middle of the year'. Yet in his memoires, Powell is unclear whether it was on his own initiative that he ordered General Hoar to devise a more muscular intervention in Somalia. He is clear, however, in saying he was not eager to get deeply involved in that imploding country, but supported the plan on humanitarian grounds. For Powell's recollections on the early stages of UNITAF, see Colin L. Powell with Joseph E. Persico, *My American Journey*, New York: Random House, 1995, pp.564–6.

39. See Hirsch and Oakley (n.8 above), p.46. Powell, it appears, was especially willing to reconsider the long-standing tradition of US troop non-involvement with UN-led peace operations in light of a *Time* article written in mid-1992. According to this piece, Powell was quoted as saying he would like to see the long-defunct Military Staff Committee (MSC) made 'more relevant' and appeared to the author as much more willing to consider placing US troops under the UN flag than many of his subordinates. See Strobe Talbott, 'America Abroad: Peacekeeping Loves Company', *Time* (US Edition), 18 May 1992, p.54.

40. See Les Aspin, 'The Use and Usefulness of Military Forces in the Post-Cold War, Post-Soviet World', address by Congressman Aspin (Chairman of the House Armed Services Committee), to the Jewish Institute for National Security Affairs, Washington DC, 21 Sept. 1992. Reprinted in Annex 3.

41. Refer to General Colin L. Powell, 'US Forces: The Challenges Ahead', *Foreign Affairs*, Vol.72, No.5, Winter 1992/93, pp.32–45.

42. This passage is found in, ibid, p.36.

43. During the PDD review process, the Pentagon's public statements did not shift a great deal. Concerns were raised by senior officials over specifics of the Somali mission, but DoD's commitment to peacekeeping was not challenged. See Keith B. Richburg, '4 US Soldiers Killed in Somalia: UN Blames Land-mine on Warlord', *Washington Post*, 9 Aug. 1993, p.A1; and John Lancaster, 'Aspin Lists US Goals in Somalia: Troop Pullout Hinges on Three Conditions: No Timetable is Set', *Washington Post*, 28 Aug. 1993, p.A1.

44. Although all these documents were produced after PDD 25, they represent the Pentagon's support for peacekeeping which resulted in the dramatic 'rethink' initiated by Cheney and Powell in late 1992. In particular, see Department of the Army, *Peace Operations FM 100-23*, Washington DC: Department of the Army, Headquarters, December 1994; Joint Chiefs of Staff, *Joint Doctrine for Military Operations Other Than War*, Washington DC:

JCS, 16 June 1995, Joint Publication 3-07; *National Military Strategy of the United States of America: A Strategy of Flexible and Selective Engagement*, Washington DC: JCS, Feb. 1995; Joint Warfighting Center, *Joint Task Force Commander's Handbook for Peace Operations*, Fort Monroe VA: JWC, 28 Feb. 1995. The policy found embedded in these documents is that the primary role of the US military is to fight and win two nearly simultaneous regional conflicts, but that peace operations are also an important role of the military, and the proper preparations must be taken for training and achieving a 'peace-keeping mentality'.

45. For examples of the arguments made by military opponents to US involvement in peace operations, see Colonel Charles J. Dunlap Jr, 'The Last American Warrior: Non-Traditional Missions and the Decline of the US Armed Forces', *The Fletcher Forum of World Affairs*, Vol.18, No.1, Winter/Spring 1994, pp.65–82; and Colonel Harry G. Summers Jr, 'US Participation in UN Peacekeeping Operations', *Strategic Review*, Fall 1993, pp.69–72.

46. For the contrary perspective, see Colonel Richard Seitz, 'The US Military and UN Peacekeeping', in *Peacemaking and Peacekeeping: Implications for the United States Military*, Panel Report of the United States Institute of Peace, Washington DC: USIP Press, May 1993, pp.25–32; and Lieutenant General Paul E. Cerjan (US Army, President, National Defense University), 'The United States and Multilateral Peacekeeping: The Challenge of Peace', in Fariborz L. Mokhtari (ed.), *Peacemaking, Peacekeeping and Coalition Warfare: The Future Role of the United Nations, Proceedings of a Conference*, Washington DC: National Defense University Press, 1994, pp.3–7. The issue of readiness was examined by the General Accounting Office in 1995. It concluded that peace operations did place a great deal of stress on support and lift units, but that the overall impact on combat units was limited. See General Accounting Office, *Peace Operations: Heavy Use of Key Capabilities May Affect Response to Regional Conflicts*, Washington DC: GAO, March 1995, GAO/NSIAD-95-51.

47. Comments of a US military officer, made to author during a personal, confidential interview in New York City, Sept. 1995.

48. See Colonel Richard Seitz (n.46 above), p.31.

49. See Les Aspin, 'Challenges to Value-Based Military Intervention', address to the Managing Chaos Conferences, reprinted in *Peaceworks*, No.3, Feb. 1995, by the United States Institute of Peace.

50. This issue was raised by two government officials during telephone interviews with the author in the spring of 1997. They requested anonymity.

51. For a good summary of the early substance of the draft PDD, see Jeffrey R. Smith and Julia Preston, 'US Evolves a New Peacekeeping Role', *Japan Times*, 21 June 1993, p.45. This piece notes that these positions were agreed to by both State and DoD staff. Given comments outlined below, however, this report must be taken with a grain of salt.

52. This suspicion shared by an anonymous DoD official during a telephone interview with the author in June 1997.

53. The foregoing account is based on a series of interviews conducted with officials involved with the review process during the spring of 1997, all of whom requested anonymity.

54. For a report on this issue as it was being played out, see Barton Gellman, 'Wider UN Police Role Supported', *Washington Post*, 5 Aug. 1993, p.A1.

55. See Gellman (n.54 above), for the Pentagon's resistance to this proposal.

56. This is based on conversations with nameless OSD and JCS officials during the spring of 1997. There is a common thread running through conversations with military officers

and Powell's autobiography, and that is the US armed forces have not forgotten Vietnam, despite proclamations by George Bush to the contrary.

57. See Eric Schmitt, 'US Set to Limit Role of Military In Peacekeeping', *New York Times*, 29 Jan. 1994, p.A2 for this aspect of the review process.

58. This brief history of the funding situation, and the problems it created between the two departments is found in, General Accounting Office, *United Nations: US Participating in Peacekeeping Operations*, Washington DC: GAO, Sept. 1992, GAO/NSIAD-92-247, pp.33–4.

59. See, for example, Ambassador Albright, 'The Clinton Administration's Policy on Reforming Multilateral Peace Operations', Statement before the Subcommittee on Foreign Operations, Export Financing and Related Programs, 5 May 1994, reprinted in *US Department of State Dispatch*, Vol.5, No.20, 16 May 1994, pp.315–18; and 'Peacekeeping Directive Designed to Impose More Discipline', transcript of remarks by Mr Lake and Lt General Weseley Clark, White House, EUR511, 6 May 1994, 5870.

FOUR

————◄〇►————

Congress into the Fray

AN OLD BATTLE RENEWED

The notion of 'separation of powers' was a key element to good government in the eyes of the framers of the US Constitution. In the area of foreign policy, this was clearly the wish of the drafters as they bestowed upon Congress the powers to declare war, ratify treaties and raise an army through taxation and spending, while reserving for the president the role of commander-in-chief of the armed forces. This constitutional arrangement has been termed 'the invitation to struggle' because it has the potential, should the two branches be in disagreement, to lead the Congress and the White House into a confrontation over a policy area in which both branches can lay a credible claim to having jurisdiction. This has been a defining characteristic of American foreign policy since 1783.[1] The number of cases of the two branches of government clashing over matters of foreign policy are many, having had, at times, very dramatic results. From this century, for instance, comes one of the more striking examples in the form of President Wilson's failure to win Senate approval for the Treaty of Versailles and the Covenant of the League of Nations contained therein. Conducting a state's foreign affairs involves a range of issues and activities. In the case of the doomed Treaty of Versailles, the Senate made its views felt by exercising its right to kill a treaty. As mentioned above, the power to ratify treaties is just one of the prerogatives Congress can employ to influence foreign policy. But have these powers been utilized with the same vigour and intensity since the founding of the Republic?

How this struggle has been played out with regard to the issue of deploying troops abroad in the years since US independence can be classified into three broad periods.[2] The first 150 years saw Congress exert the influence and control over the use of force which many writers believe the founders intended; that is to say, Congress demonstrated considerable control and influence over the conduct of the country's foreign policy. The rise of the Soviet Union as an expansionist rival at the end of the Second World War, coupled with the looming threat of nuclear war, gave way to a dramatic weakening of the influence of Congress over the use of the nation's armed forces in favour of the Executive. This aggrandizement of the Executive's powers as Commander-in-Chief almost completely subordinated Congress, and ushered in a second period known as the 'Imperial Presidency'. Not unexpectedly, this phase of Executive–Congressional relations came to another turning point in the aftermath of the Vietnam War, when a backlash swelled within Congress over what it saw as a grave mistake in forfeiting too much of its power. The *War Powers Resolution* of 1973 (passed over President Nixon's veto)[3] marked the beginning of a 'resurgent' Congress in the area of foreign policy in general, but more specifically, in the area of deploying, or indirectly using, the country's military.[4]

This 'resurgence' on the part of Congress, however, has had a very mixed, and confusing record. On the one hand, the Joint Resolution of 1973 sent a clear message to President Nixon and his successors that Congress was serious about bringing the pendulum back towards the centre, and the White House responded by complying with reports to Congress. On the other hand, the majority of those reports came after the military action in question had been taken by the president. Consultations with Congress did not occur as the Resolution envisioned, yet Congress never tried to force the issue.[5] As one Senator has lamented:

> The War Powers Resolution of 1973 was drafted to help fulfil the intent of the framers of the Constitution in that the collective judgement of both the Congress and the president would apply to the introduction of US armed forces into hostilities. In terms of this goal, the War Powers Resolution has failed.[6]

The full extent of the failure, and where most of the responsibility for that failure lies, is fully apparent in a case study by Professor Michael Rubner of the 1983 US invasion of Grenada. In his study, Professor Rubner places a large part of the burden for failure on the Senators and Representatives themselves and leaves them with four options: repeal the law; *status quo*; enforce the law more vigorously; or amend the law to make it more workable.[7] Regardless of what action Congress may take, it is apparently a law the White House has little trouble in circumventing.

Beyond its internal disorder on this issue, the Cold War with the Soviet Union was one more explanation why Congress was so quick to back away from enforcing the terms of the Resolution in that it did not want to handicap the president if he had to move quickly to counter a Soviet move. The bipartisan recognition of a common threat in the form of the Soviet Union did much to make the *War Powers Resolution* a dead letter during the 1970s and 1980s. Not surprisingly, however, the disappearance of that threat has completely reopened the debate between Congress and the White House, and within Congress itself, as to what threats exist to American interests. If a consensus could be reached regarding those threats and interests, a debate would then ensue over what measures are needed to protect US interests. In short, the bipartisan consensus of the Cold War disappeared along with the Soviet Union, and in its place is a policy void into which the Congress has made an effort to thrust itself. In many cases, this has placed the legislative body directly at odds with the White House.

It is during this period of uncertainty and change that this study falls. For the past 25 years, Congress has been trying to re-establish the intended balance of power with the Executive over the use of American military forces abroad, and other foreign policy issues. The success of Congress in reclaiming this balance had been limited largely by the weakness of its primary tool – the *War Powers Resolution* – in the Cold War context. This is no longer the case, and while the Resolution has been discarded as a vehicle for achieving some degree of balance, Congress is asserting itself in new ways, and enjoying levels of influence not seen in many years. This chapter will examine the role of Congress in the shaping of PDD 25, particularly as events in Somalia unfolded, as it defined its position and interests *vis-à-vis* the UN system in general, but more specifically regarding the US role in UN-led peace operations.

SOMALIA AND THE US CONGRESS

The Early Stages

Chapter 2 described how President Bush found himself under pressure from a number of sources to take action to ensure the delivery of relief supplies to the starving in Somalia. One of the most persistent of those sources was Congress, in particular two US Senators: Nancy Kassebaum (R-KS, who only a few years earlier drafted a funding bill designed to cut US contributions to the UN unilaterally unless it undertook a series of reform measures), and Paul Simon (D-IL). These two senators went public at the beginning of 1992 with their call for the US government to make some effort to address the famine situation in Somalia.[8] They continued their campaign through the Africa Subcommittee of the Senate Foreign Relations committee, and fact-finding missions to Somalia during January–February 1992. By the summer of 1992, a resolution adopted by both Houses called for a UN mission to be sent as soon as possible, with or without the consent of the Somali parties (which in effect, called for a Chapter VII-mandated mission).

In early December 1992, outgoing President Bush authorized the humanitarian mission which Congress had been demanding for many months. For the duration of the American-led UNITAF operation, Congress was either supportive or silent. When the time came to redefine the role of US forces in Somalia after the hand-off to the UN, both Houses passed updated resolutions (Senate Joint Resolution 45) giving their blessing to the deployment of US forces under UNOSOM II, in late May 1993. This signified Congressional acceptance of 4,000 US logistical troops operating under the control of a non-US commander (in a Chapter VII operation), in an environment where hostilities were possible. The additional 1,300 men of the QRF unit stationed off-shore, however, remained under direct US command. Just weeks later 24 Pakistani peacekeepers were killed during an ambush which passed without much discussion in either Chamber. Furthermore, one author reported that even when a draft of the policy review was leaked to the press in June with rumoured provisions allowing for an expanded role for US troops in UN missions under UN commanders, discussion remained at a minimum. One Clinton official was quoted as saying: 'We had a honeymoon. Nobody from Congress was in our face.'[9]

The Summer of Discontent

The 'honeymoon' began to show signs of being over by mid-July. One writer, who at the time was a NSC official, recalls Senator Robert Byrd taking the floor of the Senate at this point to sharply criticize the shifts in US policy in Somalia.[10] This must have been considered a bad omen for the Clinton White House for at least two reasons. One was that Senator Byrd was a Democrat and chairman of the Senate Appropriations Committee, which meant that Clinton could not depend on blind partisan support for this policy. Second, it demonstrated that high-profile members of Congress might be entertaining second thoughts about the Somali adventure and regretting that they did not pay closer attention to the terms of the transition from UNITAF to UNOSOM II when they approved the new mission in May. In late July, though, it seemed safe to say that Senator Byrd was not speaking for the majority, and that the Somali mission at that time was not yet a red-flag issue, but this would soon change.

On 8 August, four American soldiers were killed by a remote-controlled mine. In the wake of this incident, Byrd discovered that he was now leading a growing chorus of voices calling for a renewed Congressional debate on the Somali operation, and the chorus comprised members from both parties and both Houses.[11] An article in the *Washington Post* quoted then Senate Minority Leader Bob Dole as saying the time 'may be close' for a pull-out, and House Speaker Thomas Foley as saying that the attack would 'spark a heightened debate' on the Hill.[12] Ten days later, Senator Byrd took to the pages of the *New York Times* to explain his opposition to the Somali mission in particular, but also to the administration's proposed peacekeeping policy in general, which had been leaked in mid-June.[13] His concerns focused on two issues: 1) ambitious UN mandates with US troops under international command; and 2) the ever-increasing requests for paying the peacekeeping bills. With regard to the former, Byrd claimed that Congress had never approved the UNOSOM II mandate, and argued that no consensus existed to support the presence of US troops in Somalia: 'Lacking Congressional and popular support, US combat forces in Somalia should be removed as soon as possible.' With regard to the second concern, he expressed his hope that Congress would continue to be reluctant to release the peacekeeping funds requested by the State Department and White House:

> Congress's ability to support or deny financing is critical to insuring its voice in policymaking. Until a clear consensus is reached regarding the US role in all peacekeeping matters, Congress should not hand off its constitutional responsibility.[14]

Byrd's public remarks only acknowledged what many had known for years: that Congress instinctively tries to influence the policymaking process by pulling on the purse strings – a tactic employed very frequently when the UN is the policy subject.[15] Byrd's critical column also signalled that the White House and State Department would be in for a much tougher time with the draft policy directive because Byrd was intent on putting the issue on the political agenda in Washington. Peacekeeping, therefore, would not easily enter the day-to-day range of the Pentagon's duties without a full hearing in Congress.

In late September, news reports claimed that the draft policy review was undergoing significant changes, and that Congress was the reason behind them. As Byrd foreshadowed, the press noted that the problems, from the perspective of many in Congress, were the proposed provisions placing US troops under UN command, and money. One official was quoted as saying that 'I don't think the United States – I don't think the United States Congress – is ready to place US combat forces under UN command'.[16] On the financial front, the article remarked that earlier that month, Congress had rejected the requests for money to help pay for future US peacekeeping deployments and a small amount of funds to construct a UN command centre in New York. Moreover, it voted overwhelmingly to press the White House 'by November 15, to justify continued deployment of US troops to Somalia'.[17] In addition to slashing more than $60 million from the State Department's request for future operations, the House Appropriations Committee instructed the administration to notify all relevant committees about costs, funding schemes and durations of mission, before any future missions were launched.[18] With this Congressional activity as a backdrop, Clinton's very measured and cautious speech to the General Assembly, which reflected a significant 'rethink' in the administration, was taken by many as Clinton's gesture to Congress that he was willing to address its concerns in the peacekeeping policy review.[19] One senator remarked that Clinton's reversal was:

> ... a recognition of the political reality of the moment. Congress believes the American public doesn't want to get bogged down in military adventures whose benefits don't seem to justify the casualties and costs. To ignore that would be to squander political capital and goodwill that the president needs for his top domestic agenda.[20]

Despite the recognition in Congress that Clinton was now reversing the direction of his policy-review process, many of its members were still demanding more concessions from the White House. Republican Senator Bob Dole was reported as complaining that Clinton had failed to acknowledge that US interests did not include 'questionable missions' like the nation-building efforts in Somalia. Meanwhile, Democrat Representative Lee Hamilton placed the peacekeeping issue in the wider context of the debate surrounding the role for the US in the post-Cold War era, implying that neither the larger issue, nor the smaller one of peacekeeping, would be solved quickly to the satisfaction of Congress.[21]

Congress's 'Last Straw'

If Clinton was able to quell some Congressional worries with his speech to the General Assembly, it quickly became a moot point after the deaths of 18 Rangers in Mogadishu on 3 October. Members of Congress, from both Houses and parties took to the airwaves to call for the withdrawal of American troops as soon as possible, which for many meant immediately. Senate Majority Leader George Mitchell admitted that the attack would 'increase the voices demanding an American withdrawal'. Senator Sam Nunn, however, apparently represented the minority position when he argued that the mandate should be refocused on humanitarian objectives and he resisted the notion of a fixed timetable for removing the troops.[22] Jeremy Rosner has described the following week as one which produced an enormous amount of pressure on Clinton to begin the pull-out from Somalia.[23] Rosner continued by noting that on the day of his speech to Congress and the nation (7 October) Clinton finally met with Congressional leaders to discuss the situation in Somalia, the first such meeting since he had come into office. Although the President assured both Congress and the American public that the troops would be home by 31 March 1994, Congress went ahead with a number of amendments to the defence appropriations bill to limit funding for peacekeeping operations. Initially, the intent was to cut off funding for UNOSOM II immediately, but '... Congress ultimately accepted the president's proposed termination date'.[24] For now, Congress was willing to agree with the president's argument that an immediate withdrawal would do more harm than good in both the short- and the long-term.

At the start of the New Year, peacekeeping returned to the political agendas of both the Executive and Congress. Press reports of the newly revised PRD 13 seemed to indicate that the administration had moved even further from its position of the previous summer, which itself was a reaction to early Congressional complaints.[25] The revisions made to the draft policy directive during the autumn, and those reported in the press after Christmas, still did not go far enough in the eyes of many members of Congress. One of the more critical members was Senator Dole, who unveiled a new piece of proposed legislation around the same time the latest version of the PRD was being discussed in the press. Writing in the *New York Times*, Dole took the issues surrounding Somalia and other UN operations as evidence that the time had come to re-evaluate the war-powers relationship within the US government.[26] He complained that Congress had been taken completely out of the decision-making process, yet was expected to release more and more funds for these operations. Also, he was not convinced that the Clinton administration was taking the necessary precautions to keep US soldiers from being placed under UN command.[27] As his contribution to the debate, he announced his intention to table a bill, the *Peace Powers Act*, which would deal with a number of issues raised in Congress over the preceding months.[28] This proposed legislation represented a serious challenge to the established presidential prerogatives concerning the deployment of US forces while many of the financial provisions would effectively shut down UN operations, especially if other donor countries followed the American precedent. Although the bill was sent to committee for roughly a year (and eventually died on the floor), it influenced the policy review process in that many of its provisions were incorporated into the State Department Authorization Bill, and also demonstrated the determination of Congress to take on more of a role in the peacekeeping decisionmaking process, in spite of the new direction adopted by President Clinton.[29] Surprisingly though, there was one positive development to report during the spring of 1994, and that was the cooperation demonstrated by both branches in finding the money needed to bring the US out of arrears for 1994. This payment was used mostly to cover the accumulated debt and bills for 1993, and within a matter of months the US would be behind again on its payments. Furthermore, this event did not reflect a change of heart on the part of key Congressional figures, such as Robert Byrd, but simply that a number of other factors had come together in a fortuitous manner.[30]

The final version of the policy review directive was released as PDD 25, in early May, 1994. This event must have seemed anticlimatic for those involved in both branches of government. Dole's reaction to the Directive was that it did not go far enough in addressing his concerns over the command arrangements if the US were to contribute troops. House Minority whip Newt Gingrich dismissed the document because in his eyes, it '... continues to subordinate the United States to the United Nations ...'[31] Yet, it seems almost certain that these negative, even hostile, pronouncements concealed the likelihood that most Congressional leaders were feeling much less concerned about the future of American peacekeeping than just eight months earlier because the funding bottleneck, which if removed might have permitted greater peacekeeping activity, remained blocked. The 'Shared Responsibility' provisions of PDD 25, which purported to be the long-awaited solution to the funding and responsibility dispute between the State Department and DoD, died in both Houses and, thus, were never implemented. Congress balked at creating a special peacekeeping fund within the Pentagon's budget because of the strong opposition of many members to allowing defence funds be used for peacekeeping. With this proposal dead on arrival, Congress maintained the ability to release funds for peacekeeping on virtually a case-by-case basis through the State Department's much smaller budget. In the eyes of many Congressional figures, this was an effective way to keep peacekeeping under close scrutiny, and no doubt pleased them.[32]

Perhaps even more discouraging for those involved in the drafting process than the negative and critical reception from the key Republicans, and symbolic, if vain, attempt to secure more reliable funding, was the feeling that PDD 25 was irrelevant and redundant upon arrival. Rosner has quoted one congressional staffer as saying: 'The final policy was viewed as something that was OK, but somewhat peripheral. It took forever to get out. By the time it came out, it didn't have a lot to do with the decisions that were going on up on the Hill.'[33] This comment implies that many in Congress perceived a victory over the White House in respect to peacekeeping policy during the previous year. Their 'evidence' of this victory was the fact that PDD 25 was 'peripheral' in that it merely reflected the direction, tone and spirit championed by Congress, while essentially all traces of 'assertive multi-lateralism' had been purged from the government's new policy.

SUMMARY

The Bush administration was urged to act by a number of sources, but perhaps second only to television coverage, two senators were the most influential. Working for more than 11 months, Senators Simon and Kassebaum presented a strong case as to why the US should intervene in Somalia. Their pleas were so impassioned that they eventually called for an intervention which amounted to a Chapter VII-style enforcement operation. Once the operation was launched, Congress turned its attention, for the most part, elsewhere. This hands-off approach was the order of the day later in 1993 as the US-led mission turned control over to the UN-commanded UNOSOM II, despite the fact that over 4,000 US troops remained part of that UN operation.

In mid-July, however, Congress began to stir. After the deaths of 24 Pakistani peacekeepers, yet before the deaths of four American soldiers, the situation was growing more violent and Senator Byrd began to have reservations about the entire mission, not just the American involvement. Perhaps compounding his concerns were the leaked reports of the substance of the draft peacekeeping policy, then known as PRD 13. During the six weeks between the deaths of the four US soldiers in early August and the President's first speech to the UN General Assembly, Byrd led the growing number of vocal senators and representatives in attacking the administration's policy in Somalia, and its peacekeeping policy more broadly. For the first time in almost 50 years, legislation was being introduced to place limits on various aspects of US participation in peace operations. By the time Clinton made his speech, the directive was back on the drawing board, and the President's address hinted at major changes in the works.

Congress's reaction to the 3 October firefight in Mogadishu was intense and furious, as the record of speeches and statements in both Houses attests. Amendments were attached to appropriations bills for the Defense Department, and the administration began to feel the squeeze as the peacekeeping bills continued to accumulate, and its requests for funding were denied. Only by setting a date for withdrawal did President Clinton avoid the truly embarrassing situation of having to pull out the US forces because funding had been terminated. While the two branches were able to find the resources in the spring of 1994, this proved to be a shortlived example of cooperation. PDD 25 was released in May 1994, but for many it had been already overtaken, and thus rendered redundant, by the aggressive actions of Congress.

NOTES

1. This characterization of the Executive–Congressional relationship concerning foreign policy as 'an invitation to struggle' is attributed to Edward S. Crowin. See Jeremy D. Rosner, *The New Tug-of-War: Congress, the Executive Branch and National Security*, Washington DC: The Carnegie Endowment For International Peace, 1995, p.1 for the complete citation.
2. See James M. Lindsay, 'Congress and the Use of Force in the Post-Cold War Era', in Aspen Strategy Group Report, *The United States and the Use of Force in the Post-Cold War Era*, Queenstown MD: The Aspen Institute, 1995, pp.72–82, for a concise and excellent overview of the changing nature of the 'struggle' between Congress and the Executive throughout US history.
3. See *War Powers Resolution*, Public Law 93-149, 7 Nov. 1973, for the text of the binding joint resolution, and for the President's explanation of veto, see President Richard M. Nixon, 'Message from the President, Vetoing the House Joint Resolution 542, A. Joint Resolution Concerning the War Powers of Congress and the President', 24 Oct. 1973.
4. See James M. Lindsay (n.2 above), p.77 for this description.
5. For a thorough survey of presidential compliance with the Joint Resolution, see Richard F. Grimmett, *War Powers Resolution: Presidential Compliance*, CRS IB 81050, Washington DC: Congressional Research Service, 23 July 1996.
6. This passage is found in Russ Feingold, 'The Role of Congress in Deploying US Troops Abroad', *The Brown Journal of World Affairs*, Vol.3, No.1 (Winter/Spring 1996), p.306.
7. See Michael Rubner, 'The Reagan Administration, the 1973 War Powers Resolution, and the invasion of Grenada', *Political Science Quarterly*, Vol.100, No.4, Winter 1985–86, pp.627–47. His four options listed here are found with the implications and conclusions on pp.641–7.
8. An useful account of the Senators' efforts is found in John L. Hirsch and Robert B. Oakley, *Somalia and Operation Restore Hope: Reflections on Peacemaking and Peacekeeping*, Washington DC: United States Institute of Peace Press, 1995, p.36. These authors cite an article by the Senators as the start of Congressional interest in the unfolding disaster. See Hirsch and Oakley, footnote 1, p.36, or directly, Paul Simon and Nancy Kassebaum, 'Save Somalia From Itself', *New York Times*, 2 Jan. 1992. Another useful account of the role of Congress in this crisis, see Harry Johnston and Ted Dagne, 'Congress and the Somalia Crisis', in Walter Clarke and Jeffery Herbst (eds), *Learning from Somalia: Lessons of Armed Humanitarian Intervention*, Boulder CO: Westview Press, 1997.
9. Unnamed Clinton administration official quoted in Jeremy D. Rosner (n.1 above), p.70. The press report is found in, Jeffery Smith and Julia Preston, 'US Evolves a New Peacekeeping Role', *Japan Times*, 21 June 1993, p.45.

10. See Jeremy D. Rosner (n.1 above), p.71.

11. It should be noted, however, that not all of Byrd's colleagues were of the same confrontational mood. In early August, a group of 12 senators appealed to President Clinton to cooperate with them in finding a solution to the peacekeeping funding problem. Their efforts were followed by an open letter from Democrat Rep. Lee Hamilton to Clinton in which he almost pleaded with the President to make a public appeal to Congress for the money necessary to break the funding deadlock. Apparently both requests for cooperation and assistance failed. For details on these episodes, and other funding developments during the summer of 1993, see the excellent overview in Steven A. Dimoff, 'Congress's Budget-cutting Fervour Threatens US Standing at UN', *The Interdependent*, Vol.19, No.3, Fall 1993, p.6.

12. See Keith B. Richburg, '4 US Soldiers Killed in Somalia: UN Blames Land-mine on Warlord', *Washington Post*, 9 Aug. 1993, p.A1.

13. The commentary is found in, Senator Robert C. Byrd (D-W.-Virginia), 'The Perils of Peacekeeping', *New York Times*, 19 Aug. 1993, p.A26.

14. For these two quotes, see ibid.

15. Congressional refusal to pay in full, UN assessments, or to tie the payment of assessments to particular reforms or actions in the Secretariat has been a standard practice for the past 15 years. Gregg, in his *About Face: The United States and the United Nations*, outlines the use of illegal financial manipulations by Congress to extract policy shifts by the State Department, or reforms in the UN. In particular, Gregg notes that the Kassebaum Amendment to the Foreign Relations Authorization Bill is the arch-type of this sort of manipulation. The Amendment was designed to spark serious reform within the UN system by slashing the US contribution by 20%, unilaterally with the contribution remaining at that level until weighted voting practices had been implemented throughout the system. See Robert W. Gregg, *About Face? The United States and the United Nations*, Boulder CO: Lynne Rienner Publishers, 1993, Chapter 4, pp.71–2 for specific details of the Kassebaum Amendment. For a good review of how the US pays its peacekeeping bills, see Anthony McDermott, *United Nations Financing Problems and the New Generation of Peacekeeping and Peace Enforcement*, Providence RI: The Thomas J. Watson Jr Institute for International Studies, 1994, Occasional Paper #16, pp.20–1.

16. See Barton Gellman, 'US Reconsiders Putting GIs Under UN: Concern over Somalia and Bosnia Prompts Backlash in Congress', *Washington Post*, 22 Sept. 1993, p.A1, for this quote and details.

17. See ibid.

18. For these comments, see Elaine Sciolino, 'US Narrows Terms for Its Peacekeepers', *New York Times*, 23 Sept. 1993, p.A8.

19. For example, see Thomas L. Friedman, 'Clinton, at UN Lists Stiff Terms For Sending US Forces to Bosnia', *New York Times*, 28 Sept. 1993, p.A1; and John M. Goshko, 'Clinton Seen Calming Hill on Peacekeeping: Caution in Committing US Forces Said to Defuse Confrontation on Presidential Prerogatives', *Washington Post*, 2 Oct. 1993, p.A16.

20. See John M. Goshko (n.19 above).

21. See ibid.

22. These views were reported in Tom Kenworthy and John Lancaster, 'At least 5 Americans Killed in Somali Attack', *Washington Post*, 4 Oct. 1993, p.A1.

23. To illustrate the level of pressure being felt by the White House, Rosner (n.1 above) counts 67 statements in both Houses criticizing the Clinton policy in Somalia in the week following the firefight of 3 October. See p.72.

24. See ibid, pp.72–3.
25. See Eric Schmitt, 'US Set to Limit Role of Military in Peacekeeping', *New York Times*, 29 Jan. 1994, p.A2.
26. Dole's myopic view of the United Nations' role in the world is found in Bob Dole, 'Peacekeepers and Politics', *New York Times*, 24 Jan. 1994, p.A15.
27. Until it was raised as an issue during the PRD process, command and control arrangements in coalition formations were not the taboo subject Clinton's critics made them out to be during this period. US forces have served in combat situations under foreign commanders many time over the past 200 years. In relative terms, the proposed provisions of the earlier drafts of PDD 25 were very modest. For a survey of recent cases of US troops serving under non-US commanders, see Edward F. Bruner, *US Forces and Multinational Commands: PDD 25 and Precedents*, CRS 94-887 F (Washington DC: Congressional Research Service, Updated 29 Aug. 1996).
28. See *Peace Powers Act of 1995*, United States' Senate, 104th Congress, 1st Session, 4 Jan. 1995.
29. See Jeremy D. Rosner (n.1 above), p.73, for this analysis of the immediate impact of the proposed *Peace Power Act*.
30. For a fuller account of this episode, see ibid, pp.88–9.
31. For these reactions and more, see Ann Devroy, 'Clinton Signs New Guidelines for UN Peacekeeping Operations', *Washington Post*, 6 May 1994, p.A30.
32. This version of events borrows from Rosner (n.1 above), pp.83–7.
33. This passage is found in ibid, pp.73–4.

————◄◦►————

FIVE

In The Name of Public Opinion

INTRODUCTION

Roger Hilsman himself notes that the concept referred to as 'public opinion' is not a power centre in the same sense as the other three actors examined previously.[1] Unlike the president or Congress, public opinion does not write and pass laws, and unlike the principal bureaucracies, public opinion cannot influence policy decisions by virtue of direct access to the flow of information and the decisionmaking process. Moreover, this study dismissed the relevance of the 'press and media' and the 'electorate' as 'power centres' on the grounds that they were not capable of exerting political influence over this process in their own right, but that they merely influence the 'actors'.[2] Why, then, include an equally nebulous and vague notion as an actor in this adapted version of the political process model? The answer in this case is that Congress, and ultimately the White House, made 'public opinion' an actor in the process which resulted in PDD 25.

The notion that politicians should remain in touch with the public's views on important foreign-policy matters, such as overseas military deployments, has not always been a widely held conviction in American politics. Whether the political élites of the day had much faith in the wisdom of the masses, they nevertheless made an effort to portray their policies in terms which, they believed, would most likely ensure popular support. The Vietnam War changed that attitude entirely as political and military leaders watched public opinion slowly, yet overwhelmingly, turn against US policy in South East Asia with tangible political and military consequences. In the aftermath of this war, leaders in the US government and military were forced to place greater emphasis on the public's concerns relating to the use of US military forces abroad. The most explicit expression of this heightened sensitivity came with the announcement of the Weinberger Doctrine in 1984 when the public's (and Congressional) support appeared as one of the six tests to which a proposed intervention would be subject before the then Secretary of Defense, Casper Weinberger, would support the mission.[3] In subsequent years, public opinion has become a factor raised frequently in political debates by both supporters and opponents of interventions. Nowhere is this more the case than in Congress. Given their direct link and responsibility to their constituents, members of Congress are perhaps the group of public officials most inclined to cite public opinion as a justification for their positions on contentious issues. Who, after all, can argue with the will of the American people?

The debate surrounding the administration's peacekeeping policy proved to be no exception to this pattern. Through their statements and arguments, many in Congress claimed that public opinion was an influential factor guiding their positions on peacekeeping in general and US policy towards Somalia in particular. An early instance of a Congressional figure linking public opinion with the mission in Somalia came in the summer of 1993 when Senator Byrd wrote in the *New York Times* that US forces lacked Congressional and popular support and, therefore, should be withdrawn immediately.[4] His belief that the American public was so opposed to the US involvement in Somalia and with UN peace operations in general, was fully supported by many of Senator Byrd's fellow lawmakers, and even some analysts, after the 3 October 1993 firefight in Mogadishu.[5] With this example in mind the purpose of this chapter is twofold. First, it will examine the evidence available concerning American public opinion towards the Somali operation so that results of public opinion polls can be compared with the claims of politicians; and second, it will try to place this information in the larger context of the public's attitude towards peacekeeping in general, because it was also a claim of many members in Congress that the public's views on Somalia were a symptom of a deeper apprehension of UN-led peace operations, especially those where US soldiers are to serve under foreign commanders, and a broader mistrust of the UN Organization.[6]

SOMALIA AND US PUBLIC OPINION

The Mission is Launched

In the spring of 1992, the United Nations Association of the USA (UNA/USA), released the results of a Roper Poll which indicated a majority preference for conducting interventions through the UN and that in matters of internal conflict, the UN should take the lead.[7] Despite such indications that UN-led operations were the preferred response of the American public to humanitarian emergencies, President Bush only considered a unilateral course of action. Yet, it seems he was not judged negatively for that decision because it was clear from polls conducted in late 1992 that the American public was very supportive of an humanitarian mission to Somalia, even if it was US-led rather than UN-led.[8] Thanks, in part, to the efforts of Senators Simon and Kassebaum, the international media covered the unfolding of events in Somalia very closely, which left the American public well aware of the mounting crisis. By the time President Bush made the decision to intervene, there was a strong showing of support for the mission. A *Newsweek* poll found that 66 per cent of those questioned approved of the dispatch of US troops. When the troops actually hit the beaches a few weeks later, however, a *Los Angeles Times* survey discovered that the approval rating jumped to a remarkable level of 84 per cent, of whom 53 per cent were 'strongly' in favour.[9] The preference for action through the UN was first apparent in the May 1992 Roper Poll, but it then reappeared in the December poll conducted by *Newsweek*. It revealed a more surprising result, though, when the respondents were presented with the statement: 'The US should commit troops only as part of a United Nations operation.' While the US was sending troops to Somalia under US command, 87 per cent of the people polled, agreed with the proposition, a level of support even higher than the previous May.[10] The author quoting this figure remarks that it is doubtful that all 87 per cent meant that the US should abandon the option to act unilaterally, but the inclination to act through multilateral channels was undeniably very strong in early 1993.

Poll results, however, reveal a much more complicated picture of the public's perception of peacekeeping and the US's role in that activity. The average American expresses very genuine support for humanitarian interventions, but it has come to the attention of those studying this issue that this support is subject to some conditions and the product of some rather significant misunderstandings. The missions to Somalia illustrate this point very well. For example, Kohut and Toth pointed to a set of findings which emphasized the conditional nature of the seemingly strong support for the American intervention noted above. They draw our attention to a series of polls which indicated that the public had a particular understanding of the mission's mandate, and the expectations of the troops. According to a Gallup survey in December 1992, 59 per cent claimed that the mission was 'to deliver relief supplies', whereas a minority (31 per cent) thought the mission was 'also an attempt to bring a permanent end to the fighting'. Moreover, the public was expecting the mission to be brief, as two polls make plain. The first was conducted by ABC and the *Washington Post,* and reported that 62 per cent of the respondents did not anticipate the US becoming 'bogged down' in Somalia, but would rather complete the mission and leave quickly. The second, by the *Los Angeles Times*, discovered that 51 per cent believed that the mission would be over within six months and that 69 per cent expected to see the operation come to a close within a year.[11] The implication inherent in these figures is that the public's continuing support was contingent on the mission meeting a certain level of expectations which were based on the explanations and objectives furnished by the Bush administration. These expectations aside, the level of support increased as the operation entered the New Year. Furthermore, and despite the first American deaths in January in clashes with suspected followers of General Aideed, the results from a March 1993 survey showed the public was firmly behind the mission. The numbers for March actually increased one point over the January *Los Angeles Times* poll: the overall support remained steady at 84 per cent, but the 'strongly approve' category increased to 54 per cent.[12]

A Period of Benign Neglect

In the same month as this last poll, the Security Council adopted Resolution 814, which set the terms for the transition from UNITAF to UNOSOM II, and with that hand-off, the mission embarked on a new strategic direction. The objective of the operation was no longer just to ensure the delivery of humanitarian relief supplies, but also to rebuild Somalia's political, economical and social infrastructure. Kohut and Toth argued that the public was unaware that such a fundamental shift in the policy had occurred, or that their government was one of the principal sponsors of the new policy. The main reason for this lack of awareness, in their view, was that the operation was dropped as a major story throughout the winter and spring of 1993 by the media – network television news in particular. Former administration officials, on the other hand, have argued that the State Department did very little to publicize the new policy save for low profile Congressional hearings.[13] Whatever the cause, the result was clearly reflected in the polls as the number of people responding and thus closely following events in Somalia, dropped from 52 per cent in January to 16 per cent in June.[14]

UNOSOM II and the parallel US operation were largely ignored by the American public during this period, in spite of the mandate change and the rise of violence in the country. With the opening of a new session of Congress after the summer break, the issue of Somalia was claiming the sort of headlines which led many members to become uneasy with the new role of the US forces and, accordingly, with the ongoing policy review process. The polls, at this point, detected a shift in opinion regarding the American presence in Somalia. One survey found the respondents were virtually evenly split in their approval of US troops being in the racked country. A second poll conducted by Gallup reported a slight majority of 53 per cent calling for the withdrawal of US forces, while over 46 per cent argued that troops should remain in a limited peacekeeping role.[15] Furthermore, 57 per cent of the second poll's group wanted the confrontation with Aideed to end, while the first survey found that 69 per cent wanted the mission to be defined in stricter terms for food delivery. One author has attributed this decline in support for UNOSOM II, and US participation in that mission, to the perception among most Americans that the operation had already accomplished its objective of providing food for the starving.[16] This hypothesis seems to back the claim by Kohut and Toth that the public was not aware of a mandate shift in May (i.e. when the UN formally took over responsibility for the operation). Hence, the public seemed confused by the violent turn the mission had taken given the reports that the famine was, by the summer of 1993, largely under control. The general level of popular ignorance regarding the new objectives for the US military in Somalia was an unnecessary and risky oversight for a government trying to maintain a mission premised on humanitarian relief.

THE REAL IMPACT OF THE OCTOBER BATTLE

For many analysts, the October battle between US Rangers and Aideed's militia marked the turning point for US policy, not only in Somalia, but towards humanitarian interventions in general. Linda Miller provided the following assessment of the battle's legacy for US policy:

> The televised pictures of a US raid gone wrong, with 18 men killed, hardened public opinion against using American forces in the internecine quarrels of a homogeneous people in a far-away place.[17]

Most likely, one of the factors contributing to her conclusion was the week of furious debate in Congress following the deaths, during which many members called for the immediate withdrawal of all US forces. Two senators (who had already sharply criticized Clinton's policy in Somalia), claimed that their offices were flooded with calls from their constituents, with an overwhelming majority of callers demanding the immediate withdrawal of the American force.[18] Adding further urgency to an already chaotic situation, Carolyn Logan notes that polls released in early October reported public support for the mission in Somalia had dropped to as low as 33 per cent, down from the peak figure of 84 per cent less than a year earlier.[19] From this record of events, one gets the impression that Congress was not alone in its growing opposition to the administration's policy in Somalia; the public was now weighing in with a resoundingly angry voice.

Evidently the 3 October battle and accompanying 18 deaths raised two inter-related issues for the administration, and these issues took on a greater significance when it was perceived that public opinion was the driving force. The first issue was the more immediate, namely, 'what policy adjustments to make in Somalia?'. The dilemma facing the White House and the two bureaucracies was whether to withdraw immediately, or to prolong the mission somehow so as to avoid the appearance of being forced out of Somalia by General Aideed, which would send a clear, and undesirable, message to future opponents. For the US, obviously the face-saving route was the pre-ferred option. Second, the administration's peacekeeping review process was under increasingly tight scrutiny from Congress. However, it now appeared as though the concerns of the American public would have to be considered as well. The question then, is did the administration and Congress accurately read the mood of the public, and did the government follow through with policy shifts which were in line with that mood?

Immediate Concerns

With regard to the short-term problem, Clinton's decision to leave the troops in Somalia until 31 March 1994, with re-enforcements, was a sound policy move. Although a large number of Congressional members called for an immediate withdrawal, and claimed the public was of the same mind, the polls at the time reveal another story. Surveys conducted by ABC News and CNN/*USA Today*, just hours after the news of the battle and mounting casualties, found that while clear majorities wanted US forces out of Somalia, only minorities of 37 and 43 per cent respectively wanted to pull out right away.[20] Clinton's decision to add more troops to the US forces struck a chord with a majority of people polled by the same two organizations, and by a third one. CNN/*USA Today*, ABC and NBC all found majorities of, respectively, 55, 56 and 61 per cent of respondents in favour of an increased force level in Somalia for the short-term, and ABC discovered that 75 per cent of those questioned favoured the use of a 'major military attack' if US prisoners could not be freed by negotiation.[21]

Two weeks after the firefight, the Program on International Policy Attitudes (PIPA) of the University of Maryland carried out a four-day survey (15–18 October) which presented three options to the respondents. Twenty-eight per cent wanted the US to pull out immediately, 43 per cent approved of the President's decision to remain until 31 March 1994, and 27 per cent called on the US to stay in Somalia until that country was stabilized.[22] These results bear directly on the belief that the public can be expected to react very emotionally to events as they unfold. In a report publishing the survey's results, PIPA provided the average percentage of respondents wanting to pull out right away as noted by five different polls conducted in the immediate aftermath of the deaths being announced. The average percentage of people calling for an immediate withdrawal in those polls was 40.8 per cent. Less than a week later, PIPA recorded a figure of 28 per cent.[23] These numbers demonstrate that the public understood the dangers of an immediate withdrawal for American foreign policy and UNOSOM II; *ergo*, public opinion supported Clinton's plan for gradual disengagement of the United States from Somalia. The PIPA survey reached the additional conclusion that the desire for withdrawing, either immediately or in six months, 'was not simply a reaction to fatalities'. Kull argues that two factors were behind the wish to get out of Somalia: First, as mentioned above, was the general impression that the objective of the mission had already been met, namely, the famine was no longer a serious threat to the population, 'so why are the troops still there?' Second, and equally important, 58 per cent of those questioned believed that the Somalis wanted the US to leave, and of that group, 88 per cent thought that the US should withdraw from Somalia.[24]

What is undeniable from the poll results collected in the two weeks following the deaths in Mogadishu is that there was no overwhelming outcry by the public to pull out of Somalia. Rather, it appears as though many members of Congress either overestimated the public's reaction, or simply presumed what it would be. The PIPA survey conducted in the middle of October also shows that the public's reaction might not have been just against the notion of peacekeeping in Somalia, but an expression of confusion over the mandate and objectives of the mission.[25] These statistics and the argument are meant to give some insight as to what might prompt seemingly dramatic poll results, which, in turn, can be misconstrued, (intentionally) misrepresented or misunderstood by politicians and/or commentators eager to pursue their own agendas.

The Long Shadow?

Poll results collected over the following months seem to support the case put forth by the researchers at PIPA and, more pertinently, to show the disconnect between the public's perceived views on peacekeeping and the public's real (albeit complicated) attitudes. This disconnect between presumed and actual attitudes constituted the second and broader issue confronting the Clinton administration in the wake of the deaths of the US Rangers in Mogadishu: the impact of the disaster on long-term peacekeeping policy. It has been noted above that many believe the sharply negative reaction of the public to the losses in Mogadishu convinced the Clinton team that the United States should avoid humanitarian missions, especially of the enforcement kind, in the future. Once again, survey results strongly suggest that this link between the public's reaction and the policy reversal has been overstated. CBS polls in October and December 1993 showed consistent support (60 per cent both times) for the notion that the US 'did the right thing … to try and make sure shipments of food got through to the people there in Somalia'.[26] In addition, the December CBS poll cited a plurality of 48 per cent agreeing that 'the intervention was worth the "loss of American life, the financial costs and other risks involved"; while 44 per cent said it was not.'[27]

PIPA undertook a major, nationwide survey on peace operations during the winter of 1994. The results of this project represent a significant departure from the views of many in Congress, and a large number of analysts and pundits. For example, overall support for UN peacekeeping was found to be very high, at 84 per cent. With regard to specific mandates, intervening in civil wars was the least supported at 69 per cent approval, but operations to prevent or stop largescale atrocities and human right violations garnered the support of 83 and 81 per cent respectively. More to the point, PIPA found that 91 per cent of those asked 'Should the US send troops?', said yes (49 per cent 'in most cases' and 42 per cent 'only in exceptional cases').[28] Polling data confounded another common assumption that the American public would not tolerate US forces being placed under temporary command of foreign officers in a UN chain of command. In a separate study, PIPA found that 56 per cent of respondents said they found foreign commanders acceptable, while 73 per cent could accept such an arrangement if the US were to contribute only a minority of the troops involved – which is a reflection of the common misperception that the US regularly contributes a large proportion of troops to most UN missions.[29]

These consistently favourable figures, however, do not provide conclusive evidence on their own that US voters would still embrace a more proactive US peacekeeping policy; there remained the crucial matter of money. If Americans continued to be generally supportive of UN peacekeeping in the aftermath of the Mogadishu firefight at the rhetorical level, were they willing to pay their share of its unavoidable, and ever increasing, financial costs? The PIPA study examined this issue closely in the same 1994 report, and its results revealed a public remarkably uninformed, yet far more supportive than earlier suspected. As the survey concludes:

> The majority is ready to support spending substantially more on
> UN peacekeeping than the US actually now spends. (However,

this attitude may not be readily apparent because the majority imagines that the US spends much more than it does and feels that this imagined amount is too high.)[30]

In the context of opinion polls, the financial aspect of public support for UN peacekeeping is a multifaceted issue which does not lend itself to analyses based on only one or two questions. In its effort to explore this topic, the PIPA survey examined five specific issues: 1) What are the public's attitudes towards US spending on peacekeeping operations?; 2) Is there a willingness to increase personal taxes to fund peace operations?; 3) Should the US pay its UN dues in full?; 4) Is the US paying more than its fair share of peacekeeping costs?; and 5) What is the perception of one's fellow citizens' support for, and funding of, UN operations?

In trying to address the first issue, the survey asked the participants three questions concerning spending by the US government on peace operations. The results have been neatly summarized in the above passage, yet they deserve a brief elaboration here. The first question asked if the respondent believed the US was spending 'too much', 'too little' or 'about the right amount'. Given these choices, 59 per cent responded 'too much', 15 per cent thought it was 'too little' and 10 per cent offered 'about right'. Suspecting the results might be a function of a misperception concerning the actual levels of spending, the participants were then informed what the US actually spends on UN peace operations (figure for fiscal year (FY) 1994 was given as $750 million), and how this figure compared with five other government spending programmes so it could be placed in some sort of context. With the new information in hand, the participants were then asked if this amount was 'more or less than what they expected'. Fifty-five per cent responded that it was less than they had anticipated while 31 per cent reacted by saying it was a larger figure than they had expected. Next the pollsters wanted to know if the participants found the amount 'higher or lower than it should be'. Whereas 59 per cent responded to the first question that the US was paying 'too much', only 39 per cent still held that view with the new information, a 20 per cent drop. Conversely, the percentage of those finding the level of spending as insufficient increased from 15 per cent to 42 per cent after the actual amount was revealed. Next, half of the participants were asked 'how many tax dollars would you feel comfortable paying personally each year towards UN peacekeeping?'. The survey recorded a median value of $10 and an average figure of $115. The respondents were then told that the average taxpayer pays roughly $4 in taxes each year for UN peace operations. The follow-up question found that 74 per cent considered this figure to be lower than they had expected, and 62 per cent replied that it was lower than it should be.

Finally, the second half of participants was asked '… if UN peacekeeping were to be paid through the defence budget (an idea supported by 61 per cent) what percentage of the defence budget should be devoted to UN peacekeeping?' The survey found a median figure of 10 per cent, which the authors point out is 40 times greater than the figure spent in FY 1994. When told that the current level of US spending constituted just 0.25 per cent of the US defence budget, 69 per cent of the respondents claimed it was lower than expected, while 58 stated the amount of spending on UN peace operations should be higher. To correct this perceived imbalance, 62 per cent expressed their willingness to make cuts in the defence budget so that increases in peacekeeping spending could be accomodated.[31]

In a similar vein, respondents supported the notion of raising their taxes to support peace operations (issue two) by a plurality of 46 per cent, with 40 per cent opposing any increase. The proposed increases offered by the willing individuals ranged from $1 to $500. The median was calculated to be $10 which represented a 250 per cent rise over the spending levels at that time.[32] Moving from the hypothetical to a case which was potentially on the horizon in early 1994, the survey asked the participants how much they would be willing to pay through increased taxes to enable the dispatch of a peacekeeping force to help control the civil war in Burundi. The number of those opposed to any increase remained essentially the same at 39 per cent, while 42 per cent were agreeable to an increase in taxes for such a mission.

In the report's next section, the researchers presented the data related to the third main issue under consideration: payment of the American assessed contribution. As was discussed in previous chapters, the US Congress has long made the withholding of legally binding dues a common tactic in its efforts to extract concessions or reforms from the UN Secretariat or specialized agencies. Frequently, the anger or frustration of the American public is used as a justification for this approach by members of Congress trying to take a harder line *vis-à-vis* the UN. For some representatives and commentators, the US assessed contribution for peacekeeping is seen as an even more appropriate target because a different formula is used which levies a higher burden on the United States (31.7 per cent in 1994) than the assessment for the regular budget (25 per cent). On this issue, the survey found that the American public was more inclined to pay its dues than those in Washington might have expected. The findings show a majority of 55 per cent of Americans hold the belief that the US government should pay its peacekeeping assessment in full, while 34 per cent responded that the US should pay only a partial amount, and a small minority of 5 per cent said the US should pay none of its dues at all. The participants were also presented with four arguments which might be given on this topic, two presenting perspectives supportive of paying peacekeeping dues, the other two offering the contrary point of view. By clear majorities in all four cases, the poll found the majorities of the respondents agreeing with the pro-peacekeeping positions and dismissing the con arguments.[33] As a final question in this section, the respondents were asked if they agreed that 'the UN should be able to charge countries interest on the amount they owe for back dues so as to encourage them to pay sooner rather than later'. In the light of the fact that the US has been the largest debtor country to the UN for the past few years, the finding of 63 per cent supporting that statement is, indeed, very surprising and significant.

Americans' sense of fairness was the next subject of interest to the PIPA researchers when they asked the respondents whether they felt the US was being asked to pay more than its fair share of peacekeeping bills. The subject was approached in two steps. First, the participants were asked their opinion without being provided any background information as to how the dues are calculated. Based on this, 34 per cent of the respondents felt the US assessment was too high, 14 per cent believed it was too low and 32 per cent said it was about right, with 20 per cent not answering. The figures changed significantly after they were informed how the assessments were determined and that under this system the US was assessed at roughly 31.7 per cent. With the new information, the group responding felt the assessment was still too high and the poll remained virtually the same, at 33 per cent, but the percentage who felt it was about right rose to 58 per cent. The PIPA researchers go on to note, interestingly, that awareness of the assessment formula did not affect results concerning the payment of the dues in full and on time because half of the sample was asked about the payment of dues before being given the formula information and the second half was asked after the information was provided.

The last of the issues examined in the report deals with the perceptions Americans have of how their fellow citizens feel about supporting and funding UN peace operations. The respondents were presented with a scale ranging from 'strongly favour' at +2 to 'strongly oppose' at -2. They were then asked to rate the attitude of the 'average American', and then their own feelings on the topic. The average rating for fellow citizens was +0.49, while their own feelings rated an average of +1.2. Seemingly, the respondents believed that their fellow citizens were much less supportive of the UN and its peacekeeping activities than themselves. This pattern appeared again when the participants were asked to gauge the feelings of the average American, then their own, on a possible deployment to Burundi. Using the same scale, the average value of their own feelings was +0.79 while they suspected the average American's support for a possible mission to Burundi was -0.15.

Next, the participants were asked how their fellow citizens feel about US spending levels on UN peace operations and the results confirmed the trend. The scale remained as +2 to –2 but was now presented in terms of 'too much' (+2) and 'too little' (–2), and the question was posed twice; the first time without any background information being provided and the second time after the actual spending amounts were shared with the respondents. Without knowing the actual amount of money spent on peace operations, the partici- pants gave an average figure of +1.4 to describe how their fellow citizens viewed the American expenditures for peacekeeping while their feelings averaged +1.0. After being informed the actual spending levels, their average dropped into the 'too little' range of –0.05. Finally, the PIPA researchers wanted to know how the respondents viewed their fellow Americans' inclination to increase spending on UN peacekeeping. A very substantial majority of 70 per cent believed that their fellow citizens favoured spending less than themselves as compared to only 17 per cent who assumed that the general population would support higher spending than themselves and the 7 per cent who guessed the public would support the same level of spending as themselves. Quite clearly, these figures generated from the four sets of questions indicate that the public did not understand its own views on peacekeeping issues in early 1994. In the word of the researchers, '[t]his suggests that the public is misperceiving it own attitudes'.[34]

What do these figures tell us about US public opinion as it pertained to UN peacekeeping during the PRD review process and, most importantly, in the months following the American loses in Mogadishu? The most glaring result is the solid majority of support for US involvment in UN peace operations and for the timely and complete payment of dues to the UN for such missions. Moreover, the respondents signalled far more resolve than many politicians and pundits suspected to continue dangerous missions, even while taking casualties, as long as the reason for the operation and its mandate and aims are clear and perceived to be just. Yet, the research uncovers two clues as to how the media and the US government might get the impression the public is far less supportive of peace operations than it really is. First, the study found that there is a slight majority of Americans that believes the US is paying more than its fair share of costs (the number is reduced when actual spending amounts are revealed), and second, the respondents consistently underestimated the support of their fellow citizens for the UN and its peacekeeping activities. Although these results did not seriously undermine overall support for the Organization, they did highlight a serious public-relations problem for the UN and those trying to defend it from domestic criticism in the US. In its conclusion, the report admits it was unable to answer the question it set for itself (why the US supports UN peace operations but underpays its peacekeeping dues?), but states that it has provided the evidence necessary to reject the claim that reluctance to pay is the product of a 'recalcitrant public'. The authors surmised that:

> The public is, it appears, not only supportive of UN peacekeeping in principle, but is willing to make a greater contribution to UN peacekeeping than that presently being made.
> ... This suggests that the inconsistency in US policy between support for UN peacekeeping and the unwillingness to pay for it, is not necessary for the sake of the public. Rather it appears that, given the proper information, the public is ready to support a level of financial commitment that corresponds more closely to its support for UN peacekeeping operations in principle.[35]

CONCLUSIONS

Judging by the polling data discussed in this chapter, the American public emerges as a generally supportive lot when it comes to US participation in UN peace operations, in terms of both troop contribution and funding. Despite this, the United States continues to be the largest single debtor to the Organization and what was expected to be a more proactive and embracing policy review ended up producing the most restrictive and cautious position ever devised towards the UN and its peacekeeping activities. All the more puzzling is that many observers persist in arguing that the events in Somalia had such a profound impact on the American people, that Clinton was left with no alternative but to agree to a total withdrawal from the early position of assertive multilateralism and ratify that withdrawal through the terms and spirit of PDD 25. How did this perception gain such widespread currency?

One answer might be found in the earlier discussion of the public's support for the mission to Somalia being subject to certain conditions and expectations. When the proposed mission was first presented to the American people, it was cast as a purely humanitarian one and support was very high. Over the following months, the operation slipped from the nightly newscasts and, not surprisingly, the percentage of US voters following the story declined sharply. By the time the media and pollsters returned to the issue, the operation's mandate had been changed significantly and the public was very confused as to how a humanitarian mission had become a raging urban battle. Analysts such as Carolyn Logan argue that the public's support eroded dramatically in September and October because it could not reconcile the loss of life on both sides with the ambiguous objectives of the operation. The original reason for sending the troops, the famine, was, by all accounts, no longer a threat to the Somali population, so why were the forces engaged in street battles with a local warlord? Logan has concluded that the drop in support for American involvement in Somalia was not simply a function of casualties, but that the new goals of the mission were not valued highly enough, or perhaps understood enough, by the public and that it was this bewilderment which led to the sudden erosion of support. In other words, the public might consider 30 deaths as unfortunate but acceptable if they occurred during attempts to achieve a just and worthwhile goal, but 30 deaths can quickly become an unacceptable cost if the objectives are deemed unreasonable or are poorly understood. As Logan writes:

> During the Somalia intervention, the primary goal of the mission changed drastically over time, from ending the famine, to rebuilding the state, to capturing the warlord Aideed. While the public valued the first of these goals highly and tolerated costs incurred while achieving it, the latter two goals were much less important to Americans, leading to a decline in support when the goals changed and to a much lower tolerance for costs.

Evidently, this realization has a pronounced influence on how polling data can be interpreted. Yet, it appears as though the majority of those claiming that the public's staunch opposition to US involvment in UN peace operations demands a policy like PDD 25, or worse, either fail or refuse to acknowledge these complex responses. This superficial use of polls does not escape Logan's attention:

> In most analyses, however, this distinction is rarely made; public anger over the American deaths in Somalia in October 1993 is erroneously linked with the original humanitarian goals, rather than with the goals that were actually being pursued at the time of the deaths, leading to the errant conclusion that there is not sufficient US public support to take risks in pursuit of humanitarian goals.[36]

The foregoing discussion leaves very little room for those who claim the public's backlash forced Clinton's team to abandon the more activist peacekeeping policy they envisioned in early 1993 to defend their position. But one possibility does remain, and that is concerned with the perception of those officials involved with the actual drafting of the policy who did not have the benefit of this extensive polling data and analysis during the autumn and winter of 1993 while they laboured away on successive drafts of what would become PDD 25. Did they believe the media's and Congress's contentions that the public indeed demanded a much more limited and restrained relationship with the UN's peacekeeping efforts? The answer appears to be a qualified 'no'. In the early stages of the review process public opinion was not a red-flag issue as it was presumed most Americans would have few reservations with, or interest in, the substance of the policy being hammered out. This secondary concern became a primary concern in the aftermath of the October battle, but not for the reason commonly propounded. According to one official involved in the PRD evolution, the dramatic drop in popular support for UNOSOM II which was reported in the polls in early October was construed by the members of working group as a backlash against the mandate of that particular mission and the Somalis themselves. It was not interpreted as a rejection of the peacekeeping ideal, nor American support for that ideal. Instead, it was felt that the polls reflected a general shock as to why the Somalis would 'bite the hand that was feeding them' and the clear preference to bring that operation to an end.[37]

It was said at the beginning of this chapter that the power and influence of the public is a very dynamic and elusive variable in American foreign policy. In this case, it appears as though Congress and Clinton either did not recognize or did not want to recognize the distinctions and perceptions which were, and are, so imperative in understanding the public's opinion.

NOTES

1. This issue is raised in Roger Hilsman in *The Politics of Policy Making in Defense and Foreign Affairs: Conceptual Models and Bureaucratic Politics Third Edition*, Englewood Cliffs NJ: Prentice Hall, 1993, Ch.16, p.266.
2. Please see Ch.1 for more details on this issue.
3. See Annex 2 for the text of the Doctrine and its treatment of public opinion.
4. See Senator Robert C. Byrd (D, W-Virginia), 'The Perils of Peacekeeping', *New York Times*, 19 Aug. 1993, Opinion-Editorial page.
5. On the part of analysts for example, see Ivo H. Daalder, 'The United States and Military Intervention in Internal Conflict', in Michael E. Brown (ed.), *The International Dimensions of Internal Conflict*, Cambridge MA: MIT Press, 1996, p.479; and Mats R. Berdal, 'Fateful Encounter: The United States and UN Peacekeeping', *Survival*, Vol.36, No.1 (Spring 1994), p.38.
6. Senator John McCain (R-Arizona) provided a good example of this mind-set when he told a committee in early 1994 that UN peacekeeping was 'of increasing concern to policymakers and the American people'. See Senator John McCain (R-Arizona), 'US Participation in UN Peacekeeping Operations', Statement to the Subcommittee on Legislation and National Security of the House Government Operations Committee, 3 March 1994, Federal Document Clearing House, Inc. 1994, Lexis/Nexis, p.1.

7. The results of this poll were released as 'New Poll Finds Rightward Shift in Public Backing For UN', United Nations Association of the USA, *Press Release*, 11 May 1992.

8. Steven Kull, of the Program on International Policy Attitudes in Washington DC, offers a possible explanation for this result, by voicing his suspicion that the American public assumed that the mission to Somalia was UN-led from the beginning. Views expressed to the author via email in January 1998.

9. These figures have been compiled in Andrew Kohut and Robert C. Toth, 'The People, the Press and the Use of Force' in Aspen Strategy Group Report, *The United States and the Use of Force in the Post-Cold War Era*, Queenstown MD: The Aspen Institute, 1995, pp.144–7.

10. This aspect of the *Newsweek* poll is found in Steven Kull, 'What the Public Knows that Washington Doesn't', *Foreign Policy*, No.101, Winter 1995–96, p.105. By comparison, the May 1992 Roper Poll found that 58% favoured the UN over unilateral action.

11. For these figures, see Kohut and Toth (n.9 above), p.144.

12. See ibid, pp.144–5.

13. Officials, who wished to be anonymous, expressed this view during interviews with the author.

14. See Kohut and Toth (n.9 above), p.145.

15. See ibid, p.146.

16. For this reasoning, see Steven Kull, 'Misreading the Public Mood', *The Bulletin of the Atomic Scientists*, March/April 1995, p.58.

17. See Linda B. Miller, 'The Clinton Years: Reinventing US Foreign Policy', *International Affairs*, Vol.70, No.4 (1994), p.627. Another example of the linkages made between the 3 Oct. 1993 firefight and the following direction taken by the Clinton administration regarding peace operations is found in Walter Clarke and Jeffery Herbst, 'Somalia and the Future of Humanitarian Intervention', *Foreign Affairs*, Vol.75, No.2, March/April 1996, p.70.

18. Senators Bill Bradley and John McCain both reported this situation with McCain in particular claiming he received 402 calls in one day, with 400 of those demanding an immediate withdrawal. See Donald C.F. Daniel, 'The United States', in Trevor Findley (ed.), *Challenges for the New Peacekeepers*, SIPRI Research Report #12, Oxford: Oxford University Press, 1996, pp.94–5, for details of this aspect.

19. For more on Logan's figures, see Carolyn J. Logan, 'US Public Opinion and the Intervention in Somalia: Lessons for the Future of Military-Humanitarian Interventions', in *The Fletcher Forum of World Affairs*, Vol.20, No.2, Summer/Fall 1996, pp.155–80.

20. For these figures, see Kull (n.10 above), pp.111–12.

21. See ibid, p.112 for these poll results and additional commentary. These numbers could not hide the fact, though, that the US public was confused and frustrated by the turn of events. Kohut and Toth note that public confidence in the operation dropped to 44% in one poll, down from 62% some months earlier. More importantly, they quoted a NBC poll which recorded the level of support for the US presence in Somalia dropped to 34%, less than half the support the mission enjoyed earlier in 1993. Refer to Andrew Kohut and Robert C. Toth, 'Arms and the People', *Foreign Affairs*, Vol.73, No.6, Nov./Dec. 1994, p.52 for these results.

22. See Kull (n.16 above), p.58. In written correspondence with the author, Kull has pointed out that these different figures are in part due to the fact that PIPA allowed for three possible responses instead of the two options found in the other polls.

23. The survey's results were published as Steven Kull and Clay Ramsay, *US Public Attitudes*

     on US Involvement in Somalia, Program on International Policy Attitudes, University of Maryland, 26 Oct. 1993. This table of different poll results is found on p.4.

24. Kull (n.16 above) discusses these two motivations, p.58. A more detailed breakdown of the poll results on impressions of Somali desires are found in Kull and Ramsay (n.23 above), p.5.

25. Indeed, Kull notes in 'What the Public Knows that Washington Doesn't' (n.10 above), that some unnamed polls completed before October 1993, registered a decline in support for the mission because respondents believed that the objectives had been reached, and indicated opposition to any change in the mandate. See p.112.

26. See Kull (n.16 above), p.58.

27. This quote is from, Kohut and Toth, 'The People, the Press and the Use of Force' (n.9 above), p.147.

28. See Steven Kull and Clay Ramsay, *US Public Attitudes on UN Peacekeeping,* Program on International Policy Attitudes, University of Maryland, 7 March 1994, pp.6–7.

29. For these figures and further comments, see Steven Kull, I.M. Destler and Clay Ramsay, *The Foreign Policy Gap: How Policymakers Misread the Public,* Program on International Policy Attitudes, University of Maryland, Oct. 1997, p.94. It should be noted that these figures come from a survey conducted in April 1995, not during the PRD timeframe.

30. See ibid, p.8.

31. For these findings and a full commentary, see ibid, pp.8–10.

32. The report went on to note that if the percentage of people opposed to any increase in taxes was included in this calculation, the median amount of increase in taxes drops to $1, or a 25% raise over spending levels in 1994. See ibid, p.10.

33. For the full text and results of the pro and con statements, see ibid, p.11.

34. See ibid, p.14.

35. For these two passages, see ibid, p.15.

36. These two passages are found in Carolyn J. Logan, 'US Public Opinion and the Intervention in Somalia:' (n.19 above), pp.156–7.

37. These views were conveyed to the author through personal and telephone interviews during the spring of 1997. On a related point, Steven Kull suspects that the level of popular support for American involvment in Somalia had already declined sharply by September 1993 for the same reasons discussed earlier in this chapter, but this drop was not detected until after the October firefight when polling began again in earnest on this issue. This comment was shared with the author through written correspondence in January 1998.

SIX

————◄○►————

The Deciding Factor

INTRODUCTION

The previous four chapters have laid out the interests, perspectives and facts as they relate to the four power centres identified as having a role in the formulation of PDD 25. The task in this chapter is to sift through that evidence with the aim of determining the role each actor played in the formulation of PDD 25, and which, if any, exerted a dominant influence over the final version of the policy. The analysis will try to answer the central question posed in the opening pages of this book by looking at the problem from different angles, such as: Did bureaucratic 'turf' battles dictate the substance and spirit of the Directive, or did the administration cave in to a public hostile to the notion of UN peacekeeping and any form of multi-lateralism? Or is PDD 25 simply one more example of a larger battle being waged between two branches of the American government over control of the country's foreign policy in a new and very uncertain era in international politics?

By way of an initial comment, it can be stated that this study has revealed the far-reaching influence of a resurgent Congress in matters of foreign policy. The research findings indicate unambiguously that PDD 25 is the product of American domestic politics, arising from the special circum-stances which converged with the election victory of Bill Clinton as the first American, post-Cold War president meeting head on a Congress anxious to reassert its role in the making of foreign policy. Without a doubt, the terms and, especially, the spirit of the Directive were written more to address and accommodate the concerns and demands of Congress than those of any other actor involved in the process. But before elaborating on this finding, this chapter will explain why the other two power centres in this study cannot be considered as dominant influences on the final outcome of the peacekeeping review.

NARROWING THE FIELD OF CANDIDATES

Public Opinion

Throughout the debate over America's role in peacekeeping, and even its participation in the UN more broadly, public opinion was, and remains, an often-cited factor. In the majority of cases, the views of the public were held up by UN critics as undeniable justification to limit or restrict US involvement with such missions, although hard figures were rarely supplied. Of course, these fuzzy and misleading references to public opinion polls have been a regular feature of Congress rationalizing its (usually successful) efforts to withhold a large portion of the American assessed annual contribution or to deny funding for voluntary programmes. Yet, as the last chapter concluded, it is almost impossible to square these claims with the actual findings of polls conducted during the 1990s. Contradicting the assertions of many members of Congress and analysts, this section will argue that public opinion did not exert a prevailing influence on the policy review for three reasons.

First, as the figures discussed in Chapter 5 demonstrate, peacekeeping has enjoyed clear levels of majority support for the past few years, and certainly during the time frame of the review process. Moreover, this support was not limited to the abstract notion of UN peacekeeping, but also for sustaining it with the payment on time of America's assessed dues and with the US military's direct and indirect involvement, as risky as that might be at times, in worthy missions. Financially, the American public disapproved of US peacekeeping debts growing year after year, even when it imagined that peacekeeping was claiming a far greater share of the federal budget than it in fact was. Once the formulae of how peacekeeping assessments were calculated and the actual figures were explained, support for US participation and timely payment of dues increased. With regard to the use of US troops, public opinion has shown majority support for some level of involvement, with a large proportion in favour of US deployments in 'most cases'.[1] Some polls revealed the public as being a little more cautious about placing troops under UN command, but the numbers were about even during the time frame of the policy review. Other polls reported majority acceptance of the idea if the United States was contributing a minority of the troops involved. Nevertheless, this cautiousness obviously does not reflect a flat-out rejection of the idea, especially when one keeps in mind that one survey found the average American mistakenly believing that the US is normally the largest troop contributor to most operations.

Second, the public's reaction to the deaths of 18 US soldiers in Mogadishu on 3 October 1993 was not as strong as many in Congress and other observers believed. With emotions at their highest, in the hours after the news was announced, polls did not register, on average, more than 41 per cent of respondents in favour of an immediate withdrawal. After two weeks had passed this number showed a sharp decline of some 11–13 points to 28 per cent. The majority of Americans ultimately supported President Clinton's decision to pull out the troops by the end of March 1994, six months after the battle in Mogadishu. This does not substantiate the assumptions of peacekeeping's critics that the US public would not accept the human costs of peacekeeping. Moreover, this finding provides the evidence necessary to discredit the hypothesis which placed central importance on the public's negative reaction to the Mogadishu firefight in explaining the policy shift embodied in PDD 25.[2]

To be sure, Americans do not support UN peacekeeping, or US participation, without some reservations, and the drop in the polls during September and October 1993 makes that statement plainly. They, like citizens of other troop-contributing countries, want to see clear and sensible reasons for sending their men and women in uniform overseas. They expect realistic objectives and favourable chances for making a significant difference in the lives of the people they are supposed to be helping, which would constitute a success in their minds. When the approval rating for US involvement in Somalia dropped to as low as 33 per cent, the American public believed the mission was well off course from its original intentions. Nonetheless, popular support for peacekeeping and the United Nations remained high. Why? This curious dynamic is a function of the third reason why public opinion was not the driving force behind the US policy reversal, though it was widely perceived to be: the public's views on peacekeeping and the UN are more complicated and sophisticated than many would expect. As some analysts are now learning, the public is capable of making distinctions between causes they value highly enough to risk lives in pursuing, and those which simply do not warrant the trouble. For example, Logan points out that missions of a purely humanitarian nature garner the highest levels of support, while those which pursue 'nation-building' agendas are not assured the same levels of approval.[3] The twists and turns of US action in Somalia are, evidently, a case in point. It is not surprising that, when asked a simple yes/no question on Somalia in September and October 1993, many people replied they were against the mission. Certain observers then interpreted those results as a popular indictment of US participation in UN-led peace operations. This careless rush to judgment would have proved to be very misleading had those drafting PDD 25 taken the figures at face value. Some of those officials claim, however, that they perceived the drop in support for the Somali mission as an expression of the public's confusion over the change in mandate and their anger towards the Somalis for attacking the people who were there to help the country avert mass starvation. While that message was understood, the drop in support for UNOSOM II was not taken as a rejection of the peace-keeping ideal, nor as an objection to US participation in the UN and its peacekeeping activities. In short, some of the individuals responsible for the drafting of the document maintain, still to this day, that public opinion did not exert the level of pressure assumed by many others.

The Bureaucracies

Critics of PDD 25, if they realize public opinion is not to blame, might be tempted to blame the bureaucrats who crafted the document for the remark-able policy reversal contained therein. After all, the review was left in their hands for over 14 months and the only source of information on the evolving policy was through leaks to the press because the whole drafting process was conducted behind closed doors. Known for their tendency to engage in so-called 'turf wars' over what must appear to the outsider as seemingly mundane or trivial issues, the bureaucracies certainly did pose easy targets, in the days following the Directive's public release, to those who questioned the wisdom of the new policy, especially in the shadow of the misery that was Rwanda in the spring of 1994. Furthermore, many writers have identified prominent personalities among the bureaucrats as leading characters in the PDD 25 story, including the former Chairman of the Joint Chiefs of Staff, General Colin L. Powell. While not denying that the principal departments had their differences and their own agendas, this section will argue against this sort of analysis because first, it overlooks the key agreements achieved which might have cleared the way for a more positive final policy; second, it overstates those differences; and third, it unfairly casts General Powell as the spoiler, or in the view of others, the hero of the whole process.

With regard to the overlooked agreements, it is evident from the discussion in Chapter 3, that the State Department and Pentagon were able to dispense with most of their disagreements in short order, save one, or rather, two connected thorns. These two particular issues divided the State Department and Pentagon staffs very sharply, and were cited as the primary reasons for the delay in the signing of the policy during early 1994. The metaphorical thorns which caused such controversy were the inter-related issues of budget and responsibility. Unlike other differences between the departments over command issues or the earmarking of units for UN service, the funding and responsibility issues reportedly took many months to settle.[4] At the heart of the dispute was a long history of the State Department's self-serving accounting practices, and the increased control over peacekeeping policy that accompanies any increases of budgetary resources. As a compromise, the departments were given the lead roles in different types of peace operations under a plan called 'Shared Responsibility'. Under this plan, State was primarily responsible for financing America's contribution to Chapter VI missions in which no US combat units are deployed; while the Pentagon was handed financial and organizing responsibility for Chapter VII missions, or Chapter VI missions in which US combat troops were participating.[5] Unfortunately, what might have been a coup for the NSC in bringing the two departments together and finally resolving a long-standing bone of contention proved to be a moot victory for cooperation and compromise; Congress killed the deal.

These skirmishes, however, were disagreements over details of how to implement the wider policy of 'assertive multilateralism', and then later to satisfy the concerns of Congress. Both Secretaries, Christopher and Aspin, were appointed to office with similar commitments to the pro-multilateral position which Clinton had staked out as a candidate. The available evidence does not indicate an active role by either bureaucracy to initiate sweeping changes in the administration's peacekeeping policy. On the contrary, it portrays State Department and Pentagon officials as continually reacting to the political confrontation being played out between the White House and Congress. The first clear instance, and one of the more dramatic, was when the draft was sent back *twice* for revisions within a *six week period*, just as Congress was stepping up its attack on the version of the policy which was leaked to the press in mid-July 1993. Of course, by taking advantage of this confusion the JCS was able get the basic Weinberger principles of intervention inserted into the policy, but this event has been dismissed by a State Department official as merely spelling out what was already taken for granted. According to this person, the working group viewed this concession to the JCS as unnecessary because those principles would naturally factor into any decision to deploy the military and the JCS only made the request for two simple reasons: 1) to protect themselves from intervention-prone civilians; and 2) because it felt it would make the policy an easier sell to Congress with such precautions clearly written out. Apparently, the insertion of Weinberger's conditions was not perceived as a sign of JCS resistance to peacekeeping duties among the departments and agencies involved. When asked if the eagerness on the part of the JCS to include such conditions did, in fact, reflect opposition at the upper echelon of the Pentagon, a JCS officer replied: 'If Powell wanted to kill [US involvement in] peacekeeping, he could have very easily.'[6]

By the time the policy-review process was completed, the terrain was not littered with the corpses of bureaucrats slain in the bureaucratic trenches.

Without exception, the officials who shared their recollections all agreed that there was a remarkable degree of cooperation and sense of shared purpose during the committee's meetings. Certainly, there were differences of opinion, such as the OSD/JCS debate over appropriate levels of specialized peacekeeping training, and who was going to pay for what, but they were eventually resolved. And, naturally, not all of the agencies shared the same level of enthusiasm for this subject, but it seems they were committed to drafting a rather proactive policy and did not view any departmental concern or interest as an insurmountable deal-breaker. In the end, it appears that the bureaucracies were battling each other on the tactical level, while Congress and the White House struggled for control at the strategic level. Regardless of the metaphor, it is apparent that the bureaucracies were not the deciding factors which forced the policy reversal found in PDD 25.

THE INVITATION TO STRUGGLE WAS DECLINED

Jeremy Rosner points out that the foreign-policy relationship between the Executive and the Congress has been challenged by the two branches – though more usually by Congress – in the wake of major developments on the international stage, such as wars.[7] The 1990s brought just such a development: the end of the Cold War. After 50 years of defining the foreign policy of the United States, confrontation with the communist power perceived as expansionist simply disappeared from the list of mortal threats to the US. In fact, the impact of this development was perhaps much more significant for the foreign-policy relationship between the two branches than the end of the Second World War because the new direction and purpose of American foreign policy was not – and probably is still not – obvious.

In the wake of World War 2, US leaders, in both branches of government, were able to come to a bipartisan consensus on identifying threats to national security and how to deal with them. In sharp contrast to the late 1940s, however, no such consensus developed in the years after the collapse of the Soviet Union. Indeed, the 1992 presidential election seemed to indicate that political parties were unable to form any cohesive view on foreign policy internally, much less between Congress and the White House.[8] This circumstance, by itself, does not account for the policy reversal committed by Clinton in 1993/94, but it does provide the context in which Clinton attempted to establish his 'assertive multilateralism' stance, only later to back away and reverse course.

Did Clinton really 'back down' in the face of Congressional pressure? Was it a true contest of wills for control over intervention policy, notwithstanding presidential prerogatives which had been exercised and expanded for almost 50 years? Did Clinton cave in? In a word, yes. The speeches by administration officials in late-September 1993 indicate this retreat unambiguously. As one congressional staffer was quoted as saying in the press on 2 October 1993, 'Clinton just took off his [boxing] gloves, and climbed out of the ring'.[9] This being the case then, two questions now require examination: First, why did President Clinton sacrifice one of his central foreign-policy objectives in less than ten months, without an apparent effort to fight for its survival? Second, why was Congress so keen to turn this issue into a head-on confrontation when it had approved the US mission to Somalia in February, and again in May when most of the US forces were transferred to UN control? From the foregoing research results, this study can offer two reasons why Clinton gave way to Congress on the peacekeeping issue, and three reasons why Congress was so fervent in making it an issue, thereby making a collision unavoidable.

A Skittish White House

Donald Daniel provided a very succinct description of the first reason Clinton was able to desert his peacekeeping initiative so easily when he wrote: 'The key to understanding what led this particular president to issue PDD 25, as it finally appeared, is that domestic policy is by far his foremost concern.'[10] And this point cannot be overstated. In 1993, Clinton was trying to pass legislation on health-care reform, a crime bill, and other major domestic programmes which formed the foundation of his election campaign. Almost all foreign-policy issues, short of a major conflict in a strategic region, were subordinated to the domestic agenda. Knowing this, many in Congress realized that a president who was elected on a thin mandate (Clinton won the White House with a plurality vote rather than an absolute majority), would have to husband his 'political capital' and influence for the issues which really mattered to him, even though the Democrats controlled both Houses. The consequence of this predicament was that Clinton was in a very tight position on foreign policy, should Congress decide that it objected to a particular initiative. This was the case with the early programme of 'assertive multilateralism', and its peacekeeping component. Once Congress took an opposing position to Clinton's plan to expand peacekeeping, and American participation in peace operations, the range of options available to the administration was very limited. Clinton would not back up the policy vigorously if it meant expending political capital which could be better spent pushing one of his domestic policies. The dilemma facing the administration was summed up by Ivo Daalder, when he wrote: 'Only by confronting

Congress directly could Clinton have gotten his way, and this conflicted with his desire to save political capital for his domestic priorities.'[11]

Clinton's predicament would have very tangible effects on the policy review committee's efforts to reach a workable solution to the funding debate. Jeremy Rosner writes that the 'Shared Responsibility' formula in PDD 25 was not aggressively lobbied for by many of Clinton's civilian appointees in the OSD because they anticipated a losing battle against the key Congressional chairs. Rosner continues by arguing that this did not reflect a lack of support for the proposal but rather that the staffers were not keen to lobby for this proposal in the face of expected opposition from Congress because they were given no signal from the White House that this was an issue to fight for. And as Rosner notes, the repercussions were real:

> The coolness of Pentagon officials toward shared responsibility was a product not only of the heat they feared they would encounter on the Hill but also of the lack of heat they were sensing from the top of the administration. A meeting between the President and defence legislators planned for May 1994 – in part to pitch the importance of shared responsibility – was delayed and then cancelled due to conflicts with White House efforts to promote health care reform. One Pentagon official notes the ripple effect that resulted: 'The president never touched it. The involvement from top levels of DoD was half-hearted, sporadic and late. So the legislative people completely didn't push it because it was in the "too hard" category – it undermined their other priorities'.[12]

Compounding this political dynamic, was a more serious problem in the foreign-policy establishment itself. The fact that Clinton was not willing to push Congress on peacekeeping was certainly a function of domestic priorities, but also due to the lack of a clear vision regarding the role of the United Nations, and peacekeeping, in American foreign policy. In other words, there was not a strong enough commitment to 'assertive multilateralism' as a worthwhile policy doctrine to justify the fight with Congress. Observing the situation in the early period of the Clinton administration, Donald Puchala commented that the lack of a coherent foreign policy on the part of the US made it very difficult to conceive of the proper role for the UN in American thinking. He claimed that the US thought of the UN more as a 'place' than as an organization, and could not see past its day-to-day activities to the broader role it wanted the Organization to play on the strategic level.[13]

Consequently, once the administration ran into opposition over the peacekeeping issue, it lacked a singularly coherent and firm voice to argue in favour of such a policy. This implies that even if Clinton were prepared to push his policy of 'assertive multilateralism' on Congress, the fight might have been tough because of the difficulty in selling a policy which did not address the fundamental issues affecting the US–UN relationship. Somalia, after the shift to 'nation-building', was considered by many as an experiment in 'assertive multilateralism', which demonstrated the lack of thinking on the part of the administration on how to employ the UN most effectively. When the mission began to run into problems, Clinton resorted to disowning the policy of 'nation-building' rather than trying to defend it. If Clinton had pursued his policy, the ensuing battle with Congress would most likely have highlighted this lack of strategic vision in a very publicly embarrassing manner.

Congress Engages the Issue

It is clear that the Clinton administration was not inclined to defend any foreign-policy initiative if it meant diverting limited political energy away from the domestic agenda. Moreover, it lacked the strategic reasoning required, in the face of Congressional opposition, to justify a policy. These two factors by themselves, however, are not a sufficient explanation as to why PDD 25 took its ultimate form. For these to have become relevant factors, Congress had to make the policy under development in the PRD process an issue and then demonstrate a willingness to engage the White House in a contest of wills. What prompted Congress to turn around on a policy which it had been approving implicitly by authorizing the dispatch of US troops to Somalia? The answer is threefold: first, and perhaps most importantly, money; second, pride (for lack of a better expression); and third, the UN is a considered an easy 'target', by Senators and Representatives alike, for negative votes.

First, take the financial motives for Congressional opposition to a more proactive, formal policy towards UN peace operations. Budgetary oversight is the main tool, or weapon, in the Congressional arsenal, and by the summer of 1993, attention was being focused on the funding of US peacekeeping policy, present and future. Over the preceding five years, the State Department's peacekeeping budget had been one of the fastest growing expenditures in the federal budget, though still a minor sum compared with the total budget. Nevertheless, Congress took note of the fact that in FY 1989, peacekeeping cost the US $29 million. For the final year of the Bush administration (FY 1992) that figure had increased to $460 million, a 20-fold increase.[14] The

Clinton administration's first budget request was almost double that of the last one made under Bush. Some of the funds were requested as an add-on under FY 1993, while the bulk ($620 million) was requested under FY 1994, plus another add-on of $175 million to be put into a contingency fund. The total request was $913 million. The two additions were rejected by Congress, and this signalled the end of the spiralling State Department budget.

There can be little doubt that the dramatic rise in peacekeeping bills captured the attention and scrutiny of many members in Congress, at about the same time Senator Byrd was raising a critical voice over the largely ignored mission in Somalia, where the situation had become more violent during the summer of 1993. Unluckily, this was not the only problem facing the administration's budget plans. Peacekeeping funding also had the misfortune of being controlled by the Commerce, Justice and State Subcommittee, which meant it had to compete with those two domestically oriented departments for dwindling resources. In addition, the administration had indicated that its aid package to Russia was a huge programme that went through Congress before the peacekeeping request, thus claiming a big chunk of the 'foreign aid' budget. This was not helpful to those pushing for increases in peacekeeping funding because Congress had long viewed peacekeeping as another form of foreign aid which was thought of by many in Congress as a discretionary spending programme, and these programmes were taking stiff cutbacks at the height of the American recession.[15]

By the summer of 1993, as Byrd intensified his criticisms of the conduct and the purpose of the mission in Somalia, and Congress began to deal with a peacekeeping budget seemingly out of control, worries of another sort began to appear. The first draft of the PRD document was leaked in June 1993. With this, Congress was given a glimpse of how the White House planned to embark on a policy of 'assertive multilateralism'. The picture came into clearer focus during the summer as key administration officials testified before Congressional committees as to the substance and intent of the emerging policy on peacekeeping. For Congressional leaders, the already overdrawn peacekeeping account seemed to be destined for even more spectacular growth, not to mention the proposals for placing US troops under UN command. In the eyes of Congress, the administration's plans for peacekeeping were growing very ambitious, which was all the more alarming with a possible mission to Bosnia looming on the horizon.

While money is often a convincing motive in its own right, members of Congress may have had an added incentive: pride. Although 'pride' may not be the most accurate term to use, it conveys the point well enough. Clinton, in early 1993, was learning his way around Washington just as were the majority of his advisors, so it should not have been unexpected to watch the new administration make a series of mistakes as it tried to establish it relationship with Congress. With regard to the PRD policy review, however, it appears as though the ball was dropped a number of times and that these fumbles did not help the White House as it endeavoured to craft new peacekeeping guidelines.

These mistakes, for the most part, fall under the umbrella heading of 'insufficient consultations'. During the first eight months of the review process, no formal briefings were conducted for members of Congress on how the Directive was taking shape or what the objectives for the review were. Sure, members of Congress were aware of the PRD process but very few, if any, knew what the scope of the discussion was or what the White House intended to produce as a final policy. Instead of direct communication, Congress came to rely on leaks through the press and staff rumours as its primary sources of information. If members found certain aspects suspect, their primary avenues for response were either through the media or in Congressional debates, both of which are public forums. This, in turn, would give the debate a much higher profile than if disagreements were first aired in closed briefings, thereby making it more difficult to back away from stated positions. Perhaps the most damaging error was the administration's failure to establish ties to sympathetic members who might have been able to lobby on behalf of the White House during important votes. One glaring missed opportunity was Clinton waiting over eight months before meeting with a group of Congressional figures who were, early in the debate, interested in finding a solution to the funding issue. Many of the officials who worked on PDD 25 acknowledge that the administration completely overlooked the views of Congress in the initial stages of the review and neglected to bridge that divide in time.[16] This was a critical error in dealing with a Congress only too eager to leave its mark on a foreign-policy decision early in the term of a new president.

One would be correct to point out, however, that Congress could have found much larger spending programmes to focus on during Clinton's first year in office. After all, as has been mentioned earlier in this discussion, the total amount of US expenditures for UN-related spending was less than 0.5 per cent of the Pentagon budget in FY 1994, hardly a large sum in Washington's terms. As for the issue of a perceived snub, surely the novice Clintonites put more than a few noses out of joint during 1993, especially among members of Congress. So, perhaps, on their own merits, these two explanations amount to less than convincing evidence that Congress was the most influential actor in the PDD 25 development. While this might be true, the third and final reason will suggest that, in conjunction with the two factors outlined above, UN peacekeeping, or the entire UN Organization for that matter was, and remains, a target too tempting to resist for a majority of American legislators.

In October 1997, the Program on International Policy Attitudes released a report dealing with the gap between what the public would like to see as foreign policy and what the élite (i.e. members of Congress, the Executive, media and NGOs) believe the public wants.[17] The results of the report are startling to say the least. In many of the cases, members of Congress and/or their staff members are completely out of touch with what the polls indicate are popular preferences, and usually more so than the other so-called 'élites'. Nowhere is this more obvious than over UN-related issues. For example, when members of Congress were asked how the average American citizen felt about the UN, 82 per cent said 'negative'. Similarly, when asked how Americans felt about paying UN dues, 82 per cent replied 'generally negative'. As for questions pertaining to peacekeeping, the results were equally pessimistic. A full 80 per cent of members responded that the American public viewed UN peacekeeping in a 'generally negative' light, while 71 per cent believed the US public wanted to withdraw immediately from Somalia in the aftermath of the Mogadishu firefight.[18] But it is obvious, keeping in mind the data presented in Chapter 5, that these members of Congress grossly underestimate the support their fellow citizens extend to the UN and peacekeeping. Maybe they can be forgiven this level of ignorance if research has shown that the public underestimates its own level of support, but this impression, coupled with the fact that UN spending, like other foreign-policy programmes, does not have a natural domestic base of support, leaves it a difficult programme to defend in times of fiscal austerity. In other words, if members of Congress are faced with reducing spending on a domestic programme, with its unavoidable consequences for American voters in particular districts or states, or withholding funds from an international organization many believe the American people do not support anyway, the decision is easy. The commonly held perception is that a vote against the UN in the House or Senate will not cost a member votes the next time he or she is up for re-election; it is, in effect, a cost-free negative vote.

These three factors coalesced during the summer of 1993 to ensure that peacekeeping would be given a rough ride in Congress, and that rough ride began in August with the publication of Byrd's opinion piece in the *New York Times*. The results of Byrd's campaign, and other vocal action from Congress, appear to have forced the first major rounds of revisions in late July and August 1993. This apparently speedy reaction of the administration to the complaints of Congress was quickly recognized as a reluctance to be drawn into a foreign-policy battle. This was perceived as a lack of backbone on the part of the White House and led many members of Congress to conclude that they could take the initiative in crafting the peace operations policy if they so desired. In a sense, Congress was showing its willingness to engage in a struggle over foreign policy, but by the end of September 1993 it was clear that Clinton was declining the invitation.

The result of Clinton revealing his unwillingness to fight for his expanded peacekeeping policy was Congress assuming the *de facto* lead and defining position in the process, without actually being a party to the review committee. Rosner notes that as the two branches interacted over peace-keeping, it became clear that Congress was the driving force.[19] By the end of September, Congress was willing to push the issue further, despite the indications that the administration was drastically scaling back its policy, because many members saw the chance to influence the policy's substance, and not just its financial aspects. The 3 October 1993 firefight which left 18 Rangers dead, allowed Congress to push its demands even further, and forced the White House to continue drafting a set of stringent conditions for peacekeeping. The course of the process leading to PDD 25, however, was already determined by September 1993 due to the efforts of an activist Congress.

NOTES

1. See Steven Kull and Clay Ramsay, *US Public Attitudes on UN Peacekeeping*, Program on International Policy Attitudes, University of Maryland, 7 March 1994, pp. 6–7.
2. This is referred to as the first hypothesis in the Introduction to this book. Please see p.xxii.
3. Carolyn J. Logan discusses this aspect at length in her 'US Public Opinion and the Inter-vention in Somalia: Lessons for the Future of Military-Humanitarian Interventions', *The Fletcher Forum of World Affairs*, Vol.20, No.2, Summer/Fall 1996, pp.169–77.
4. See General Accounting Office, United Nations: *US Participating in Peacekeeping Operations*, Washington DC: GAO, Sept. 1992, GAO/NSIAD-92-247, pp.33–4.
5. See White House, *The Clinton Administration's Policy on Reforming Multilateral Peace Operations (PDD 25)*, *USUN Press Release* 74-(94), Annex 1, 12–13 for the rationale behind this division of responsibility.
6. Interview with author, July 1997.
7. Rosner offers this observation in *The New Tug-of-War: Congress, the Executive Branch and National Security*, Washington DC: The Carnegie Endowment For International Peace, 1995, pp.3–4.
8. An interesting overview of the 1992 election is provided in Leon V. Sigal, 'The Last Cold War Election', *Foreign Affairs*, Vol.72, No.5, Winter 1992/93, pp.1–15.
9. The last week of September 1993, Clinton signalled the end of the fight with Congress over peacekeeping with his speech to the General Assembly, and speeches by Christopher, Lake and Albright. 'Assertive Multilateralism' was dead as an official policy by 1 October. This quote was printed in John M. Goshko, 'Clinton Seen Calming Hill on Peacekeeping: Caution in Committing US Forces Said to Defuse Confrontation on Presidential

Prerogatives', *Washington Post*, 2 Oct. 1993, p.A16, the day *before* the battle in Mogadishu, which killed 18 US soldiers.

10. See Donald C.F. Daniel, 'The United States', in Trevor Findley (ed.), *Challenges for the New Peacekeepers*, SIPRI Research Report #12, Oxford: Oxford University Press, 1996, p.89.

11. See Ivo H. Daalder, 'The United States and Military Intervention in Internal Conflict', in Michael E. Brown (ed.), *The International Dimensions of Internal Conflict*, Cambridge, MA: MIT Press, 1996, p.464.

12. Rosner lays out this argument on pp.86–7 of his *The New Tug of War* (n.7 above). This passage is found on p.87.

13. See Donald J. Puchala, 'Outsiders, Insiders, and UN Reform', *The Washington Quarterly*, Vol.17, No.4, pp.169–70 for this argument. The same sentiment is expressed in Edward C. Luck, 'The United Nations, Multilateralism and US Interests', in Charles William Maynes and Richard S. Williams (eds), *US Foreign Policy and the United Nations System*, New York: W.W. Norton and Company, 1996, pp.27–53.

14. These figures are quoted in Rosner, *The New Tug-of-War* (n.7 above), pp.76–7.

15. Refer to ibid, Ch.3, for the full discussion on the range of obstacles working against peacekeeping funding in Congress in the early 1990s.

16. Each government official interviewed for this book conceded this point, and said they considered it one of the more significant mistakes committed by the White House. Of course, this could also be interpreted as just one more sign that Clinton was not willing to exert much energy on this topic.

17. See Steven Kull, I.M. Destler and Clay Ramsay, *The Foreign Policy Gap: How Policy-makers Misread the Public*, Program of International Policy Attitudes, University of Maryland, Oct. 1997.

18. For a discussion of these figures, and other data, see ibid, Chs 3 and 4.

19. See Rosner (n.7 above), p.68.

————◆◇◆————

SEVEN

Conclusions and Implications

The analysis offered in the previous chapter has suggested a conclusion that can only be considered disappointing for those who anticipated a leading role for the United States in the post-Cold War era which would emphasize the rule of law in the conduct of international relations. And the central position given to the United Nations in much of the rhetoric seemed to foreshadow the renewed prominence of that organization in American thinking. It was this style of leadership that Clinton seemed to promise in 1992, but it did not play out according to that script. The purpose of this chapter is twofold. First, it will review the findings drawn from the analysis regarding the nature of the US policymaking process towards UN peacekeeping with the aim of placing PDD 25 in this political context. Second, the implications of this policymaking process will be considered *vis-à-vis* how they affected two dimensions of the US–UN relationship: 1) peacekeeping; and 2) the nature of the broader dimension of US policy at the United Nations.

This book has argued that the final substance and spirit of PDD 25 were largely the result of a self-perpetuating cycle of confrontation and conciliation played out between the White House and Congress. Weaknesses in US policy towards Somalia led to Congressional criticism of the Somali mission, but also of US policy taking shape under the label of assertive multilateralism. Congressional pressures designed to satisfy various agendas, and the concomitant failure of the Clinton administration to remain faithful to its original intentions in the face of mounting Congressional opposition, signified an opportunity for Congress to influence a foreign-policy decision in the very early stages of the first administration in the new epoch of international affairs. Because the cost to domestic policy initiatives was perceived to have been too high by the domestically oriented White House, the harder Congress pushed, the more pliable the Executive appeared to be. Therefore, by September 1993, the substance of the policy under consideration had taken on a much more accommodating nature as far as the complaints emanating from Congress were concerned. In this light, PDD 25 does not appear as the tool to 'improve', or 'fix', peacekeeping as administration officials claimed when they released the public version of the document in 1994.[1] The belief that this policy directive would benefit peacekeeping might have been held by a few officials at the time, but it is now clear that the principal intent of the Directive was to mollify a motivated and aggressive Congress. Rather than being designed to strengthen peacekeeping, PDD 25 was designed to avoid any future confrontations with Congress over US support of a UN mission, or participation in such a mission.

The terms of the Directive make it plain that tough questions will be asked, and that no single answer will determine US support or participation. Instead, an analysis of the full body of these factors will be considered. As one senior UN official remarked, this allows the administration to justify any decision with the terms of the Directive, on a case-by-case basis.[2] This suspicion appears to be well grounded when one recalls the press conference given by National Security Advisor, Anthony Lake, which unveiled PDD 25. During the question-and-answer session, reporters tried repeatedly to get Lake to indicate which of the 18 current missions would qualify under the new criteria, especially why the US was intervening in Haiti and not in Rwanda. He refused to comment.[3] His reluctance to explain how the new policy would be applied in practice leaves the impression that he did not say because he did not know. The Directive's terms were flexible enough so that the administration could act under them when it felt it had to defend a particular American interest, but at the same time, the three tiers of questions could be used to justify blocking any action it did not want to pursue, or if the White House knew Congressional support would not be forthcoming. And this final point of Congressional support is critical to understanding Lake's reluctance to comment on current missions and just how involved the United States might be in the future because, if nothing else, PDD 25 ensures a great deal of Congressional control over any future peace operation. By killing the shared responsibility provisions of the policy, Congress secured for itself an extra-ordinary measure of *de facto* control over the approval, or denial, of any proposed mission because it eliminated any possibility of funding within the annual DoD budget, consequently forcing funding requests to be made for each individual case as it arises. In other words, if shared responsibility was implemented, a peacekeeping account would have been created within the Pentagon's budget allowing for operations to be funded during the course of the fiscal year without having the express approval of Congress. Yes, Congress would have had to authorize the funds in the budget for that fiscal year but, once the funds were approved, Congress would have lost direct control over them until the next budget appropriations the following year.

What does this suggest about American leadership in efforts to enhance the UN's ability to meet the increasing challenges of the new era? One author has come to the conclusion that the prognosis is bleak because domestic politics have led the US to become a 'self-restrained' power.[4] The White House is now leery of any involvement with peacekeeping operations, especially if direct US military support is requested. This posture, however, has inherent dangers of its own, as Waltraud Morales pointed out after the Directive was announced:

> By discrediting UN multilateralism for domestic expediency, the Clinton administration could find it harder, especially when no vital US national interests are engaged, to forge a New World Order in which UN multilateralism replaces the US as the world policeman. When vital US foreign policy goals are involved but unilateral US intervention is not desirable or feasible, the UN could more effectively provide the legal and moral framework for intervention, and the basis for domestic and international support.[5]

From this vantage point, PDD 25 contains a supposed formula for heading off Congressional attacks, and for keeping peacekeeping bills down, but it also contains the seeds for potentially larger problems, and costs, for the US government.

IMPLICATIONS

At the outset of this study, it was hoped that an analysis of the decisionmaking process towards peacekeeping might help us better understand the shifts in both US peacekeeping policy, and American policy at the UN in general. With this in mind, this discussion may have provided some insight into the motivations behind the decisions made by the Clinton administration concerning the United Nations and, in the process, have revealed a link between the process leading to PDD 25, and how American policy towards the United Nations might develop in the future. Although a thorough examination of the implications of the defining characteristics behind the PDD 25 process on American UN policy would entail a separate study in its own right, two examples can be discussed briefly here.

PDD 25's First Application: Rwanda

In terms of peacekeeping policy, the impact of PDD 25 was felt almost immediately in the spring of 1994, when ethnic tensions erupted into a horrific episode of genocide in Rwanda. The killings were largely committed during April and May of that year, just as the Directive was being released publicly. Despite the press reports detailing the dire situation in the country, the US was one of the most vocal opponents to any increase of the existing UN force.[6] By mid-May, the American position was widely seen as the main reason why the UN force was being downsized, rather than increased, as the UN General in Rwanda was requesting.[7] The motivation for this position was that the government 'intends to apply its rigid new constraints on peacekeeping to all United Nations operations, not just the ones in which the United States might play a central role'.[8] The criticism this decision generated within the human-rights organizations, and even some sections of UN Headquarters, was intense, but Congress was silent with not one member calling for American action.[9]

In the early days of June, 1994, the Clinton administration went one step further in trying to avoid involvement by denying that the violence in Rwanda was genocide. If the acts of aggression by the Hutus against the Tutsis were declared to be genocide, the parties to the 1948 Genocide Convention would be morally and legally bound to respond with the aim of stopping the genocide, and punishing those responsible. This included the United States which signed the treaty in 1989, some 41 years after the treaty was first offered for signature. Rather than acknowledge its responsibilities under the treaty and act to fulfil them, the administration, instead, instructed its officials to avoid the term 'genocide' when discussing the situation in Rwanda.[10] As one reporter wrote: 'Trying to avoid the rise of moral pressure to stop the mass killing in Rwanda, the Clinton administration has instructed its spokesmen not to describe the deaths there as genocide, even though some senior officials believe that is exactly what they represent.'[11] Meanwhile, in the Security Council, administration officials echoed the language they used to disengage their government from Somalia as the reason not to take action in Rwanda: 'But whatever efforts the United Nations may undertake, the true key to the problems in Rwanda is in the hands of the Rwandese people.'[12] This argument has not attracted many believers over the years as it was clear to many then, and now, that the mayhem was well beyond the ability of the Rwandans to control in any way, shape or form. Among the more disappointed was probably General Roméo Dallaire, UN commander in Rwanda during the crisis, because he has consistently argued that if he had been given just a few thousand more properly trained and equipped soldiers he could have saved tens of thousands of lives, or more. The international community and Security Council abandoned not only him and his soldiers, but Rwanda itself, and this is a belief he still holds today.[13]

Less diplomatic analysts, however, place the responsibility for the terribly deficient UN response squarely on the United States and its PDD 25-guided policy. General Dallaire is correct to blame the Security Council, but he is overlooking, intentionally or not, the enormous influence the US exerts on that body's actions. While it is true than none of the countries which had supplied the UN with lists of earmarked military units came forward to answer the pleas for troops with generous and timely offers, the fact that the American delegation was so openly opposed to the dispatch of additional troops must be treated as a mitigating circumstance when judging the decisions of those countries. For many states, the lack of US support, be it financial, logistical or military, signifies greater chances of failure and much higher costs than would otherwise be the case in such complex and risky operations. This reality has led to the point where US involvement is almost a prerequisite for other governments attempting to respond to a cry for help, especially in cases of complex emergencies. It was in this context, and in the face of undeniable genocide, that the United States imposed its uncompromising view on the Security Council with dire results:

> ... the US chose Rwanda as a chance to 'draw a line in the sand' and forcefully enunciated and implemented Presidential Decision Directive 25 (PDD 25). ... PDD 25 itself is a group of good peacekeeping principles and ideas. In many ways it only repeats what many other troop contributing nations have been saying, and this resonates in their own official and off-the-record concerns about UNAMIR and other ongoing peacekeeping missions. However, in the Rwandan crisis post 6 April, PDD 25 was pushed too far and applied inflexibly so as to become an impediment to rapid and effective conflict resolution and intervention into what was a humanitarian disaster.[14]

It was only a matter of time before the warning of Morales came to be, and the press started asking whether the administration had allowed a far greater problem to develop by refusing to deal with the crisis at an earlier stage. By late July, one journalist came to the conclusion that the answer was 'yes' – Clinton's opposition to responding forcefully in April and May led to the immense humanitarian crisis.[15] The article noted that the US was forced to address the mounting crisis with the dispatch of over 2,000 troops and a $250 million relief effort. Administration officials, however, refused to admit to a policy failure, even in the face of the gathering evidence that the rigid application of PDD 25 was largely responsible for the greater US involvement after the killings had stopped – both in terms of money and a troop presence – than was originally proposed when the crisis first burst on to the scene.

The suffering of the Rwandan people, of course, did not end with the victory of the Tutsi rebel army (the RPF) in the summer of 1994. Millions of Hutus fled the country, fearing reprisals at the hands of the new Tutsi-led government, to neighbouring countries where refugee camps were established. The majority of the Rwandans found themselves in either Zaire or Tanzania where the camps soon acquired an air of permanency as the Hutu militia members and soldiers of the defeated former Rwandan army, who were responsible for the genocide, set about regrouping and organizing the camps to act as launching bases for strikes back into Rwanda. Quickly, the refugees became pawns in the ongoing conflict merely by virtue of their plight; the militias intimidated the refugees from returning to Rwanda so as to ensure the continued flow of relief supplies into the camps which, in turn, sustained their ability to conduct operations against the new Rwandan government. International relief agencies worked under these conditions without the ability to challenge the militias' control over the camps and inhabitants. Tensions were especially high in eastern Zaire, where the Hutu militias also encountered Tutsi populations native to the region who were wary of both the Hutu newcomers and the Mobutu regime in Kinshasa.[16] For more than two years, this dismal situation remained unchanged as the region awaited the inevitable violence to begin anew.

The endgame was set in motion in the autumn of 1996, ironically, by the Zairean government when it declared that Tutsis living in the eastern part of the country (most of whom had arrived over 200 years ago) would have to leave Zaire. What happened next surprised many foreign observers: the indigenous Tutsis took up arms and engaged the local government garrisons, successfully.[17] Yet, as events unfolded, it became clear that the rebel forces were well organized and intent on doing more than just defending their homes from Mobutu's troops. The rebel movement entered into fierce battles with the Hutu militias operating out of the refugee camps in cooperation with Zairean government troops. Caught in this confusing, dangerous and escalating situation were the Rwandan Hutus who had only one feasible option if they did not want to die in the camps: leave the camps and flee further into Zaire to escape the fighting because they believed the border was out of reach. In November, Canada came forward to offer its leadership to a multinational relief effort aiming to get food and supplies to the refugees, and guide them home in the process. In the middle of November, just as American officials signed on to the mission, the Tutsi rebels (along with units of the Rwandan army) attacked one of the main refugee camps forcing the Hutu militia to retreat westward into Zaire. With their oppressors on the run in the other direction, the refugees themselves were able to gather their belongings and walk the short distance to the Rwandan border in a series of mass movements over the subsequent weeks. At that point, the Rwandan government declared that the international intervention force was no longer needed in eastern Zaire but, if scaled down, could be of some help as the refugees resettled. The United States quickly agreed and the momentum behind the relief force evaporated, despite several reports that an almost equal number of Hutus were either unaccounted for in the region or were moving deeper into Zaire, as international concern shifted to the fate of Zaire itself.[18]

During this period, it might have appeared to the casual observer that the crisis had indeed passed. Press reports stressed the large numbers of returning refugees, in apparently good health, and the fact that almost everyone, save the Hutu militias, was celebrating the closing of the large refugee camps which had engendered such regional tension and instability. Moreover, the intended recipient government in Kigali repeatedly called for the mission to be either called off or significantly refocused to assist solely those refugees who had made it back to Rwanda. In the wake of the first mass movement back to Rwanda, the United States publicly began to question the urgency of the force and argued for a reassessment of the needs in the area. By the time the intervention plan was completely shelved only a few weeks later, only 500 or so Western troops had been deployed. Yet, more than a year later, there was growing speculation and second-guessing that the decision to abort the operation may have been premature as evidence of massacres of Hutu refugees in eastern Zaire became well documented.[19] As the evidence mounted in what was eastern Zaire and ethnic conflict continued to plague Rwanda, questions such as, 'did the international community abort its mission too quickly, and if so, why?', naturally came to mind. The answers, on the other hand, are less forthcoming.

As far as wondering if the multinational force (MNF) folded its tent too early, the scale of the atrocities being uncovered in eastern Zaire seems to indicate an unequivocal response of 'yes', the mission was aborted prematurely. But, having said that, it is much more difficult to ascertain the answer to the second part of the question, 'why?' The trouble lies in trying to separate the multitude of motives and agendas behind the involvement of different governments in the crisis. One western government official commented that the permanent members of the Security Council (the P5) all recognized the limitations of Canada in leading an MNF without the firm support of the United States and, accordingly, used the Steering Group either to conceal their genuine lack of interest in a deployment to Africa or to influence the process for their own ends. If the political will was lacking, then given the right excuse, it was easy to walk away from Zaire. In this context, true intentions are hard to identify, thus making it even more difficult to lay responsibility for the deaths of these people at the feet of any one government; but, just as two years earlier, there still seems to be enough blame to go around. Having said that, however, what is clear is that PDD 25, and its concomitant mind-set, went a long way to letting this situation develop, and this leads to the reason why the force never fully deployed or adjusted to meet the changing conditions in the field.

Many people hoped that, with Clinton's agreement, there would be an acceleration in the planning and deployment to eastern Zaire. American participation, however, did not speed up the process; rather it slowed it down, to the dismay of many partner governments.[20] The US set out to draft a limited mandate for the mission which, in many respects, did not complement the type of operation envisioned by the Canadians. As one Western official described the early stages of planning, the US came with a long list of 'don'ts'.[21] The press reported these demands as being concerned with the duration of the mission (the US wanted no more than four months, the Canadians anticipated six); predetermined funding arrangements for the African contingents; no disarming of militias or rebels and no separation of militias from general refugee populations was to be attempted; a ceasefire was to be in effect before any coalition forces entered the area; and refugees escorted back on a voluntary basis only, using supplies inside the Rwandan border as an incentive. Given the volatile situation on the ground, these concerns may have been justified, but on the other hand, they can be seen as an excessive cautiousness which effectively stalled the operation (though it should be noted that the ceasefire demand was dropped). While circumstances changed further on the ground, the Steering Group was left in a chronic state of limbo as it repeatedly put off any decision on how to alter the mandate to meet the new conditions. The official explanation was that the situation was too confusing and chaotic, *ergo*, the mandate could not be reconsidered if the needs, let alone location, of any remaining refugees could not be identified. The only straightforward response from the United States and its partners was a replay of the Security Council's response to the original crisis in Rwanda two years earlier: scale down the size and scope of the proposed mission; just as UNAMIR was reduced in size at the very moment it was needed most.

Throughout the second half of November and into December, all the press could do was report the hesitation of the troop-contributing nations to deployment into the region, in spite of the persistent claims by the UN and relief organizations that hundreds of thousands were still in Zaire and more vulnerable than ever because they were without the relative safety of the camps.[22] Eventually, the operation was aborted but some of the advance units did remain to assist the returning refugees inside Rwanda. Unfortunately, those who never made it out of Zaire, however, were essentially ignored. It is right to point out (as the Tutsi-led Rwandan government often did) that ignoring these people was made easier by the fact that many of the Rwandan Hutus who had run west rather than east when the camps were 'liberated' by the Zairean rebels ran in that direction for a reason: they were the ones most responsible for the planning and implementation of the genocide in 1994 and, consequently, feared reprisals upon their homecoming. But the majority of those going westward were not guilty of genocide. These people were Hutus unable to reach the Rwandan border without help, or they were honestly afraid to return to their homeland because they believed the militias' claims that those who returned would be killed. For many, it seemed to be a no-win situation. Without help from the outside world, it is now painfully true that thousands of Rwandans suffered the same fate as so many of their compatriots just two years earlier.

Is PDD 25 responsible for this failure of international will? The answer would have to be a qualified 'yes'. The cautious, risk-averse attitude towards peace operations found in PDD 25 was directly responsible for the very constrained US posture in the planning sessions even before the refugee camps were attacked. Once the Rwandans were scattered in the aftermath of those attacks and the proposed relief mission became much more complicated, the already narrowly defined operation was found to be unworkable in the new circumstances. As soon as this realization was made, there was obviously no interest on the part of the United States to reopen the negotiations with the aim of being involved in a humanitarian mission with peace enforcement overtones. The Clinton administration was determined to avoid being dragged into a more aggressive mission in Zaire because it knew that such a mission would not attract the support of Congress, as some members, such as Jesse Helms, were already sending that message.[23] In short, Rwandans were denied international help when their plight was most dire because the United States could not bring itself to sign on to a more complicated, and possibly more dangerous, rescue mission as events on the ground overtook the politically sensitive parameters of PDD 25. Just as the US was only too willing to accept the view that the violence in Rwanda was incompatible with the terms of PDD 25 in 1994, the Clinton administration was only too eager to concur with Kigali that all of the legitimate refugees were safely home in Rwanda. In both cases, the US either lobbied for a reduction in the UN force, or simply argued that the need for an intervention force had passed. In both cases, the US was wrong.

There is, of course, a caveat in this qualified conclusion, and that concerns the other parties to this aborted venture. It was argued above that the inability of Canada to firmly lead a coalition without the support of the US allowed many other important countries to hide their individual lack of resolve behind the inaction of the faceless 'Steering Group' and, ultimately, the US itself, because they knew the mandate would be of a very restricted nature so as to avoid undue risk for the Clinton administration. The reluctance of the US, however, should not absolve these other countries completely of their responsibility. With the exception of some African states, most of the participants were OECD members, or, more to the point, NATO members, which means that, presumably, they have some military capabilities in their own right. In fact, France had proved its capacity to quickly deploy a force to Rwanda during the original crisis in 1994 and managed to establish a safe haven which protected a large number of potential victims (and perpetrators as well). Why, then, were these countries so dependent on American involvement? Naturally, US participation enables a larger-scale response and reduces the risks and costs, but given the numbers of lives at stake, and if the motives were purely humanitarian as claimed, should not some effort have been made to help the Hutus? Although the PDD 25 mind-set appears to have a firm hold over American decisionmakers, it is a less compelling excuse in other capitals. For this reason, and also that perhaps no operation could have saved the westward-bound refugees, it would be unfair to label PDD 25 as the sole reason why Rwandans were abandoned twice in two years, only to be killed in such ugly and unnecessary circumstances. After having granted this concession, however, there is little doubt that PDD 25 was the leading culprit in this disaster.

From the tragedy of Rwanda and its legacy in eastern Zaire, PDD 25 in practice does little to reassure the international community that the United States is willing to provide the necessary leadership in times of need, or worse, can perhaps even cause efforts by others to answer a call for help to be blocked. At a time when the United Nations' capacity for responding to more frequent, and complicated calls for help needs steady support, PDD 25's subservience to domestic politics leaves it as anything but certain that the support needed will be forthcoming. This does not mean that the US has, or will, turn its back on UN peace operations altogether. For example, American support was a significant factor in the launching of UN missions in the former Yugoslavia and then backing up that support by contributing ground troops.[24] But these operations were in the traditional style of peacekeeping, and were conducted under the protective and overpowering wing of an ongoing NATO operation. As such, while signifying a continuing endorsement of the UN's Chapter VI-mandated activities, American support in these cases does not constitute a sign of faith in more aggressive peace-enforcement operations launched under Chapter VII of the UN Charter. In this respect, PDD 25 has all but ruled out US participation in, and perhaps even support for, UN-led peace-enforcement operations, and this has not gone unnoticed by the Organization's leadership, or other member states.

In a letter to the then President of the Security Council on 18 September 1995, UN Secretary-General Boutros-Ghali indicated that he had come to the realization that Chapter VII-mandated enforcement operations are beyond the UN's competence.[25] He based this conclusion on a number of factors, chief among them the Organization's trouble in securing sufficient troop and civilian contributions for missions, the stress placed on the Organization due to its chronic cash-crunch, and finally, the UN's limited ability to manage large-scale missions, especially those launched under Chapter VII which have a chance of involving combat. This, on the surface, may appear to be a redundant finding, but it reflects the lasting legacy of PDD 25. Clinton launched the policy review in 1993 to address, *inter alia*, this particular issue, namely, how to help the UN develop into a more capable and effective organization. By September 1995 (if not sooner), it had become clear to the Secretary-General that not only had the US failed to craft a policy designed to better the UN, but that PDD 25 essentially eliminated that type of mission from the UN's range of responses to international conflict and humanitarian disasters. In the PDD 25 era, the notion of 'subcontracting' potentially dangerous missions to coalitions of like-minded states would become the norm, rather than the exception, if any mission were launched at all.[26]

More discouraging than this blunt assessment of the new situation, however, were the remarks by Ambassador Albright a year after the 1994 Rwandan disaster, which implied that PDD 25 was considered a success by the Clinton administration after its first year, simply because the number of missions had decreased (and that the costs had been reduced as well).[27] This sort of comment leaves one with the discouraging impression that the lessons of Rwanda have not been taken to heart by those who make the decisions. Furthermore, the retreat from peace operations is being sounded even over missions deemed successful and those which have been conducted outside of the UN framework. One reporter interviewed the current Secretary of Defense, William Cohen, after his first trip abroad as head of the Pentagon and discovered that, while he acknowledged the positive contribution of American forces to the advancement of peace in the Balkans, he was nonetheless committed to pulling all US personnel out of the mission by June 1998, regardless of the mission's status.[28] The reason for this puzzling position, the Secretary explained, was an unsupportive Congress. But the reporter added that Cohen is unlikely to push the administration to confront Congress over this, and other issues, just as Clinton is not keen to rock relations with the legislative houses. As the journalist concluded:

> Mr Cohen will not be pulling and tugging at the president to take
> bold steps abroad that would cost money and cause him trouble
> with Congress as Mr Clinton felt some aides did in his first term.
> The two men meet on a common ground of caution, of observing
> limits and of desiring above all peace on the home front.

If the US persists in judging the value and effectiveness of peacekeeping in terms of fiscal responsibility and exit strategies, and continues to be held by the whims of Congress, then it will be a long time before the shortcomings observed by Boutros-Ghali will be addressed in good faith. The future of peacekeeping in the PDD 25 era, given the Rwanda/eastern Zaire model and the UN's exclusion from Chapter VII peace operations, seems destined to be even more ineffective and *ad hoc* than ever before.[29]

US Domestic Politics Spill-over

It is difficult to make a full analysis of the impact of PDD 25 on the broader level of US relations with the UN system as a whole, but there is evidence that the Beltway politics which so clearly drove the US peacekeeping policy review, has also infected the American policy towards the UN Organization. To illustrate this connection, this section will review the controversy surrounding Clinton's very public and high profile campaign to veto the re-election bid of former UN Secretary-General, Boutros Boutros-Ghali.

The US relationship with the newly elected Secretary-General began on an awkward note in late 1991 when the US, confident that Boutros-Ghali would not win the necessary nine votes (and no vetoes) in the Security Council, abstained on the Egyptian's candidacy while the Bush administration was actively considering other contenders.[30] When Boutros-Ghali won the Council's backing, the Americans were surprised and perhaps disappointed, but quickly stated their support for the new UN leader. Speculation at the time contended that the Bush administration was very sensitive to publicly opposing the national of a key Arab ally, especially in the wake of the Gulf War. The hope was that Boutros-Ghali's nomination would not be able to garner the requisite number of votes, then flounder until a more popular candidate was identified. Despite this miscalculation, the US set out to work with the new Secretary-General with a particular focus on reform issues.

By the end of 1993, the Clinton administration found fault in Boutros-Ghali over two key issues: 1) the lack of coherent management of the Somali mission; and 2) the perceived stalling of the reform initiatives after his first year in office. These criticisms, however, had an air of implausibility about them because, as we now know, Boutros-Ghali was unfairly cited as the reason why UNOSOM II ended in such failure, and the lack of progress on the reform front was often overstated. As one journalist noticed: 'US critics of Boutros-Ghali always liked to accuse him of blocking UN reform, but that charge was unfair. Boutros-Ghali actually cut the Secretariat staff from 12,000 to 9,000 and presided over the Organization's first-ever zero-growth budgets.'[31] Boutros-Ghali could also lay claim to other reform measures, but it was evident that his critics in Washington were not prepared to grant him a fair appraisal. Clinton and his foreign-policy advisors, for the most part, continued to declare their confidence in the Secretary-General and, into early 1996, gave no indication that they were planning to move against him. When Boutros-Ghali first learned of the administration's intention to bar him from a second term, he admitted to an interviewer that he was stunned and failed to understand the sudden reversal.[32] In the context of American domestic politics during a presidential election campaign, nothing should have surprised the Secretary-General of the United Nations.

The administration had for some time had certain frustrations with Dr Boutros-Ghali, but the decision to block his attempt at another five-year term came only after Republican presidential candidates made the Secretary-General an issue during the Republican Party's primaries. Subsequently, the issue was raised with vigour in Congress.[33] During an election year, Clinton decided he could not take a chance in allowing the man accused of 'dictating US foreign policy' to remain at the head of the Organization, and give the Republicans in the campaign, or in Congress, something they could use to their political advantage, as distorted as it was. The desire to remove this apparent political liability was so strong, that the administration publicly moved against the Secretary-General, after a secret offer to stay on for just one more year was refused by the, perhaps, too-proud former university professor. By late September, the administration had expressed its position so emphatically, it appeared highly unlikely it would change course.[34] Moreover, Clinton irritated a vast number of UN member states by making this decision despite the fact that a majority of them did not oppose the Secretary-General's re-election, and also that Clinton did not have another candidate in mind to replace Boutros-Ghali when he committed himself to the latter's eviction.[35]

In the denouement of this undiplomatic drama, Clinton carried the day. Boutros-Ghali, after the first voting rounds in which he repeatedly encountered the American veto, 'suspended' his candidacy so that other Africans could come forward for consideration. After a number of straw polls, it became a concern among African states that unless they threw their support behind one person, they risked a deadlock which might result in losing the post to another region. Out of this scenario, the then Under-Secretary-General for the Department of Peacekeeping Operations, Kofi Annan, was elected – a two-point victory for the US in that they wanted Boutros-Ghali out, and Kofi Annan was their favourite possible replacement. But the victory did not come cost free, as was evident immediately following the announcement of Annan's selection when many African leaders spoke out against the American hard-ball tactics and the fact that the first UN Secretary-General to be denied a second term, over the unanimous endorsement of the region's governments, was an African.[36] As for the UN itself, a former senior staff member wrote that it was a 'humiliation' for the Organization which raised a number of important issues regarding how the leading powers viewed the UN and what the long-term repercussions of those perspectives might be.[37] Apparently, Clinton was more concerned with the views of his Congressional opponents than he was with diplomatic manners and any long-term damage to the UN; two myopic attitudes which may only frustrate American initiatives in the future.

FINAL REMARKS

One might argue that Clinton's tactics regarding the ousting of Boutros-Ghali were used only because of unusual circumstances and that this type of hard-nosed veto-wielding was an isolated incident. There is, however, a strong chance that the pattern of Congressional influence so apparent in the political process leading to PDD 25 has become a standard ingredient in the US decisionmaking on policy to be pursued at the United Nations. The current cast of characters in Washington, both in Congress and the White House has done very little to suggest otherwise. The leading antagonist is the elderly Chairman of the Senate Foreign Relations Committee, Jesse Helms of North Carolina, who would consider it a personal victory if the UN were to be slowly starved into bankruptcy.[38] Senator Helms has demonstrated, time and again, the enormous amount of influence he and his like-minded colleagues can bring to bear on any issue of interest. The threats to sink the Chemical Weapons Treaty and his single-handed, successful campaign to torpedo the nomination of another Republican for the post of Ambassador to Mexico are only recent examples of the very assertive posture Helms, and others in Congress, are eager to play in the foreign-policy arena. So it should have come as no surprise when Congress made its boldest move yet in its efforts to advance its agenda by withdrawing its support for a deal on US arrears to the UN over a domestic issue. In November 1997, Congress voted to kill provisions of a foreign-spending bill which allowed for, *inter alia*, the partial payment of over $900 million of US arrears, because

Republican Congressional leaders were unable to reach an agreement with the White House over a policy on family planning and abortion, a totally unrelated, and essentially, domestic issue.[39] Once again, the UN and foreign aid had proved to be an irresistible target for members of Congress, but they outdid themselves in the sense that they were able to take a swipe at the UN although the point of contention with the White House was in no way connected to the work of the Organization.[40] The one positive result of this fiasco is that perhaps, finally, one member of the Clinton cabinet has had enough. In the fallout with Congress over this spending bill, Secretary of State Madeleine Albright issued the sternest condemnation yet of Congress's actions *vis-à-vis* the UN, claiming that Congress was engaging in 'legislative blackmail' with little regard for its consequences.[41] Foremost in her mind is the further eroding of US leadership at the UN as the debts continue to pile up but American legislators fail to treat the problem seriously. Although it is promising to see the Secretary of State try to highlight the role of Congress in undermining US efforts at the UN, and ultimately, the UN's effectiveness, it is clear she is unlikely to make a profound difference on her own. She will need help, and this brings us back to President Clinton.

During the 1992 presidential campaign, then Governor Clinton happily rode the wave of optimism surrounding the future role of the United Nations in the post-Cold War era. He even tried to raise the bar of expectations on the master himself, President Bush – the man who ushered in the vague, but attractive New World Order vision in the aftermath of the Gulf War and his rediscovery of the UN. Upon winning the White House, Clinton gave every indication of wanting to transform those ambitious ideas into policy, but soon Congress showed signs of wanting a fight, and Clinton turned away. Eventually, Clinton would leave the false impression that the UN was to blame for the deaths of American soldiers in Somalia, before signing a peacekeeping policy document which confirmed his preference to weaken the UN rather than strengthen it in the face of domestic opposition. Hardly a staunch ally, Clinton has instead proved himself to be a fairweather friend to the UN, which leaves the Organization, and the millions of people who depend on it, in a chronically precarious position. Clinton, and the aloof American posture he codified in PDD 25, will continue to undermine not only peacekeeping efforts but the overall capacity of the UN for the foreseeable future.

NOTES

1. The author has been assured by a number of knowledgeable officials that the public version and the classified document differ only slightly.
2. Personal correspondence with a UN official, who wished to remain anonymous.

3. See Anthony Lake (National Security Advisor), 'Peacekeeping Directive Designed to Impose More Discipline', transcript of remarks by Mr Lake and Lt General Weseley Clark, White House, EUR511, 6 May 1994, 5870.

4. For this reasoning, see Stanley R. Sloan, *The United States and the Use of Force in the Post-Cold War World: Toward Self-Restraint?*, CRS 94-581 S, Washington DC: Congressional Research Service, 20 July 1994, pp.16–17. For the similar views of a journalist as the policy shift became apparent to the public, see Thomas L. Friedman, 'Theory vs. Practice: Clinton's Stated Foreign Policy Turns Into More Modest "Self-Containment"', *New York Times*, 1 Oct. 1993, p.A3.

5. This passage is found in Waltraud Queiser Morales, 'US Intervention and the New World Order: Lessons from Cold War and Post-Cold War Cases', *Third World Quarterly*, Vol.15, No.1, 1994, p.91.

6. For an example of press accounts of the situation as the bulk of the UN force pulled out in mid-April, see Reuters, 'UN Force Nears Collapse in Chaotic Rwanda', *Washington Post*, 21 April 1994, p.A26.

7. To be fair, it must be noted that the US was not the only country unwilling to rush to the rescue of Rwanda; the level of collective guilt is high indeed. For example, a report commissioned by the Canadian government casts the UK and Russia as supporting the American effort to reduce the size of UNAMIR in Security Council deliberations. See Paul LaRose-Edwards, *The Rwandan Crisis of April 1994: The Lessons Learned*, Ottawa: Department of Foreign Affairs and International Trade, 30 Nov. 1994, p.63. Furthermore, Canada and the other so-called middle powers, long the traditional source of the best trained and equipped peacekeepers, did not dispatch the numbers of soldiers requested by Dallaire. More shocking are the accusations that a Western government was actually involved in the campaign of genocide. See William Pfaff, 'An Active French Role in the 1994 Genocide in Rwanda', *International Herald Tribune*, 17 Jan. 1998 Editorial-Opinion page, IHT Website.

8. See Douglas Jehl, 'US Showing New Caution On UN Peacekeeping Missions', *New York Times*, 18 May 1994, p.A1.

9. See ibid.

10. It is worth noting that the administration's bobbing and weaving around the term 'genocide' might have been an acknowledgment of the fact that the American people held a moral conviction that such an act should be stopped. PIPA, in a July 1994 survey asking if the US should act with the UN to stop genocidal conflict, reported that 31% said 'always', 34% believed 'in most cases', 23% replied 'only when US interests are involved, and 6% stated 'never'. Regarding Rwanda and Bosnia specifically, the respondents were asked how 'they would feel if a UN commission determined that genocide was occurring' in those countries. Eighty per cent replied 'they would favour intervention in both cases'. Perhaps the government was worried that if it did concede that the Tutsis were the targets of genocide, public opinion might have demanded a forceful intervention. See Steven Kull, I.M. Destler and Clay Ramsay, *The Foreign Policy Gap: How Policymakers Misread the Public*, Program of International Policy Attitudes, University of Maryland, Oct. 1997, pp.78–9, for more on these figures.

11. This summary of the policy of denial is found in Douglas Jehl, 'Officials Told to Avoid Calling Rwanda Killings "Genocide"', *New York Times*, 10 June 1994, p.A8; and Thomas W. Lippman, 'Administration Sidesteps Genocide Label in Rwanda', *Washington Post*, 11 June 1994, p.A1.

12. Comments by the American deputy-representative in the Security Council. See United

Nations Document, Provisional Verbatim, S/PV.3377, United States Representative Inderfurth's statement to the Security Council, 16 May 1994, p.13.

13. On these views and the ongoing finger-pointing between the UN and various member states and NGOs as to who is ultimately responsible for the Organization's feeble response to the crisis, see Paul Knox, 'UN States Blamed', *Globe and Mail* (Toronto), 5 Dec. 1997, p.A16; Jeff Sallot, 'Dallaire Stands by Actions in Rwanda', *Globe and Mail* (Toronto), 13 Dec. 1997, p.A6; Scott Straus, 'UN Ignored my Pleas: Dallaire', and Jeff Sallot, 'Stint in Rwanda Seared General's Soul', both in *Globe and Mail* (Toronto), 26 Feb. 1998, pp.A1 and A9.

14. For this passage see LaRose-Edwards, *The Rwandan Crisis of April 1994* (n.7 above), p.15.

15. See Douglas Jehl, 'The Rwanda Disaster: Did US Err on Rwanda', *New York Times*, 23 July 1994, p.A1.

16. In this discussion, the name 'Zaire' will be used as it was the official name during the period under consideration. After a successful military campaign, the new rulers of the country changed the name to the 'Democratic Republic of the Congo' in May 1997.

17. A full telling of the story, with its overlapping and competing agendas and multitude of characters and secondary players, along with suspected foreign connections, is beyond the scope of this discussion. For an excellent account and useful background information, refer to the series of articles printed in *The Economist*: 'Death Shadows Africa's Great Lakes', Vol.341, No.7988, 19 Oct. 1996, pp.51–3; 'Behind the Zairean Shambles', Vol. 341, No.7990, 2 Nov. 1996, p.47; 'Someone Else's Doing, Someone Else's Problem', Vol.341, No.7991, 9 Nov. 1996, p.57; 'The World Makes up its Mind(s) about Zaire', Vol.341, No.7992, 16 Nov. 1996, p.55; and 'The Great Escape', Vol.341, No.7993, 23 Nov. 1996, p.53.

18. For a report on the number debate surrounding the Hutus remaining in Zaire after the first major exodus back to Rwanda, see Bradley Graham and Stephen Buckley, 'US sharply Cuts Back Africa Force', *Washington Post*, 20 Nov. 1996, pp.A1 and A24. As for attention shifting away from the refugee crisis to the political stability of Zaire, see Thomas W. Lippman, 'US Remains Uncertain on Response in Zaire', *Washington Post*, 8 Dec. 1996, p.A34.

19. For example, see Anne McIlroy, 'Proof Surfaces of Long Trek to Death in Congo', *Globe and Mail* (Toronto), 17 Nov. 1997, p.A8.

20. The press reported widely that the Clinton administration was not keen on joining the mission, but agreed only after pressure was applied by Canada, France and the UN Secretary-General. See Thomas W. Lippman, 'US May Send up to 5,000 Troops to Africa', *Washington Post*, 14 Nov. 1996, pp.A1 and A25; Alison Mitchell, 'Clinton Offers US Troops to Help Refugees in Zaire', *New York Times*, 14 Nov. 1996, pp.A1 and A14; Barbara Crossette, 'US Sets Conditions for Using Troops to Aid Refugees in Zaire', *New York Times*, 15 Nov. 1996, p.A7; and Thomas W. Lippman and Dana Priest, 'Pentagon Wants Cease-fire Pledge in Zaire', *Washington Post*, 15 Nov. 1996, pp.A1 and A28.

21. Comment expressed during a interview in March 1998 with an official of a Western government involved in the planning of the operation, who wishes to remain nameless.

22. To get a sense of the paralysis in the Steering Group, and the progressive scaling back of the mission, see R. Jeffery Smith, 'US Military Role May Be Scaled Back', *Washington Post*, 18 Nov. 1996, p.A16; Thomas W. Lippman, 'US Ground Troops May not go to Zaire', *Washington Post*, 19 Nov. 1996, pp.A1 and A17; James Bennet, 'Size of US Force Bound for Africa is Cut Below 1,000', *New York Times*, 20 Nov. 1996, pp.A1 and A11; Bradley Graham and Stephen Buckley, 'US Sharply Cuts Back Africa Force: Number

of Refugees in Zaire Disputed', *Washington Post*, 20 Nov. 1996, pp.A1 and A24; and Thomas W. Lippman, 'US Remains Uncertain on Response in Zaire', *Washington Post*, 8 Dec. 1996, p.A34.

23. For a sample of Helms's views, see Alison Mitchell (n.20 above), p.A14; and for other negative feedback from Congress, see Otto Kreisher, 'US Troops for Bosnia and Africa OK'd', *Copley News Service*, 16 Nov. 1996, Lexis/Nexis.

24. American support in the Security Council allowed for the creation of many UN missions in the former Yugoslavia since the signing of PDD 25, and in the following examples, the US contributed troops: UNPROFOR, UNCRO, UNPREDEP and UNMIBH. For a listing of missions supported by the US, and which ones enjoyed a US troop contribution, as of late 1996, see United Nations, *The Blue Helmets*, Third Edition, New York: United Nations, DPI, 1996.

25. My thanks to a Canadian government official for drawing my attention to this letter.

26. As this book was in the early stages of final production by the publisher, the US was leading a NATO force in a bombing campaign designed to compel the Serbian government into allowing ethnic-Albanian Kosovars back into their province and end the persecution against that population. Although the bombing has ended, the operation, as of July 1999, is not yet finished as NATO troops remain in the province and the UN is beginning to deploy a civil administration and police mission. Despite the uncertain conclusion to this operation, one fact seems very apparent at this point and this is the fact that the NATO intervention in Kosovo has little direct bearing on the issues under discussion in this book because PDD 25 had little bearing on the US decision to bypass the UN Security Council. The decision to intervene in Kosovo through a NATO force mostly likely had more to do with the very public opposition of Russia and China to UN enforcement action in Kosovo than the terms of PDD 25. Better litmus tests of PDD 25's enduring influence over UN peacekeeping operations might arise out of the possible requests for UN action in the Democratic Republic of the Congo and Sierra Leone, or how the current mission to East Timor develops in the late summer and autumn of 1999.

27. See Ambassador Albright, 'The United States and the United Nations: What's In It For Us', address to the Chicago Mid-America Committee, Chicago, 23 June 1995, *USUN Press Release*, #98-(95).

28. See Jim Hoagland, 'Less Appetite for Military Involvement Abroad', *International Herald Tribune*, 13 March 1997, p.8.

29. Michael N. Barnett has argued that the UN's ineffective response to the Rwanda crisis was out of a sense that it could not afford to get involved with another 'losing' situation, because its reputation could not withstand another public-relations disaster. His argument is well made, but I would add that the fear of another public-relations disaster was a reaction to pressure coming from the US Congress and the perspective that came to the fore through the PRD process. See his 'The UN Security Council, Indifference, and Genocide in Rwanda', *Cultural Anthropology*, Vol.12, No.4, pp.551–78.

30. See Boutros Boutros-Ghali, *Unvanquished: A US–UN Saga*, New York: Random House, 1999, p.12, for this account of the US position during the election. The reader should note, however, that the Security Council does not maintain any records of the voting in elections for the position of Secretary-General, thereby making it difficult to confirm this, or any, account of how the votes were cast.

31. For these comments, see Carroll Bogart, 'Most Likely to Succeed', *Newsweek*, Vol.128, No.26, 23 Dec. 1996, pp.10–12.

32. Boutros-Ghali expressed these views in a lengthy interview late in his term in office in

which he responded to many of the more common criticisms levelled at him in the US. See Arnaud de Borchgrave, 'The Change in the Administration's Position is a Mystery', *Washington Times*, 11 Nov. 1996, Lexis/Nexis.

33. For an account of this development, and an overview of the rather paranoid views of the extreme right wing of America's political spectrum, see John M. Goshko, 'America 1996: Looking Inward: Among Conservatives, a Deep Suspicion of United Nations', *International Herald Tribune*, 24 Sept. 1996, pp.1 and 8.

34. See Craig Turner and Stanley Meisler, 'UN Chief Must Step Down, Clinton insists: Diplomacy: Boutros-Ghali's Supporters Say he will Fight for Second Term as Secretary-General Despite Opposition', *Los Angeles Times*, 25 Sept. 1996, Lexis/Nexis, for the hardening Clinton position.

35. This fact was reported in Barbara Crossette, 'Christopher Scours Africa and the UN is Watching', *International Herald Tribune*, 11 Oct. 1996, pp.1 and 8.

36. As one example, see the views of the Ivory Coast's president in James Rupert, 'Ivory Coast Chief Criticizes UN Wrangle', *International Herald Tribune*, 16 Dec. 1996, p.6.

37. See Sir Brian Urquhart, 'Momentous Humiliation for the United Nations', *International Herald Tribune*, 11 Dec. 1996, p.10.

38. Senator Helms tried his best to convey his exceptionally conservative views on the UN in a reasonable light in his, 'Saving the UN: A Challenge to the Next Secretary-General', *Foreign Affairs*, Vol.75, No.5, Sept./Oct. 1996, pp.2–7.

39. For more on this incident, see Eric Pianin and Thomas W. Lippman, 'Republicans Withhold funds for UN and IMF', *International Herald Tribune*, 14 Nov. 1997, IHT Website; Barbara Crossette, 'UN Chief Assails US Congress for Killing Plan to Pay Dues', *International Herald Tribune*, 15 Nov. 1997, IHT Website; and *Washington Post* editorial, 'Holding up Foreign Aid', *International Herald Tribune*, 28 Feb. 1998, IHT Website. Secretary-General Kofi Annan made a statement on this issue, see UN Press Release SG/SM/6393, 14 Nov. 1997.

40. It should be noted that this proposed bill contained almost 40 other conditions, beyond the abortion issue, which rendered it totally unacceptable to the White House.

41. See Andrew Cohen, 'Albright Accuses Congress of Blackmail', *Globe and Mail* (Toronto), 14 Jan. 1998, p.A8.

———◄o►———

Clinton Administration Policy on Reforming Multilateral Peace Operations (PDD 25)

Released on the World-Wide Web by the Bureau of International Organizational Affairs, US Department of State, 22 February 1996

EXECUTIVE SUMMARY

Last year, President Clinton ordered an inter-agency review of our nation's peacekeeping policies and programs in order to develop a comprehensive policy framework suited to the realities of the post-Cold War period. This policy review has resulted in a Presidential Decision Directive (PDD 25). The President signed this directive, following the completion of extensive consultations with Members of Congress. This paper summarizes the key elements of that directive.

As specified in the 'Bottom-Up Review', the primary mission of the US Armed Forces remains to be prepared to fight and win two simultaneous regional conflicts. In this context, peacekeeping can be one useful tool to help prevent and resolve such conflicts before they pose direct threats to our national security. Peacekeeping can also serve US interests by promoting democracy, regional security, and economic growth.

The policy directive (PDD) addresses six major issues of reform and improvement:

1. Making disciplined and coherent choices about which peace operations to support – both when we vote in the Security Council for UN peace operations and when we participate in such operations with US troops.

To achieve this goal, the policy directive sets forth three increasingly rigorous standards of review for US support for or participation in peace operations, with the most stringent applying to US participation in missions that may involve combat. The policy directive affirms that peacekeeping can be a useful tool for advancing US national security interests in some circumstances, but both US and UN involvement in peacekeeping must be selective and more effective.

2. Reducing US costs for UN peace operations, both the percentage our nation pays for each operation and the cost of the operations themselves.

To achieve this goal, the policy directive orders that we work to reduce our peacekeeping assessment percentage from the current 31.7% to 25% by January 1, 1996, and proposes a number of specific steps to reduce the cost of UN peace operations.

3. Defining clearly our policy regarding the command and control of American military forces in UN peace operations.

The policy directive underscores the fact that the President will never relinquish command of US forces. However, as Commander-in-Chief, the President has the authority to place US forces under the operational control of a foreign commander when doing so serves American security interests, just as American leaders have done numerous times since the Revolutionary War, including in Operation Desert Storm.

The greater the anticipated US military role, the less likely it will be that the US will agree to have a UN commander exercise overall operational control over US forces. Any large scale participation of US forces in a major peace enforcement operation that is likely to involve combat should ordinarily be conducted under US command and operational control or through competent regional organizations such as NATO or ad hoc coalitions.

4. Reforming and improving the UN's capability to manage peace operations.

The policy recommends 11 steps to strengthen UN management of peace operations and directs US support for strengthening the UN's planning, logistics, information and command and control capabilities.

5. Improving the way the US government manages and funds peace operations.

The policy directive creates a new 'shared responsibility' approach to managing and funding UN peace operations within the US Government. Under this approach, the Department of Defense will take lead management and funding responsibility for those UN operations that involve US combat units and those that are likely to involve combat, whether or not US troops are involved. This approach will ensure that military expertise is brought to bear on those operations that have a significant military component.

The State Department will retain lead management and funding responsibility for traditional peacekeeping operations that do not involve US combat units. In all cases, the State Department remains responsible for the conduct of diplomacy and instructions to embassies and our UN Mission in New York.

6. Creating better forms of cooperation between the Executive, the Congress and the American public on peace operations.

The policy directive sets out seven proposals for increasing and regularizing the flow of information and consultation between the executive branch and Congress; the President believes US support for and participation in UN peace operations can only succeed over the long term with the bipartisan support of Congress and the American people.

KEY ELEMENTS OF THE CLINTON ADMINISTRATION'S POLICY
ON REFORMING MULTILATERAL PEACE OPERATIONS
(AS SPECIFIED IN PDD 25, MAY 1994)

Introduction: The Role of Peace Operations in US Foreign Policy

Serious threats to the security of the United States still exist in the post-Cold War era. New threats will emerge. The United States remains committed to meeting such threats.

When our interests dictate, the US must be willing and able to fight and win wars, unilaterally whenever necessary. To do so, we must create the required capabilities and maintain them ready to use. UN peace operations cannot substitute for this requirement. (Note: For simplicity, the term peace operations is used in this document to cover the entire spectrum of activities from traditional peacekeeping to peace enforcement aimed at defusing and resolving international conflicts.)

Circumstances will arise, however, when multilateral action best serves US interests in preserving or restoring peace. In such cases, the UN can be an important instrument for collective action. UN peace operations can also provide a 'force multiplier' in our efforts to promote peace and stability.

During the Cold War, the United Nations could resort to multilateral peace operations only in the few cases when the interests of the Soviet Union and the West did not conflict. In the new strategic environment such operations can serve more often as a cost-effective tool to advance American as well as collective interests in maintaining peace in key regions and create global burden-sharing for peace.

Territorial disputes, armed ethnic conflicts, civil wars (many of which could spill across international borders) and the collapse of governmental authority in some states are among the current threats to peace. While many of these conflicts may not directly threaten American interests, their cumulative effect is significant. The UN has sought to play a constructive role in such situations by mediating disputes and obtaining agreement to cease-fires and political settlements. Where such agreements have been reached, the interposition of neutral forces under UN auspices has, in many cases, helped facilitate lasting peace.

UN peace operations have served important US national interests. In Cambodia, UN efforts led to an election protected by peacekeepers, the return of hundreds of thousands of refugees and the end of a destabilizing regional conflict. In El Salvador, the UN sponsored elections and is helping to end a long and bitter civil war. The UN's supervision of Namibia's transition to independence removed a potential source of conflict in strategic southern Africa and promoted democracy. The UN in Cyprus has prevented the outbreak of war between two NATO allies. Peacekeeping on the Golan Heights has helped preserve peace between Israel and Syria. In Former Yugoslavia, the UN has provided badly-needed humanitarian assistance and helped prevent the conflict from spreading to other parts of the region. UN-imposed sanctions against Iraq, coupled with the peacekeeping operation on the Kuwait border, are constraining Iraq's ability to threaten its neighbors.

Need for Reform

While serving US interests, UN peace operations continue to require improvement and reform. Currently, each operation is created and managed separately, and economies of scale are lost. Likewise, further organizational changes at UN Headquarters would improve efficiency and effectiveness. A fully independent office of Inspector General should be established immediately. The US assessment rate should be reduced to 25 per cent.

Since it is in our interest at times to support UN peace operations, it is also in our interest to seek to strengthen UN peacekeeping capabilities and to make operations less expensive and peacekeeping management more accountable. Similarly, it is in our interest to identify clearly and quickly those peace operations we will support and those we will not. Our policy establishes clear guidelines for making such decisions.

Role in US Foreign Policy

UN and other multilateral peace operations will at times offer the best way to prevent, contain or resolve conflicts that could otherwise be more costly and deadly. In such cases, the US benefits from having to bear only a share of the burden. We also benefit by being able to invoke the voice of the community of nations on behalf of a cause we support. Thus, establishment of a capability to conduct multilateral peace operations is part of our National Security Strategy and National Military Strategy.

While the President never relinquishes command of US forces, the participation of US military personnel in UN operations can, in particular circumstances, serve US interests. First, US military participation may, at times, be necessary to persuade others to participate in operations that serve US interests. Second, US participation may be one way to exercise US influence over an important UN mission, without unilaterally bearing the burden. Third, the US may be called upon and choose to provide unique capabilities to important operations that other countries cannot.

In improving our capabilities for peace operations, we will not discard or weaken other tools for achieving US objectives. If US participation in a peace operation were to interfere with our basic military strategy, winning two major regional conflicts nearly simultaneously (as established in the Bottom Up Review), we would place our national interest uppermost. The US will maintain the capability to act unilaterally or in coalitions when our most significant interests and those of our friends and allies are at stake. Multilateral peace operations must, therefore, be placed in proper perspective among the instruments of US foreign policy.

The US does not support a standing UN army, nor will we earmark specific US military units for participation in UN operations. We will provide information about US capabilities for data bases and planning purposes.

It is not US policy to seek to expand either the number of UN peace operations or US involvement in such operations. Instead, this policy, which builds upon work begun by previous administrations and is informed by the concerns of the Congress and our experience in recent peace operations, aims to ensure that our use of peacekeeping is selective and more effective. Congress must also be actively involved in the continuing implementation of US policy on peacekeeping.

I. SUPPORTING THE RIGHT PEACE OPERATIONS

i. *Voting for Peace Operations*

The US will support well-defined peace operations, generally, as a tool to provide finite windows of opportunity to allow combatants to resolve their differences and failed societies to begin to reconstitute themselves. Peace operations should not be open-ended commitments but instead linked to concrete political solutions; otherwise, they normally should not be undertaken. To the greatest extent possible, each UN peace operation should have a specified timeframe tied to intermediate or final objectives, an integrated political/military strategy well-coordinated with humanitarian assistance efforts, specified troop levels, and a firm budget estimate. The US will continue to urge the UN Secretariat and Security Council members to engage in rigorous, standard evaluations of all proposed new peace operations.

The Administration will consider the factors below when deciding whether to vote for a proposed new UN peace operation (Chapter VI or Chapter VII) or to support a regionally-sponsored peace operation:

• UN involvement advances US interests, and there is an international community of interest for dealing with the problem on a multilateral basis.

- There is a threat to or breach of international peace and security, often of a regional character, defined as one or a combination of the following:

  - International aggression, or;
  - Urgent humanitarian disaster coupled with violence;
  - Sudden interruption of established democracy or gross violation of human rights coupled with violence, or threat of violence.

- There are clear objectives and an understanding of where the mission fits on the spectrum between traditional peacekeeping and peace enforcement.
- For traditional (Chapter VI) peacekeeping operations, a ceasefire should be in place and the consent of the parties obtained before the force is deployed.
- For peace enforcement (Chapter VII) operations, the threat to international peace and security is considered significant.
- The means to accomplish the mission are available, including the forces, financing and mandate appropriate to the mission.
- The political, economic and humanitarian consequences of inaction by the international community have been weighed and are considered unacceptable.
- The operation's anticipated duration is tied to clear objectives and realistic criteria for ending the operation.

These factors are an aid in decisionmaking; they do not by themselves constitute a prescriptive device. Decisions have been and will be based on the cumulative weight of the factors, with no single factor necessarily being an absolute determinant.

In addition, using the factors above, the US will continue to scrutinize closely all existing peace operations when they come up for regular renewal by the Security Council to assess the value of continuing them. In appropriate cases, the US will seek voluntary contributions by beneficiary nations or enhanced host nation support to reduce or cover, at least partially, the costs of certain UN operations. The US will also consider voting against renewal of certain long-standing peace operations that are failing to meet established objectives in order to free military and financial resources for more pressing UN missions.

ii. Participating in UN and Other Peace Operations

The Administration will continue to apply even stricter standards when it assesses whether to recommend to the President that US personnel participate in a given peace operation. In addition to the factors listed above, we will consider the following factors:

- Participation advances US interests and both the unique and general risks to American personnel have been weighed and are considered acceptable.

- Personnel, funds and other resources are available;
- US participation is necessary for operation's success;
- The role of US forces is tied to clear objectives and an endpoint for US participation can be identified;
- Domestic and Congressional support exists or can be marshalled;
- Command and control arrangements are acceptable.

Additional, even more rigorous factors will be applied when there is the possibility of significant US participation in Chapter VII operations that are likely to involve combat:

- There exists a determination to commit sufficient forces to achieve clearly defined objectives;
- There exists a plan to achieve those objectives decisively;
- There exists a commitment to reassess and adjust, as necessary, the size, composition and disposition of our forces to achieve our objectives.

Any recommendation to the President will be based on the cumulative weight of the above factors, with no single factor necessarily being an absolute determinant.

II. THE ROLE OF REGIONAL ORGANIZATIONS

In some cases, the appropriate way to perform peace operations will be to involve regional organizations. The US will continue to emphasize the UN as the primary international body with the authority to conduct peacekeeping operations. At the same time, the US will support efforts to improve regional organizations' peacekeeping capabilities.

When regional organizations or groupings seek to conduct peacekeeping with UNSC endorsement, US support will be conditioned on adherence to the principles of the UN Charter and meeting established UNSC criteria, including neutrality, consent of the conflicting parties, formal UNSC oversight and finite, renewal mandates.

With respect to the question of peacekeeping in the territory of the former Soviet Union, requests for 'traditional' UN blue-helmeted operations will be considered on the same basis as other requests, using the factors previously outlined (e.g., a threat to international peace and security, clear objectives, etc.). US support for these operations will, as with other such requests, be conditioned on adherence to the principles of the UN Charter and established UNSC criteria.

III. REDUCING COSTS

Although peacekeeping can be a good investment for the US, it would be better and more sustainable if it cost less. The Administration is committed to reducing the US share of peacekeeping costs to 25% by January 1, 1996, down from the current rate of 31.7%. We will also inform the UN of Congress's likely refusal to fund US peacekeeping assessments at a rate higher than 25% after Fiscal Year 1995.

The Administration remains concerned that the UN has not rectified management inefficiencies that result in excessive costs and, on occasion, fraud and abuse. As a matter of priority, the US will continue to press for dramatic administrative and management improvements in the UN system. In particular, the US is working hard to ensure that new and on-going peace operations are cost-effective and properly managed. Towards this end, the US is pursuing a number of finance and budget management reforms, including:

- immediate establishment of a permanent, fully independent office of Inspector General with oversight responsibility that includes peacekeeping;

- unified budget for all peace operations, with a contingency fund, financed by a single annual peacekeeping assessment;

- standing cadre of professional budget experts from member states, particularly top contributing countries, to assist the UN in developing credible budgets and financial plans;

- enlargement of the revolving peacekeeping reserve fund to $500 million, using voluntary contributions;

- required status of forces/mission agreements that provide preferential host nation support to peacekeeping operations;

- prohibit UN 'borrowing' from peacekeeping funds to finance cash shortfalls in regular UN administrative operations;

- revise the special peacekeeping scale of assessments to base it on a 3-year average of national income and rationalize Group C so that higher income countries pay their regular budget rate.

Moreover, the US will use its voice and vote in the Fifth Committee of the General Assembly of the United Nations to contain costs of UN peace operations once they are underway.

IV. STRENGTHENING THE UN

If peace operations are to be effective and efficient when the US believes they are necessary, the UN must improve the way peace operations are managed. Our goal is not to create a global high command but to enable the UN to manage its existing load more effectively. At present each UN operation is created and managed separately by a still somewhat understaffed UN Department of Peacekeeping Operations (DPKO). As a result, support to the field may suffer, economies of scale are lost, and work is duplicated. Moreover, the UN's command and control capabilities, particularly in complex operations, need substantial improvement. Structural changes at UN Headquarters, some of which are already underway, would make a positive difference.

A. The US proposals include the reconfiguration and expansion of the staff for the Department of Peacekeeping Operations to create:

• Plans Division to conduct adequate advance planning and preparation for new and on-going operation;

• Information and Research Division linked to field operations to obtain and provide current information, manage a 24 hour watch center, and monitor open source material and non-sensitive information submitted by governments;

• Operations Division with a modern command, control and communications (C^3) architecture based on commercial systems;

• Logistics Division to manage both competitive commercial contracts (which should be re-bid regularly on the basis of price and performance) and a cost-effective logistics computer network to link the UN DPKO with logistics offices in participating member nations. This system would enable the UN to request price and availability data and to order material from participating states;

• Small Public Affairs cell dedicated to supporting on-going peace operations and disseminating information within host countries in order to reduce the risks to UN personnel and increase the potential for mission success;

• Small Civilian Police Cell to manage police missions, plan for the establishment of police and judicial institutions, and develop standard procedures, doctrine and training.

B. To eliminate lengthy, potentially disastrous delays after a mission has been authorized, the UN should establish:

- a rapidly deployable headquarters team, a composite initial logistics support unit, and open, pre-negotiated commercial contracts for logistics support in new mission;
- data base of specific, potentially available forces or capabilities that nations could provide for the full range of peacekeeping and humanitarian operations;
- trained civilian reserve corps to serve as a ready, external talent pool to assist in the administration, management and execution of UN peace operations;
- modest airlift capability available through pre-negotiated contracts with commercial firms or member states to support urgent deployments.

C. Finally, the UN should establish a professional Peace Operations Training Program for commanders and other military and civilian personnel.

D. Consistent with the specific proposals outlined above, the US will actively support efforts in the Fifth Committee of the General Assembly to redeploy resources within the UN to enable the effective augmentation of the UN DPKO along the lines outlined above. In addition, the US is prepared to undertake the following, primarily on a reimbursable basis:

- detail appropriate numbers of civilian and military personnel to DPKO in New York in advisory or support roles;
- share information, as appropriate, while ensuring full protection of sources and methods;
- offer to design a command, control, and communications systems architecture for the Operations Division, using commercially available systems and software;
- offer to assist DPKO to establish an improved, cost-effective logistics system to support UN peacekeeping operations;
- offer to help design the database of military forces or capabilities and to notify DPKO to establish an improved, cost-effective logistics system to support UN peacekeeping operations;
- offer to help design the database of military forces or capabilities and to notify DPKO, for inclusion in the database, of specific US capabilities that could be made available for the full spectrum of peacekeeping or humanitarian operations. US notification in no way implies a commitment to provide those capabilities, if asked by the UN;
- detail public affairs specialists to the UN;
- offer to help create and establish a training program, participate in peacekeeping training efforts and offer the use of US facilities for training purposes.

V. COMMAND AND CONTROL OF US FORCES

A. Our Policy: The President retains and will never relinquish command authority over US forces. On a case by case basis, the President will consider placing appropriate US forces under the operational control of a competent UN commander for specific UN operations authorized by the Security Council. The greater the US military role, the less likely it will be that the US will agree to have a UN commander exercise overall operational control over US forces. Any large scale participation of US forces in a major peace enforcement mission that is likely to involve combat should ordinarily be conducted under US command and operational control or through competent regional organizations such as NATO or ad hoc coalitions.

There is nothing new about this Administration's policy regarding the command and control of US forces. US military personnel have participated in UN peace operations since 1948. American forces have served under the operational control of foreign commanders since the Revolutionary War, including in World War I, World War II, Operation Desert Storm and in NATO since its inception. We have done so and will continue to do so when the President determines it serves US national interests.

Since the end of the Cold War, US military personnel have begun serving in UN operations in greater numbers. President Bush sent a large US field hospital unit to Croatia and observers to Cambodia, Kuwait and Western Sahara. President Clinton has deployed two US infantry companies to Macedonia in a monitoring capacity and logisticians to the UN operation in Somalia.

B. Definition of Command: No President has ever relinquished command over US forces. Command constitutes the authority to issue orders covering every aspect of military operations and administration. The sole source of legitimacy for US commanders originates from the US Constitution, federal law and the Uniform Code of Military Justice and flows from the President to the lowest US commander in the field. The chain of command from the President to the lowest US commander in the field remains inviolate.

C. Definition of Operational Control: It is sometimes prudent or advantageous (for reasons such as maximizing military effectiveness and ensuring unity of command) to place US forces under the operational control of a foreign commander to achieve specified military objectives. In making this determination, factors such as the mission, the size of the proposed US force, the risks involved, anticipated duration, and rules of engagement will be carefully considered.

Operational control is a subset of command. It is given for a specific time frame or mission and includes the authority to assign tasks to US forces already deployed by the President, and assign tasks to US units led by US officers. Within the limits of operational control, a foreign UN commander cannot: change the mission or deploy US forces outside the area of responsibility agreed to by the President, separate units, divide their supplies, administer discipline, promote anyone, or change their internal organization.

D. Fundamental Elements of US Command Always Apply: If it is to our advantage to place US forces under the operational control of a UN commander, the fundamental elements of US command still apply. US commanders will maintain the capability to report separately to higher US military authorities, as well as the UN commander. Commanders of US military units participating in UN operations will refer to higher US authorities orders that are illegal under US or international law, or are outside the mandate of the mission to which the US agreed with the UN, if they are unable to resolve the matter with the UN commander. The US reserves the right to terminate participation at any time and to take whatever actions it deems necessary to protect US forces if they are endangered.

There is no intention to use these conditions to subvert the operational chain of command. Unity of command remains a vital concern. Questions of legality, mission mandate, and prudence will continue to be worked out 'on the ground' before the orders are issued. The US will continue to work with the UN and other member states to streamline command and control procedures and maximize effective coordination on the ground.

E. Protection of US Peacekeepers: The US remains concerned that in some cases, captured UN peacekeepers and UN peace enforcers may not have adequate protection under international law. The US believes that individuals captured while performing UN peacekeeping or UN peace enforcement activities, whether as members of a UN force or a US force executing a UN Security Council mandate, should, as a matter of policy, be immediately released to UN officials; until released, at a minimum they should be accorded protections identical to those afforded prisoners of war under the 1949 Geneva Convention III (GPW). The US will generally seek to incorporate appropriate language into UN Security Council resolutions that establish or extend peace operations in order to provide adequate legal protection to captured UN peacekeepers. In appropriate cases, the US would seek assurances that US forces assisting the UN are treated as experts on mission for the United Nations, and thus are entitled to appropriate privileges and immunities and are subject to immediate release when captured. Moreover, the Administration is actively involved in negotiating a draft international convention at the United Nations to provide a special international convention at the United Nations to provide a special international status for individuals serving in peacekeeping and peace enforcement operations under a UN mandate. Finally, the Administration will take appropriate steps to ensure that any US military personnel captured while serving as part of a multinational peacekeeping force or peace enforcement effort are immediately released to UN authorities.

VI. STRENGTHENING US SUPPORT FOR MULTILATERAL PEACE OPERATIONS

Peace operations have changed since the end of the Cold War. They are no longer limited to the interposition of small numbers of passive, unarmed observers. Today, they also include more complex and sometimes more robust uses of military resources to achieve a range of political and humanitarian objectives.

The post-Cold War world has also witnessed the emergence of peace enforcement operations involving the threat or use of force. These missions have been considerably more challenging than traditional peacekeeping operations, yet the US and the UN are only now beginning to change sufficiently the way they manage peace operations. The expansion of peacekeeping operations without a commensurate expansion of capabilities has contributed to noticeable setbacks. If the US is to support the full range of peace operations effectively, when it is in our interests to do so, our government, not just the UN, must adapt.

It is no longer sufficient to view peace operations solely through a political prism. It is critical also to bring a clear military perspective to bear, particularly on those missions that are likely to involve the use of force or the participation of US combat units. Thus, the Department of Defense should join the Department of State in assuming both policy and funding responsibility for appropriate peace operations. We call this policy 'shared responsibility.'

A. Shared Responsibility: DoD will assume new responsibilities for managing and funding those UN peace operations that are likely to involve combat and all operations in which US combat units are participating. The military requirements of these operations demand DoD's leadership in coordinating US oversight and management. Professional military judgement increases the prospects of success of such operations. Moreover, with policy management responsibility comes funding responsibility.

DoD will pay the UN assessment for those traditional UN peacekeeping missions (so called 'Chapter VI' operations, because they operate under Chapter VI of the UN Charter) in which US combat units are participating, e.g. Macedonia. DoD will also pay the UN assessment for all UN peace enforcement missions (so called 'Chapter VII' operations), e.g. Bosnia and Somalia. State will continue to manage and pay for traditional peacekeeping missions in which there are no US combat units participating, e.g. Golan Heights, El Salvador, Cambodia.

When US military personnel, goods or services are used for UN peace operations, DoD will receive direct and full reimbursement; reimbursement can only be waived in exceptional circumstances, and only by the President.

Our Shared Responsibility policy states: 'Unless the President determines otherwise, at the request of one of the Principals:

- The State Department will have lead responsibility for the oversight and management of those traditional peacekeeping operations (Chapter VI) in which US combat units are not participating. The Administration will seek to fund the assessments for these operations through the existing State Contributions for International Peacekeeping Activities account, and;

- The Defense Department will have lead responsibility for the oversight and management of those Chapter VI operations in which there are US combat units and for all peace enforcement (Chapter VII) peace operations. The Administration will seek to fund the assessments for these operations through the establishment of a new account within DoD established to pay UN assessments. Once such an account is established, DoD may receive direct reimbursement from the UN for contributions of goods, services and troops to UN peace operations.'

The Administration will submit legislation to Congress creating a new peace-keeping assessment account for DoD and implementing the shared responsibility concept. The legislation will stipulate that, in all cases, the agency with lead responsibility for a given operation will be responsible for assessments associated with the operation.

Since peace operations are neither wholly military nor wholly political in nature, consisting instead of military, political, humanitarian and developmental elements in varying degrees, no one agency alone can manage all facets of an operation effectively. Therefore, the designated lead agencies will engage in full and regular interagency consultation as they manage US support for peace operations.

In all cases, State remains responsible for the conduct of diplomacy and instructions to embassies and our UN Mission in New York. DoD is responsible for military assessments and activities. NSC facilitates interagency coordination.

B. Reimbursements from the UN: Under the shared responsibility policy, and the proposed accompanying legal authorities, DoD would receive and retain direct reimbursement for its contributions of troops, goods and services to the UN. An important advantage will be to limit any adverse impact on DoD Operations and Maintenance funds, which are essential to the US military readiness. As our draft legislation stipulates, the US will seek full reimbursement from the UN for US contributions of troops, goods and services. The US will first apply reimbursements against DoD incremental costs. Any remaining excess after the Services have been made whole would be credited to DoD's proposed peace-keeping account when it is a DoD-led operation or to State's CIPA account when it is a State-led operation. The President may choose to waive UN reimbursement only in exceptional circumstances.

C. US Funding of UN Peace Operations: In the short term, the Administration will seek Congressional support for funding the USG's projected UN peace-keeping arrears. Over the long run, we view the shared responsibility approach outlined above as the best means of ensuring improved management and adequate funding of UN peace operations. Moreover, the Administration will make every effort to budget for known peacekeeping assessments and seek Congressional support to fund, in the annual appropriation, assessments for clearly anticipated contingencies.

D. US Training: The Armed Services will include appropriate peacekeeping/emergency humanitarian assistance training in DoD training programs. Training US forces to fight and decisively win wars will, however, continue to be the highest training priority.

VII. CONGRESS AND THE AMERICAN PEOPLE

To sustain US support for UN peace operations, Congress and the American people must understand and accept the potential value of such operations as tools of US interests. Congress and the American people must also be genuine participants in the processes that support US decisionmaking on new and on-going peace operations.

Traditionally, the Executive branch has not solicited the involvement of Congress or the American people on matters related to UN peacekeeping. This lack of communication is not desirable in an era when peace operations have become more numerous, complex and expensive. The Clinton Administration is committed to working with Congress to improve and regularize communication and consultation on these important issues. Specifically, the Administration will:

- Regularize recently-initiated periodic consultations with bipartisan Congressional leaders on foreign policy engagements that might involve US forces, including possible deployments of US military units in UN peace operations.

- Continue recently-initiated monthly staff briefings on the UN's upcoming calendar, including current, new, and expanded peace operations.

- Inform Congress as soon as possible of unanticipated votes in the UNSC on new or expanded peace operations.

- Inform Congress of UN command and control arrangements when US military units participate in UN operations.

- Provide UN documents to appropriate committees on a timely basis.

- Submit to Congress a comprehensive annual report on UN peace operations.

- Support legislation along the lines of that introduced by Senators Mitchell, Nunn, Byrd and Warner to amend the War Powers Resolution to introduce a consultative mechanism and to eliminate the 60-day withdrawal provisions.

CONCLUSION

Properly constituted, peace operations can be one useful tool to advance American national interests and pursue our national security objectives. The US cannot be the world's policeman. Nor can we ignore the increase in armed ethnic conflicts, civil wars and the collapse of governmental authority in some states – crises that individually and cumulatively may affect US interests. This policy is designed to impose discipline on both the UN and the US to make peace operations a more effective instrument of collective security.

US Department of State Publication Number 10161
Released by the Bureau of International Organization Affairs
May 1994

ANNEX 2

—◀◦▶—

'The Uses of Military Power'
Secretary of Defense, Caspar W. Weinberger

Excerpts from address given to the National Press Club, Washington DC, 28 November 1984

... Of all the many policies our citizens deserve – and need – to understand, none is so important as those related to our topic today – the uses of military power. Deterrence will work only if the Soviets understand our firm commitment to keeping the peace ... and only from a well-informed public can we expect to have that national will and commitment.

So today, I want to discuss with you perhaps the most important question concerning keeping the peace. Under what circumstances, and by what means, does a great democracy such as ours reach the painful decision that the use of military force is necessary to protect our interests or to carry out our national policy?

National power has many components, some tangible – like economic wealth, technical pre-eminence. Other components are intangible – such as moral force, or strong national will. Military forces, when they are strong and ready and modern, are a credible – and tangible – addition to a nation's power. When both the intangible national will and those forces are forged into one instrument, national power becomes effective ... .

Aware of the consequences of any mis-step, yet convinced of the precious worth of the freedom we enjoy, we seek to avoid conflict, while maintaining strong defenses. Our policy has always been to work hard for peace, but to be prepared if war comes. Yet, so blurred have the lines become between open conflict and half-hidden hostile acts that we cannot confidently predict where, or when, or how, or from what direction aggression may arrive. We must be prepared, at any moment, to meet threats ranging in intensity from isolated terrorist acts, to guerilla action, to full-scale military confrontation.

Alexander Hamilton, writing in the *Federalist Papers*, said that 'it is impossible to foresee or define the extent and variety of national exigencies, or the correspondent extent and variety of the means which may be necessary to satisfy them.' If it was true then, how much more true it is today, when we must remain ready to consider the means to meet such serious indirect challenges to the peace as proxy wars and individual terrorist action. And how much more important is it now, considering the consequences of failing to deter conflict at the lowest level possible. While the use of military force to defend territory has never been questioned when a democracy has been attacked and its very survival threatened, most democracies have rejected the unilateral aggressive use of force to invade, conquer or subjugate other nations. The extent to which the use of force is acceptable remains unresolved for the host of other situations which fall between these extremes of defensive and aggressive use of force.

We find ourselves, then, face to face with a modern paradox: The most likely challenge to the peace – the gray area conflicts – are precisely the most difficult challenges to which a democracy must respond. Yet, while the source and nature of today's challenges are uncertain, our response must be clear and under-standable. Unless we are certain that force is essential, we run the risk of inadequate national will to apply the resources needed.

Because we face a spectrum of threats – from covert aggression, terrorism and subversion, to overt intimidation, to use of brute force – choosing the appro-priate level of our response is difficult. Flexible response does not mean just any response is appropriate. But once a decision to employ some degree of force has been made, and the purpose clarified, our government must have the clear mandate to carry out, and continue to carry out, that decision until the purpose has been achieved. That, too, has been difficult to accomplish.

The issue of which branch of government has authority to define that mandate and make decisions on using force is now being strongly contended. Beginning in the 1970s Congress demanded, and assumed, a far more active role in the making of foreign policy and in the decisionmaking process for the employment of military forces abroad than had been thought appropriate and practical before. As a result, the centrality of decisionmaking authority in the executive branch has been compromised by the legislative branch to an extent that actively interferes with that process. At the same time, there has not been a corresponding acceptance of responsibility by Congress for the outcome of decisions concern-ing the employment of military forces.

Yet the outcome of decisions on whether – and when, and to what degree – to use combat forces abroad has never been more important than it is today. While we do not seek to deter or settle all the world's conflicts, we must recognize that, as a major power, our responsibilities and interests are now of such scope that there are few troubled areas we can afford to ignore. So we must be prepared to deal with a range of possibilities, a spectrum of crises, from local insurgency to global conflict. We prefer, of course, to limit any conflict in its early stages, to contain and control it – but to do that our military forces must be deployed in a timely manner, and be fully supported and prepared *before* they are engaged, because many of those difficult decisions must be made extremely quickly.

Some on the national scene think they can always avoid making tough decisions. Some reject entirely the question of whether any force can ever be used abroad. They want to avoid grappling with a complex issue because, despite clever rhetoric disguising their purpose, these people are in fact advocating a return to post-World War I isolationism. While they may maintain in principle that military force has a role in foreign policy, they are never willing to name the circumstance or the place where it would apply.

On the other side, some theorists argue that military force can be brought to bear in any crisis. Some of these proponents of force are eager to advocate its use even in limited amounts simply because they believe that if there are American forces of any size present they will somehow solve the problem.

Neither of these two extremes offers us any lasting or satisfactory solutions. The first – undue reserve – would lead us ultimately to withdraw from international events that require free nations to defend their interests from the aggressive use of force. We would be abdicating our responsibilities as the leader of the free world – responsibilities more or less thrust upon us in the aftermath of World War II – a war incidentally that isolationism did nothing to deter. These are responsibilities we must fulfill unless we desire the Soviet Union to keep expanding its influence unchecked throughout the world. In an international system based on mutual interdependence among nations, and alliances between friends, stark isolationism quickly would lead to a far more dangerous situation for the United States: We would be without allies and faced by many hostile or indifferent nations.

The second alternative – employing our forces almost indiscriminately and as a regular and customary part of our diplomatic efforts – would surely plunge us headlong into the sort of domestic turmoil we experienced during the Vietnam War, without accomplishing the goal for which we committed our forces. Such policies might very well tear at the fabric of our society, endangering the single, most critical element of a successful democracy: *a strong consensus of support and agreement for our basic purposes.*

Policies formed without a clear understanding of what we hope to achieve would also earn us the scorn of our troops, who would have an understandable opposition to being used – in every sense of the word – casually and without intent to support them fully. Ultimately this course would reduce their morale and their effectiveness for engagements we must win. And if the military were to distrust its civilian leadership, recruitment would fall off and I fear an end to the all-volunteer system would be upon us, requiring a return to a draft, sowing the seeds of riot and discontent that so wracked the country in the 60s ... .

In today's world where minutes count, such decisive leadership is more important than ever before. Regardless of whether conflicts are limited, or threats are ill-defined, we must be capable of quickly determining that the threats and conflicts either *do or do not* affect the vital interests of the United States and our allies ... and then responding appropriately.

Those threats may not entail an immediate, direct attack on our territory, and our response may not necessarily require the immediate or direct defense of our homeland. But when our vital national interests and those of our allies *are* at stake, we cannot ignore our safety, or forsake our allies.

At the same time, recent history has proven that we cannot assume unilaterally the role of the world's defender. We have learned that there are limits to how much of our spirit and blood and treasure we can afford to forfeit in meeting our responsibility to keep peace and freedom. So while we may and should offer substantial amounts of economic and military assistance to our allies in their time of need, and help them maintain forces to deter attacks against them, usually we cannot substitute our troops or our will for theirs.

We should only engage our troops if we must do so as a matter of our own vital national interest. We cannot assume for other sovereign nations the responsibility to defend their territory – without their strong invitation – when our own freedom is not threatened.

On the other hand, there have been recent cases where the United States has seen the need to join forces with other nations to try to preserve the peace by helping with negotiations, and by separating warring parties, and thus enabling those warring nations to withdraw from hostilities safely. In the Middle East, which has been torn by conflict for millennia, we have sent our troops in recent years both to the Sinai and to Lebanon, for just such a peacekeeping mission. But we did not configure or equip those forces for combat – they were armed only for their self-defense. Their mission required them to be – and to be recognized as – peacekeepers. We knew that if conditions deteriorated so they were in danger, or if because of the actions of the warring nations, their peacekeeping mission could not be realized, then it would be necessary either to add sufficiently to the number and arms of our troops – in short to equip them for combat ... or to withdraw them. And so in Lebanon, when we faced just such a choice, because the warring nations did not enter into withdrawal or peace agreements, the President properly withdrew forces equipped only for peacekeeping.

In those cases where our national interests require us to commit combat forces, we must never let there be doubt of our resolution. When it is necessary for our troops to be committed to combat, we must commit them, in sufficient numbers and we must support them, as effectively and resolutely as our strength permits. When we commit our troops to combat we must do so with the sole object of winning.

Once it is clear our troops are required, because our vital interests are at stake, then we must have the firm national resolve to commit every ounce of strength necessary to win the fight to achieve our objectives. In Grenada we did just that.

Just as clearly, there are other situations where United States combat forces should not be used. I believe the postwar period has taught us several lessons, and from them I have developed six major tests to be applied when we are weighing the use of US combat forces abroad. Let me now share them with you: (1) *First*, the United States should not commit forces to combat overseas unless the particular engagement or occasion is deemed vital to our national interest or that of our allies. That emphatically does not mean that we should *declare* beforehand, as we did with Korea in 1950, that a particular area is outside our strategic perimeter.

(2) *Second*, if we decide it is necessary to put combat troops into a given situation, we should do so wholeheartedly, and with the clear intention of winning. If we are unwilling to commit the forces or resources necessary to achieve our objectives, we should not commit them at all. Of course if the particular situation requires only limited force to win our objectives, then we should not hesitate to commit forces sized accordingly. When Hitler broke treaties and remilitarized the Rhineland, small combat forces then could perhaps have prevented the holocaust of World War II.

(3) *Third*, if we *do* decide to commit forces to combat overseas, we should have clearly defined political and military objectives. And we should know precisely how our forces can accomplish those clearly defined objectives. And we should have and send the forces needed to do just that. As Clausewitz wrote, 'No one starts a war – or rather, no one in his senses ought to do so – without first being clear in his mind what he intends to achieve by that war, and how be intends to conduct it.'

War may be different today than in Clausewitz's time, but the need for well-defined objectives and a consistent strategy is still essential. If we determine that a combat mission has become necessary for our vital national interests, then we must send forces capable to do the job – and not assign a combat mission to a force configured for peacekeeping.

(4) *Fourth*, the relationship between our objectives and the forces we have committed – their size, composition and disposition – must be continually reassessed and adjusted if necessary. Conditions and objectives invariably change during the course of a conflict. When they do change, then so must our combat requirements. We must continuously keep as a beacon light before us the basic questions: 'Is this conflict in our national interest?' 'Does our national interest require us to fight, to use force of arms?' if the answers are 'yes', then we must win. If the answers are 'no', then we should not be in combat.

(5) *Fifth*, before the US commits combat forces abroad, there must be some reasonable assurance we will have the support of the American people and their elected representatives in Congress. This support cannot be achieved unless we are candid in making clear the threats we face; the support cannot be sustained without continuing and close consultation. We cannot fight a battle with the

Congress at home while asking our troops to win a war overseas or, as in the case of Vietnam, in effect asking our troops not to win, but just to be there.

(6) *Finally*, the commitment of US forces to combat should be a last resort.

I believe that these tests can be helpful in deciding whether or not we should commit our troops to combat in the months and years ahead. The point we must all keep uppermost in our minds is that if we ever decide to commit forces to combat, we must support those forces to the fullest extent of our national will for as long as it takes to win. So we must have in mind objectives that are clearly defined and understood and supported by the widest possible number of our citizens. And those objectives must be vital to our survival as a free nation and to the fulfillment of our responsibilities as a world power. We must also be farsighted enough to sense when immediate and strong reactions to apparently small events can prevent lion-like responses that may be required later. We must never forget those isolationists in Europe who shrugged that 'Danzig is not worth a war,' and 'why should we fight to keep the Rhineland demilitarized?'

These tests I have just mentioned have been phrased negatively for a purpose – they are intended to sound a note of caution that we must observe prior to committing forces to combat overseas. When we ask our military forces to risk their very lives in such situations, a note of caution is not only prudent, it is morally required.

In many situations we may apply these tests and conclude that a combatant role is not appropriate. Yet no one should interpret what I am saying here today as an abdication of America's responsibilities, either to its own citizens or to its allies. Nor should these remarks be misread as a signal that this country, or this Administration, is unwilling to commit forces to combat overseas.

We have demonstrated in the past that, when our vital interests or those of our allies are threatened, we are ready to use force, and use it decisively, to protect those interests. Let no one entertain any illusions – if our vital interests are involved, we are prepared to fight. And we are resolved that if we must fight, we must win.

So, while these tests are drawn from lessons we have learned from the past, they also can – and should – be applied to the future. For example, the problems confronting us in Central America today are difficult. The possibility of more extensive Soviet and Soviet-proxy penetration into this hemisphere in months ahead is something we should recognize. If this happens we will clearly need more economic and military assistance and training to help those who want democracy.

The President will not allow our military forces to creep – or be drawn gradually – into a combat role in Central America or any other place in the world. And indeed our policy is designed to prevent the need for direct American involvement. This means we will need sustained congressional support to back and give confidence to our friends in the region.

I believe that the tests I have enunciated here today can, if applied carefully, avoid the danger of this gradualist incremental approach which almost always means the use of insufficient force. These tests can help us to avoid being drawn inexorably into an endless morass, where it is not vital to our national interest to fight ... .

Source: Richard N. Haass, 'Intervention: The Use of American Military Force in the Post-Cold War World', Washington DC: The Carnegie Endowment for International Peace, 1994

'The Use and Usefulness of Military Forces in the Post-Cold War, Post-Soviet World'
Representative Les Aspin

Excerpts from an address by the Chairman of the House Armed Services Committee to the Jewish Institute for National Security Affairs, Washington, DC, 21 September 1992.

... I'd like to take just a few minutes to discuss with you a question that I think will be central to our national defense in the new post-Soviet, post-Cold War world. The question is, how are our military forces going to be used in the future? Now, we have, of course, had debates about the use of military force by the United States before. In particular, we had a debate after the bombing of the Marine barracks in Beirut in the middle 80s. Where is this debate going in the new era? I think there are going to be a few new twists, but at the moment we have more questions than answers. I think now is the time to start asking those questions and I think this is the right kind of informed, interested citizens group that should be considering this issue.

The debate on the use of force has been fueled by what many say were ill-considered military ventures. Following those events, a number of people tried to design a set of rules of thumb by which we could judge ahead of time whether the use of military force would be a good idea. Kind of a check-list, if you will.

Senator Gary Hart attempted such a list, as did Secretary of Defense Caspar Weinberger. On 2 November 1984, Secretary Weinberger outlined a six-point check-list to govern the decision on the use of force. Three of those tests concerned when to use force. He argued that one, force should be used in the defense of our vital interests; two, only with the support of the American people and Congress; and three, only as a last resort. The other three Weinberger tests dealt with how force ought to be used: first, with the clear intention of winning; second, when military objectives can be clearly defined; and third, only so long as the objectives were worth the risk.

There was a lot of discussion not only about the points, but about whether such a check-list helped or simply raised more questions. One particularly troublesome point was the question of public support. Some said that it was not known whether there would be support beforehand, and, besides, the purpose of leadership was to create support. In fact, most wars start out to be popular and may become unpopular if they drag on. Ultimately, there is no guarantee that the American people simply won't change their minds.

Weinberger was not the last word. Similar sentiments about the need for a high threshold for the use of force have been heard very recently. President Bush stated before the Gulf War that, and I quote, 'I will not as Commander-in-Chief ever put somebody into a military assessed situation that we do not win ... there is not going to be any drawn out agony like Vietnam.' This debate was not only conducted among civilian officials, defense analysts, columnists and editorial writers alone. There was another level of debate, one that was very important. That debate was in the officer corps of the US military. The men who carried the burden of battle developed their own views of when military force should be used.

They spent more time thinking about it and they gradually developed – and recently honed – the concept. By the beginning of this decade, 1990 I would say, the view of the US military came down to four propositions on when it is appropriate to use force.

NUMBER ONE: Force should only be used as a last resort. Diplomatic and economic solutions should be tried first.

NUMBER TWO: Military force should only be used when there is a clear-cut military objective. We should not send military forces to achieve vague political goals.

NUMBER THREE: Military forces should be used only when we can measure that the military objective has been achieved. In other words, we need to know when we can bring the troops back home.

NUMBER FOUR: Probably the most important. Military force should be used only in an overwhelming fashion. We should get it done quickly and with little loss of life and therefore, with overwhelming force.

What all this reveals is that there is a substantial block of very expert opinion that says this is the way to go. This camp says that if we ignore these prescriptions we are likely to end with another Vietnam or another Beirut. We have learned through bitter experience, they say and we should not make the same mistakes again. We can call this the 'all or nothing' school. If you want a name associated with it, it would be Colin Powell – he is a believer in this. This school says if you aren't willing to put the pedal to the floor, don't start the engine.

This school would also say that this checklist avoids the problem of maintaining public support. It allows the troops to go in, get the job done and get out quickly. And because it is done with overwhelming force you don't run into the problem of public support. All wars are popular at the beginning and all wars are popular if they don't result in a lot of American lives lost. [It] Gets around the problem very nicely.

And, in fact, these criteria – although only recently fully formulated – have served us extraordinarily well. The two most recent examples of the use of force followed this formula almost exactly – Operation Just Cause and Operation Desert Storm. The formula worked in both cases. And with those successes a lot of people believe that the thorny problem of the use of American military force has been finally solved. Just follow the formula, this four-part formula, and we will avoid Vietnams and Beiruts, and we will only have Operation Just Causes and Operation Desert Storms.

But just when we might think we've got the problem solved, it becomes clear that this brand new world of ours is a world of turmoil and agitation. And that agitation has provoked calls for the use of military force in a whole range of circumstances that don't fit the old [world] I've just described.

Right now the US military is either already involved in or may soon be involved in the following: One, enforcing a no-fly zone in southern Iraq. Two, helping deliver humanitarian aid to Bosnia and/or pressuring Serbia to leave its neighbors alone. Three, delivering humanitarian aid to Somalia in the face of roving gangs that want to steal and sell the aid. And four, providing emergency relief for the victims of hurricanes in Florida, Louisiana and Hawaii. None of these situations fall within the 'Colin Powell' categories I've just outlined.

So there we are. Just when we thought we had the problem solved. Just when we thought we had a check-list that would tell us when to use military force and military assets and when not to use them, we enter into a world where there is serious public opinion in favor of using the military in situations when the categories don't apply.

Now some would say, as Yogi Berra has, 'it's just *déjà vu* all over again.' If the categories don't fit, military force and military assets should not be used. Acting Secretary of State Larry Eagleburger said in late August that he was 'horrified' by what he called the 'arm chair strategists and generals' calling for US military involvement in the Yugoslavian conflict.

Eagleburger has said he was not prepared to accept the argument that there was a level of successful involvement somewhere between that which we had in Vietnam and doing nothing. He asserted that when there is no clear purpose and no clear end, the result can be a situation like Vietnam. He claims there is no middle ground. Here are his words: 'It's again what has got us into Vietnam. You do a little bit and it doesn't work, what do you do next?' End quote.

But those who disagree with the all-or-nothing school are unwilling to accept the notion that military force can't be used prudently short of all-out war. They go further to suggest this new world we live in is going to demand it. We can call this camp the opposite camp, the limited objectives school. The argument made by this school has two main parts, one dealing with results, the other with process. The name that goes with this school is Mrs Thatcher.

The limited objectives school wants the kind of results that often require military action or at least the credible threat of military action. Today, the examples are Iraq and Bosnia. This school says we should use military force if necessary to enforce UN resolutions against Iraq, particularly those to get rid of Iraq's weapons of mass destruction. Otherwise, they argue, Operation Desert Storm will become a hollow victory and Saddam will continue his nuclear, chemical and biological weapons programs. This school also wants to do something to stop the ethnic cleansing in Bosnia. If we do not, they say, others may follow these horrific practices. And there is no scarcity of candidates.

The debates over Iraq and Bosnia, incidentally, have scrambled the political spectrum in this country pretty well and jumbled the views of both isolationists and internationalists. Many of our citizens are clearly upset that Saddam Hussein is thumbing his nose at UN resolutions after Operation Desert Storm; others are upset with what they see going on in Bosnia. Some people wanted to use force in Iraq and Bosnia, some in neither, some in Iraq but not Bosnia, some in Bosnia and not Iraq.

So, we can see the break up of the Eastern Bloc has opened up the possibility of ethnic or nationalist conflicts in many parts of the world. Therefore, a signal should be sent to deter such behavior. Contrary to the all-or-nothing school, the US military is likely to be used very, very rarely. The limited objectives camp says the military will become, in fact, very much like the nuclear weapons during the Cold War – important, expensive but not useful. It will not be a useful tool for achieving the objectives if it's only going to be used in the extreme cases. And therefore, this argument goes, support for it will diminish and it will become basically irrelevant to the problems that the United States faces on a day-to-day basis in the post-Cold War world.

There is a related argument that can be made here. It concerns the willingness of the American people to pay $250 billion or even $200 billion a year for a military that is not very useful. It may be that to maintain a military for the extreme contingencies, it will be necessary to show that it is useful in lesser contingencies, too.

What the existence of these conflicting camp means, I think, is that we will face a debate over the use of force every time fate sends a recalcitrant Iraq or a Bosnia our way.

The debate in each case will hinge on two questions – one, something called escalation and, two, something called compellence.

First escalation. Is escalation inevitable? In other words, is every military action with a limited objective a potential quagmire? The all-or-nothing school would answer yes. Escalation is the central fear of this school. As Larry Eagleburger said, and again I'm quoting, 'You do a little bit and it doesn't work. What do you do next?' End quote. They would cite Vietnam as the prime example of escalation gone wrong.

But there has been one very big development since Vietnam – the Soviet Union has dissolved. The superpower rivalry is no more. The stakes do not automatically go up every time the United States decides to use force. In Vietnam, American policymakers kept escalating our involvement because they were afraid of what our allies and adversaries would think – and do – if we withdrew. If we failed to keep our commitment, we would embolden our adversaries and cause our allies to question our commitment to them. During the Cold War you could not just walk away.

That's not to say we don't have to worry about signals and outcomes today. There are still aggressors out there and we don't want them to get any wrong ideas. And US presidents have to worry about winning and losing. The American electorate does not like anything that looks like a lost war.

But on the whole, the escalation argument has been affected by the collapse of the Soviet Union. So, escalation is the first question in the debate. The second question is about something called 'compellence.' Compellence is the use of military force against an adversary to influence his behavior elsewhere.

The issue of compellence is at the heart of the argument made by the limited objectives camp. What we are really talking about here is striking military targets or assets to influence behavior elsewhere, most often air strikes in one place to convince someone to change their behavior in another place. Airpower is the heart of this limited objectives argument.

Let's look at the record, which has been mixed. Compellence did not work very well in Vietnam. Earlier, the bombing of cities in Britain and Germany during World War II seemed to strengthen rather than weaken resolve. On the other side, the bombing of Libya worked. Quadafi cut back his export of terrorism.

But World War II, Vietnam, even Libya, are old news. The most important question we can ask today is what has happened that bears on use of compellence, as a policy objective of the US military. There are two sets of developments to look at here. One concerns sophisticated technology and the other sophisticated targeting.

As far as technology goes, we are living in a different world than we did even as we bombed the targets in Libya. We have stealthy aircraft and we have stealthy planes and precision guided munitions, some provided by Israel. Let's look at some Air Force figures to see how much has changed. In World War II, if we wanted to have a 90 percent chance of knocking out a medium-sized target, we had to plan to drop 9,000 bombs on it. In Vietnam, the figure was about 175 bombs. In Operation Desert Storm, we are talking about numbers in the single digits.

What this means is that we have technology which has improved our ability to make air strikes with little, if any, loss of US lives and with a minimum of collateral damage and loss of civilian lives on the other side. This is a big, big change.

But we've also become more sophisticated about targeting at a time when our adversaries have become more dependent on the kinds of things we can target. We can target communications nodes, power grids, and command and control assets. These things are the kinds of targets that national leadership and military commands hold dear.

So what do all these developments mean for the use of military force in the future?

I think we are still going to have to decide the question of the use of force case by case. Nothing has happened that would lead us to say on the one hand that we're never going to use force short of the all-out war, as in the case of Desert Storm, or on the other hand, that we're going to be the cop on the beat for the whole world.

I do think one thing has happened to weaken the all-or-nothing or Colin Powell school and one thing has happened to strengthen the limited objectives or Maggie Thatcher school. The all-or-nothing school was weakened when the collapse of the Soviet Union removed some – not all – but some of the pressure for escalation that accompanied any limited military venture.

The limited objectives school has been strengthened as technological developments have improved our ability to achieve compellence.

I think these things are going to tilt future debates somewhat in the direction of the limited objectives school or Mrs Thatcher's point of view, but it has by no means been decided. Stay tuned for the case-by-case debates.

I also think these developments send a signal here at home. It's a signal that we'd better be careful how we structure our military in the future. We have to make sure that our forces are flexible enough to do a number of simultaneous, smaller contingencies. We want these case-by-case debates settled on the merits, not predetermined because our forces lack flexibility ...

Source: Richard Haass, 'Intervention: The Use of American Military Force in the Post-Cold War World', Washington DC: The Carnegie Endowment for International Peace, 1994

————◄○►————

'Myths of Peacekeeping'
Madeleine K. Albright, US Permanent
Representative to the United Nations

Statement before the Subcommittee on International Security, International Organizations, and Human Rights of the House Committee on Foreign Affairs, Washington, DC, 24 June 1993

Mr Chairman and distinguished members of the subcommittee, it is a great pleasure to appear before you again. During my last visit to this subcommittee, on May 3, we discussed the American stake in a system of collective security. Much has occurred since early May to make that subject even more relevant today. I am submitting for the record my speech before the Council on Foreign Relations on June 11 because its discussion of collective security and UN reform should be of particular interest to this subcommittee.

Today, however, I want to review peacekeeping operations in Somalia, Cambodia, and Mozambique and describe recent Security Council action on Haiti. But I want to spend some time dispelling what I believe are some serious misperceptions about UN peacekeeping and the US role in it.

Let me begin by noting that I have spoken in other forums in recent weeks about four categories of states that are emerging at the United Nations. They include:

- A significant number of states that have a stake in the United Nations and the international community as a whole;

- Emerging democracies trying to play a constructive role but struggling with internal political and economic turmoil;

- Other states and factions that are at war with international norms and institutions and which I call the 'defiant regimes'; and finally,

- The failed societies – the ones where effective government has collapsed, or anarchy reigns, or the economy is hopeless, or a humanitarian calamity overwhelms the country and the people are sliding into an abyss. These failed societies cry out for help from the international community.

Much of our credibility as a superpower – and we must, in my view remain one – will depend upon our ability to manage our approach to these four groups. Though sometimes we will act alone, our foreign policy will necessarily point toward multilateral engagement. But unless the United States also exercises leadership within collective bodies like the United Nations, there is a risk that multilateralism will not serve our national interest well – in fact, it may undermine our interests.

These two realities – multilateral engagement and US leadership collective bodies – require an 'assertive multilateralism' that advances US foreign policy goals. Preventive diplomacy is the linchpin of assertive multilateralism. We are going to have to open our minds to broader strategies, multilateral forums. We need to project our leadership where it counts long before a smoldering dispute has a chance to flare into the crisis of the week. But we have inherited many conflicts that the United Nations is deeply involved in resolving. In recent weeks several failed societies have required assertive multilateral action in the interests of their people and of international peace and security.

SOMALIA

In Somalia, the United Nations took over from the US-led UNITAF operation on May 4. From a peak of 25,800 American troops in mid-January, the US contingent now comprises a ground logistics force of about 3,000 troops in the UN peacekeeping force in Somalia, UNOSOM II, and a separate quick reaction force of about 1,100 troops. The total multinational force in UNOSOM II is currently about 20,000 troops from 22 countries. The United Nations has troop commitments from additional countries which should permit it to reach its target of about 28,000 troops by the end of July.

The US role thus has been vastly reduced. Other nations' troops carry the greater burden on the ground, as the events of the last two weeks have clearly shown. A true multinational coalition of forces has gathered under the UN flag. Rather than pay most of the cost – as we did for the UNITAF operation – the United States now will pay its share of the regular assessment for the UN peace-keeping force.

The brutal attack on UN troops on June 5 left 23 Pakistani peacekeepers dead and 59 wounded. Three American soldiers also were wounded. This occurred while the UN troops were carrying out operations specifically within their mandate authorized in Security Council Resolution 814 of the 26th of March. The Security Council determined, in Resolution 837 on June 5, that law and order must be restored in Mogadishu and that the perpetrators of the killings of June 6 be apprehended, detained, and prosecuted. The UN envoy in Somalia, Admiral Jonathan Howe, issued an arrest warrant for General Aideed in connection with the shooting of Pakistani troops.

The unprecedented and decisive actions of UNOSOM II since June 12 against General Aideed's armed militia, their arms depots, and their strongholds were essential for the restoration of law and order in Mogadishu; the elimination of heavy weapons in the Mogadishu area; the resumption of humanitarian aid deliveries; the eventual resumption of discussion on political reconciliation; and the fulfillment of Resolution 837's mandate.

US forces participated in the UN action with critical air and limited ground support. We can all be proud of our soldiers' measured and professional performance as part of the UN operation. About 1,400 UN peacekeepers from four other countries – Morocco, Pakistan, Italy, and France – were heavily engaged on the ground earlier this month. Four Moroccans and one Pakistani lost their lives, and dozens of peacekeepers were wounded.

If General Aideed and other perpetrators of the June 5 killings are apprehended, the Security Council will ensure that they are held accountable under the rule of law. In any event, the arrest warrant against General Aideed greatly restricts his mobility and effectiveness as a rogue leader, something I believe the vast majority of Somalis desperately want. As Admiral Howe has aptly stated, 'People are sick of rule by the gun and extortion.' As UNOSOM II succeeds in disarming factions and heavy weapons are destroyed, the average Somali will be able to participate, without fear, in recreating a civil society. UNOSOM's prospects for promoting a durable political settlement will then improve.

There may well be further challenges to the authority of the UN peacekeeping force in Somalia. Rebuilding Somali society and promoting democracy in that strife-torn nation are difficult endeavors. But after the enormous effort made by the United States and other nations in the UNITAF operation to reverse famine in Somalia, it would be folly now to permit conditions to deteriorate again. Had there not been a UN response to the June 5 killings, the UN's credibility in Somalia would have been fatally undermined.

CAMBODIA

The UN-organized elections in Cambodia were remarkably successful, with a 90% turnout of the registered voters. The UN peacekeeping operation in Cambodia (UNTAC) deserves considerable credit for this success. We believe that the Cambodian people have spoken with unmistakable clarity in saying they want an end to warfare. They want peace. The process of reconciliation has already begun. I sincerely hope we have finally reached a stage where Cambodia is beginning to emerge from the category of 'failed societies.'

At our initiative, the Security Council recently endorsed the results of the election, which has been certified as free and fair by the United Nations, and requested UNTAC to continue to play its role during the transition period in accordance with the Paris agreements. The Council also requested the Secretary-General to report by mid-July on the possible future role for the United Nations and its specialized agencies after UNTAC's mandate expires.

The newly elected constituent assembly has begun its work of drawing up a constitution, and will transform itself into a legislative assembly with the establishment of a new government for Cambodia. We believe Prince Sihanouk is playing a vital and constructive role working with the leaders of the political parties that won seats in the elections. Last weekend, the government party (CPP) and the royalist opposition (FUNCINPEC) tentatively agreed to a power-sharing arrangement during the transition period.

Cambodia and the United Nations have now entered a critical stage in the transition to peace and democracy. There remains a serious risk that the Khmer Rouge will continue attempting to disrupt the peace process. The elected Cambodian leaders must ultimately decide on the composition of their own government. It is difficult, however, to see how the international community could support a government that included the Khmer Rouge or others who would seek to disrupt the peace process by means of violence.

We have come so far in Cambodia and it is essential that we stand by the Cambodian people and UNTAC and give democracy a chance to work there. We should anticipate that the United Nations will need to respond quickly and decisively to any attempt by any party to reverse the historic achievement of the elections. Finally, we must also work with the United Nations and others to create the economic and social conditions under which peace and democracy can flourish.

MOZAMBIQUE

The United Nations is also involved in moving war-torn Mozambique toward lasting peace and multi-party democracy. The ambitious UN peacekeeping operation in Mozambique (OMUMOZ) is charged with coordinating several major aspects of the transition to peace, including monitoring of the cease-fire, demobilization of combatants, preparation for and monitoring of elections, and the crucial humanitarian assistance effort. Despite some early administrative and logistical problems, the UN operation is now fully operational, with over 6,000 'blue helmet' forces deployed from two dozen countries.

We have been encouraged by the commitment of the government and

RENAMO to uphold the cease-fire. However, we are concerned about delays in beginning the all-important demobilization process. We are urging both parties to overcome differences over details, so that demobilization can begin smartly, and preparations can get underway for elections, which are expected to be held before October 1994.

The United States participates actively in three UN-chaired commissions overseeing implementation of the Mozambique peace agreement. We are working with the UN Secretariat to determine what types of assistance the United States can provide at this very important time. We are encouraged that this is a devastated society that can be resurrected, in large part because of a viable peacekeeping presence.

HAITI

The people of Haiti have waited a long time for the re-establishment of a democratic government. The international community's political will to press for a settlement to restore democracy was evidenced in the tough UN sanctions resolution (841) that went into effect yesterday. The Security Council acted to stop the flow of oil and arms to Haiti through mandatory, legally binding, worldwide sanctions. The resolution breaks new ground in a number of areas. This is the first time UN sanctions of this kind have been imposed on a country in this hemisphere. It is the first time Chapter VII sanctions have been imposed on a country not in civil conflict or at war with a neighbor. And it marks a new level of cooperation between the United Nations and a regional organization – in this case the Organization of American States. The United States is committed to seeing that international oil suppliers comply fully with Resolution 841.

SOME MYTHS ABOUT UN PEACEKEEPING

These four examples alone show the complexities and modern requirements of UN peacekeeping and enforcement actions. There are many more. But I want to focus now on some misperceptions about the United Nations and peacekeeping that continue to shape – erroneously in my opinion – our public discourse on this country's role in the United Nations. There are, in short, myths about the United Nations that need to be exposed before they lead us in the wrong direction during this turbulent new era of world politics:

Myth No. 1: UN peacekeeping has nothing to do with US national interest. I trust that my testimony before this subcommittee on May 3 dispensed with this myth. Peacekeeping has become instrumental in meeting three fundamental imperatives of our national interest: economic, political, and humanitarian. The world continues to be a dangerous place.

And yet consider for a moment what the world and the US defense budgets would be today if there were no UN peacekeeping operations and the resultant power vacuums invited intervention by neighbors or would-be regional powers. Increasingly, we are faced with an often violent eruption of local or regional disputes that require the world's attention. And it is in this new world that peacekeeping and the modern responsibilities of collective security are essential to our security.

Myth No. 2: When the United Nations takes over a security operation, the United States can bail out. When the refrain is, 'Let the UN handle it', that cannot mean a 'pass' for the United States. This country is a part of the United Nations – in fact we are and should remain a very senior partner – and our participation and leadership are vital to its work. The alternatives – blissful isolation or costly duty as the world's cop – are unrealistic and unacceptable. The Somalia operation is a good example of how a continued US role – minor compared to our initial UNITAF deployment – is part and parcel of letting 'the UN' handle it.

Myth No. 3: Peacekeeping operations are consensual, avoid the risks, and only prolong conflicts between governments. Many peacekeeping operations, particularly today in connection with failed societies, are deployed into internal conflicts or anarchy, and thus are not dependent on conventional notions of consent from each warring party. Nor, by any measure, are peacekeeping operations risk-free: 925 peacekeeping soldiers have been killed in action in the course of UN history, and 528 of those have died in on-going operations; 53 British, 49 French, 43 Irish, 35 Canadians, and 10 Americans have died in the line of duty. In the former Yugoslavia, 43 peacekeepers have been killed; 186 peacekeepers have sacrificed their lives in Cyprus. The Somalia massacre of June 5 was a stark reminder of how exposed some peacekeepers are in the very hostile environments into which they are deployed.

Half (14) of the 28 UN peacekeeping operations in UN history have been terminated, most within 1 or 2 years of their creation. While some peacekeeping operations may indeed encourage stalemate, the alternative often would be a bloody and costly conflict – with severe risks of escalation – that no one desires.

Myth No. 4: Peacekeeping is too expensive and ridden with fraud and mismanagement. I have testified and spoken out often about the ad hoc approaches that dominate peacekeeping operations. 'Improvisation' is the single word that might best evoke the problems of peacekeeping. And while the potential for fraud and mismanagement exists, as it does in any large organization, the most pressing problems in UN peacekeeping relate to the sheer improvisational character of the system. This produces major gaps in institutional capacity on one hand and inefficiencies on the other. In fact, the small peacekeeping staff at UN headquarters is superlative, and steps are now being taken to increase its size and effectiveness. The millions that are spent on peacekeeping operations – totaling more than $3 billion in 1993 – must be measured against the much higher costs that result if conflicts are left to fester and explode.

I would like to add that the Administration is taking the lead to enhance UN peacekeeping through implementation of important initiatives at the United Nations and within our own government. On May 28 the Security Council reached consensus on a list of peacekeeping reforms, and plans for implementing them will be reported to us by the Secretary-General in September. Within our government the Administration has been conducting an intensive inter-agency review since February of both the US role in peacekeeping and the planning and managerial capabilities of the United Nations for peacekeeping. We anticipate that review process to be concluded soon. Finally, in September we hope there will be a ministerial-level session of the Security Council to review peacekeeping.

Myth No. 5: The US domestic agenda prevents us from leading and shaping a free and secure world. This is faulty logic at best, and disastrous public policy at worst. The stability of the world economy and of regional and world politics is deeply integrated with US interests and our economy. If we pursue a domestic agenda with blinders on, refusing to recognize the carnage to our left and the distant conflict to our right, eventually the cost of that disengagement, at a minimum, will be an additional financial burden we must bear. More likely, the costs will include US forces with attendant potential loss of life. President Clinton and Secretary Christopher have always recognized that the foreign agenda is inseparable from the domestic agenda. The sooner we all grasp that fundamental fact the sooner we will recognize UN peacekeeping as one small, but important, piece in the overall effort to achieve global stability and prosperity and to advance democracies and their typically market-oriented economies.

All of this points to the fact that we are engaged in a great dialogue, the conclusion of which no one can yet predict with certainty. In our effort to plot what role the United States should fill in this new era, we cannot abandon the responsibilities of a superpower.

We cannot apply 'old think' to how we judge peacekeeping operations and missions today and into the future. A whole new platter of issues confronts contributing nations, including deployments into internal conflicts and to protect humanitarian aid convoys. We need more minds pole-vaulting over the conventions of the past and directing this nation's power into the 21st century.

Source: US Department of State Dispatch, 28 June 1993, Vol.4, No.26

'Use of Force in a Post-Cold War World' Madeleine K. Albright, US Permanent Representative to the United Nations

Address at the National War College, National Defense University, Fort McNair, Washington DC, 23 September 1993

To me, this auditorium – this military institution – is the right place to discuss the Clinton Administration's foreign policy goals and address that most crucial of topics: the use of military force in the post Cold War world. I believe that our national dialogue must ensure that this nation's foreign policy is clearly understood by those who might be asked to risk their lives in its behalf. And policymakers must not only explain but listen – take the time to hear the concerns and answer the questions of our military personnel.

For almost half a century, whenever we talked foreign policy, we did so within a Cold War context. A whole new vocabulary was established of containment and deterrence, throw weights and missile gaps, subversion and domino theories. And US military action was almost always related – directly or indirectly – to the Soviet threat. The world was a chessboard, and the two superpowers moved the pieces.

But then our chess rival left the table. The game has changed and the rules to the new one are still being written. Most of us do not for a minute mourn the Cold War era. But now there are those from all parts of the political spectrum for whom the new world is more confusing than gratifying. They can conceive of no threats to America that are not Cold War threats. They look at that empty chair on the other side of the chess table and counsel us to sit back, put our feet up, and lose interest in the outside world.

Obviously, America is safer and more secure than it was. Anyone who feels nostalgia for the Cold War ought to have his or her head examined. But anyone who concludes that foreign adversaries, conflicts, and disasters do not affect us misreads the past, misunderstands the present, and will miss the boat in the future.

Indeed, President Clinton has talked often about the similarity between this historical moment and the early days of the Truman Administration immediately following World War II. Then, as now, a new President saw a dramatically altered world, sought to redefine America's interests in that new world, and acted to protect those interests from a rising tide of isolationist thinking. And then, as now, the President's decisions were based on an analysis of new threats, a recognition of our enduring interests, and the imperative of engagement. So what are these new threats, and what should be America's response?

The Cold War is gone, but weapons of mass destruction are not. The possible aggressive use of such weapons remains perhaps the greatest threat to international peace and our security. Revelations about Iraq's weapons programs should have shocked even the most complacent among us. Besides Iraq, serious proliferation threats exist from states that fear the future, like North Korea; states that have fallen prey to the extremes of intolerance, such as Iran; and states that are engulfed by regional tension, such as in South Asia.

Beyond the destructive weapons, there are the destructive hatreds. Less than two months ago, the FBI apprehended a group with apparent foreign connections planning to blow up the building in which I work. The recent Middle East agreement is sure to enrage further those whose insecurities and extremism have made them blind to the promise of peace and open to the use of terror. The terrorist threat is aggravated by advances in technology and by the availability of weapons of every description. I know we remain vulnerable to terrorism, and I know it can affect our most vital of interests – our fathers, mothers, spouses, daughters, and sons.

We also face increasing ethnic and subnational violence. Wherever we turn, someone is fighting or threatening to fight someone else. These disputes may be far removed from our borders, but in today's global village, chaos is an infectious disease. Although violence in a failed state such as Somalia may seem trivial to some, when combined with unrest in Sudan, Rwanda, Liberia, Bosnia, Georgia, and so on, our attention and our interest – whether political or humanitarian cannot help but be engaged.

When a democratic government was ousted in Haiti, drug trafficking skyrocketed, repression increased, and the risk of a massive new influx of refugees to America grew. In Somalia, we have indications that a tactical alliance may be forming between Aideed's faction, terrorists based in Sudan, and the Government of Iran. The current violence in Azerbaijan threatens to bring Turkey, Iran, and Russia into conflict in ways that could well threaten our interests directly. And the possibility remains that the war in former Yugoslavia will spread to neighboring regions and nations, swelling further the flow of refugees, straining the economic vigor of Europe, and threatening the security of key European allies.

There is also a moral dimension to these conflicts, dramatized most hauntingly by the brave people of Sarajevo and Mostar but embodied, as well, by the millions of others who suffer the depredations of violence off camera, out of sight, every day.

Obviously, neither we nor anyone else can right every wrong, nor would it make sense for us to try. But let us never become so preoccupied with day-to-day concerns that we lose sight of our own most basic interest, which is the preservation not simply of American leadership but of American purpose.

Ten days ago, in Washington, I attended a lunch to celebrate the signing of an agreement between Israel and the PLO – a day I will remember all my life. I will remember, in particular, a comment by Israeli Foreign Minister Shimon Peres about America's purpose. When the history books are written, he said:

> Nobody will understand the United States, really: You have so much force, and you didn't conquer the land of anybody; you have so much power, and you didn't dominate another people; you have problems of your own, and you have never turned your back on the problems of others.

We should be proud that so much of the world sees America the way Foreign Minister Peres sees America, for our leadership today rests on the same solid foundation of principles and values – the same enlightened self interest – that has made service to America from Valley Forge to Desert Storm a badge not only of courage but of honor.

As Secretary Christopher and National Security Adviser Tony Lake have said this week, American foreign policy has four overarching goals: first, to strengthen the bonds among those countries that make up the growing community of major market democracies; second, to help emerging democracies get on their feet; third, to reform or isolate the rogue states that act to undermine the stability and prosperity of the larger community; and, fourth, to contain the chaos and ease the suffering in regions of greatest humanitarian concern. Taken together, our strategy looks to the enlargement of democracy and markets abroad.

To achieve these goals, some say we must make rigid choices between unilateral and multilateral, global and regional, force and diplomacy. But that is not true. We have the flexibility in this new era to steer a reasoned course between the counsel of those who would have us intervene everywhere and of those who see no American purpose anywhere. We have a full range of foreign policy tools with which to work, and we will choose those that will be most effective in each case.

As America's permanent representative to the United Nations, I have made it clear that we remain committed to the cause of peace and to the principle of resolving conflicts without violence whenever that is possible. The end of the Cold War has provided us with new and important opportunities in this regard. Cooperation, not confrontation, is now the norm at the UN Security Council.

As a result of our assertive diplomacy, we have been able to muster global support for sanctions against Libya for shielding the alleged saboteurs of Pan Am 103, against Iraq for its continued failure to meet its obligations following the Persian Gulf war, and against Haiti prior to the agreement reached recently to restore democratic rule. The use of sanctions has also arisen in the case of Angola, where our goal is to encourage an armed opposition group to abide by the results of a free election, and, of course, in Serbia, where they have drastically weakened the economy of an aggressor state.

Diplomacy will always be America's first choice, and the possibilities for diplomatic achievements today are ample. But history teaches us that there will always be times when words are not enough, when sanctions are not enough, when diplomacy is not enough.

The foremost mission of our government – its constitutional duty – is to protect our nation's territory, people, and way of life. We cannot fulfill that mission unless we have both the capacity to use force effectively and the will to do so when necessary. When neither our ability to fight nor our resolve to fight are in doubt, we can be most certain not only of defeating those who threaten us but of deterring those who are tempted to take such action.

Under the leadership of Secretary Aspin, I am confident that we will maintain military forces that are modern, versatile, ready, and strong. It is Department of Defense policy to maintain a military capable enough, in concert with local allies, to fight and win two major regional wars. The existence of such a force – and the credible threat to use it – is the surest way to prevent our interests from being threatened in the first place.

For years, a debate has raged about whether it is necessary to spell out a set of specific circumstances – a checklist – describing when America will or will not contemplate the use of military force. This Administration has wisely avoided the temptation to devise a precise list of the circumstances under which military force might be used or of repeating the State Department's mistake concerning Korea 43 years ago when it defined too narrowly the scope of America's interests and concerns. Too much precision in public, however well intentioned, can impinge on the flexibility of the commander in chief or generate dangerous miscalculations abroad. But let no one doubt that this President is willing to use force unilaterally when necessary.

Last June, the President ordered a strike against Saddam Hussein's military intelligence headquarters in response to Iraq's plot to kill former President Bush. We didn't seek anyone's permission to carry out that raid. We didn't ask anyone's help. We did it using our own forces exercising our own right of self-defense. The President said in his inaugural speech that America would act militarily with others when possible but 'alone when we must.' That commitment was true then; it is true today.

In the future, if America's vital economic interests are at risk – as they were in the Gulf – or if the lives of American citizens are in danger – as they were in

Panama – or if terrorists need to be tracked down – as when President Reagan ordered the use of force to apprehend the hijackers of the *Achille Lauro* – President Clinton will not hesitate to act as a commander in chief must act to protect America and Americans.

The President's inaugural statement also indicated that we support the use of force on a multilateral basis when it is in our interests to do so. As Secretary Christopher put it, we see 'multilateralism as a means, not an end.' No one understands the potential advantages of multilateralism better than the United States. That's why we proposed NATO and helped create the United Nations. The underlying thesis of the post-World War II strategy of containment, the legacy of such leaders as President Truman, General Marshall, and General Eisenhower, was that American strength is made even greater when cemented by strong alliances and joint endeavors with other nations in pursuit of common objectives.

The history of the Persian Gulf over the past three years is a classic modern example of this. I know that some of you here today helped to plan and execute operations during that war, including perhaps the most decisive air operation in history, along with the complex passage to the front lines of large combat units from different countries with different languages. I salute you for your skill and professionalism in this most effective coalition campaign. In the Gulf, American leadership benefited greatly from the support of other states before, during, and after the war. UN sanctions strengthened our cause politically, allied support spread the burden militarily, and contributions from Arab states, Germany, and Japan reduced the costs of the war and its aftermath financially.

The end of the Cold War has opened up another avenue for multilateral cooperation that had long been limited by the US–Soviet rivalry, and that is UN peacekeeping. In recent years, there has been a dramatic increase in requests for UN assistance in resolving ethnic and other conflicts. The statistics by now are familiar: more peacekeeping operations in the past five years than in the previous 43; a sevenfold increase in troops; a tenfold increase in budget; and a dramatic but immeasurable increase in danger and complexity.

At their best, UN peacekeeping operations can be very effective. Obviously, they cannot be a substitute for fighting or winning our own wars, nor should we allow the existence of a collective peacekeeping capability to lessen our own military strength. But UN efforts have the potential to act as a 'force multiplier' in promoting the interests in peace and stability that we share with other nations.

As I said earlier, territorial disputes, armed ethnic conflicts, civil wars, and the total collapse of governmental authority in some states are now among the principal threats to world peace. The UN is playing a constructive role in many such situations by mediating disputes, obtaining cease-fires, and, in some cases, achieving comprehensive peace agreements. This often requires the presence of UN peacekeepers or observers either to help arrange a peace or to help keep it.

Past UN peace missions have achieved important goals in places as diverse as the Middle East, Namibia, El Salvador, and Cambodia. To the extent that future peacekeeping missions succeed, they will lift from the shoulders of American servicemen and servicewomen and the taxpayers a great share of the burden of collective security operations around the globe. Particularly when circumstances arise where there is a threat to international peace that affects us but does not immediately threaten our citizens or territory, it will be in our interests to proceed in partnership with the UN or other appropriate groupings to respond to the threat involved and, hopefully, eliminate it. In such cases, we will benefit not only from the burden-sharing aspects but from the ability to invoke the voice of the community of nations in behalf of a cause that we support.

At the same time, as America's representative to the UN, I know that UN capabilities have not kept pace with its responsibilities – and I have discussed this problem on many prior occasions. Those who support the goals of the UN do it no favors if they fail to speak out when its reach begins repeatedly to exceed its grasp. The UN emerged from 40 years of Cold War rivalry overweight and out of shape. Today, UN peacekeepers need reformed budget procedures, more dependable sources of military and civilian personnel, better training, better intelligence, better command and control, better equipment, and more money. These limitations are not inherent; they are correctable, and the Administration is doing its part to see that they are corrected.

We believe, for example, that the UN decisionmaking process on peacekeeping must be overhauled. When deciding whether or not to support a UN peace-keeping or peacemaking resolution, we are insisting that certain fundamental questions be asked before, not after, new obligations are undertaken. These questions include the following:

- Is there a real threat to international peace and security – whether caused by international aggression; or by humanitarian disaster accompanied by violence; or by the sudden, unexpected, and violent interruption of an established democracy?

- Does the proposed peacekeeping mission have clear objectives, and can its scope be clearly defined?

- Is a cease-fire in place, and have the parties to the conflict agreed to a UN presence?

- Are the financial and human resources that will be needed to accomplish the mission available to be used for that purpose?

- Can an end point to UN participation be identified?

These questions illustrate the kind of consistent criteria – which do not now exist – that we are proposing that the UN take into account when contemplating new peacekeeping operations. And we are preparing guidelines for American participation that will promise greatest assistance in specialized areas such as logistics, training, intelligence, communications, and public affairs.

And although the Administration has not yet fully completed its review of our policy toward UN peacekeeping, I can assure you of one thing: This Administration believes that whether an operation is multilateral or unilateral, whether the troops are US or foreign, young men and women should not be sent in harm's way without a clear mission, competent commanders, sensible rules of engagement, and the means required to get the job done. The credibility of UN peace operations should hinge not on how many missions there are but on the quality of planning, the degree of professionalism demonstrated, and the extent to which mission objectives are achieved.

America under President Clinton will be a strong supporter of the UN. We take seriously President Truman's pledge to the first UN General Assembly that America will work to help the UN 'not as a temporary expedient but as a permanent partnership.'

At the same time, we understand that there are limits to what that partnership can achieve for the United States. Adlai Stevenson used to refer to the UN as the 'meeting house of the family of man,' which it is, but it is a very large family. It is the ultimate committee. It reflects the broadest possible diversity of viewpoints. As Americans, we command enormous influence there because of our power and the power of our ideals. But we cannot rely on the UN as a substitute guarantor for the vital interests of the United States. The Berlin Wall would be upright today if we had relied on the UN to contain communism. That ceremony on the front lawn of the White House two weeks ago would never have taken place if America had subcontracted to others the job of helping Israel to survive.

Sending American military forces into dangerous situations is the most difficult decision any President can make. History teaches us that public support for such decisions is essential and that in each such circumstance Americans are entitled to the facts.

The Administration has welcomed and takes very seriously the Senate's recent request to review our policy in Somalia. We have also begun, and will continue, a regular series of close consultations with the Congress and a dialogue with the public on our policy toward Bosnia.

I have spoken at length in public speeches and congressional testimony about both issues, and both are about to enter a new phase. Bosnia may be witness to a negotiated peace that will present the international community with its most daunting peacekeeping task ever. Yesterday, the Security Council approved a resolution setting out clearly that the UN's principal goal in Somalia is to bring about the political reconciliation of that long-suffering country, in part through the establishment of basic civic institutions, such as a functioning judiciary and police. In the weeks ahead, we will continue our consultations on Somalia, Bosnia, and the full range of national security and peacekeeping issues.

Now, let me summarize my message here today. The world has changed, and the Cold War national security framework is now obsolete. The Clinton Administration is fashioning a new framework that is more diverse and flexible than the old – a framework that will advance American interests, promote American values, and preserve American leadership. We will choose the means to implement this framework on a case-by-case basis, relying on diplomacy whenever possible, on force when absolutely necessary. If American servicemen and servicewomen are sent into combat, they will go with the training, the equipment, the support, and the leadership they need to get the job done.

Recognizing that global solutions are required to global problems, the tools that America will use to carry out its foreign policy will be both unilateral and multilateral. Other nations and institutions can and should be asked to bear a substantial part of the burden of advancing common interests. We have strong reason to help build a United Nations that is increasingly able and effective. But America will never entrust its destiny to other than American hands.

Finally, in keeping with a bipartisan tradition that stretches back a half-century, America will remain engaged in the world. It was 50 years ago this month that the Republican congressional leadership, mindful of what America's periodic tendency toward isolationism had done to the League of Nations, first went on record in support of an international organization 'to prevent military aggression and attain permanent peace.' Senator Arthur Vandenberg sponsored that resolution, in his words:

> To end the miserable notion ... that the Republican Party will return
> to its foxhole when the last shot in this war has been fired and will
> blindly let the world rot in its own anarchy.

Under the Clinton Administration, our nation will not retreat into a post-Cold War foxhole. Under the President's leadership, we will be called upon to work together, Republican and Democrat, civilian and military, public official and private citizen, to protect America and build a better world.

Source: US Department of State Dispatch, Vol.4, No.39, 27 September 1993.

———◄◦►———

Address by President William Clinton To The 48th Session Of The United Nations General Assembly

The United Nations, New York, 27 September 1993

Thank you very much, Mr President, and let me congratulate you on your election as president of this General Assembly.

Mr Secretary-General, distinguished delegates and guests, it is an honor to address you and to stand in this great Chamber, which symbolizes so much of the 20th century – its darkest crises and its brightest aspirations.

I come before you as the first American president born after the founding of the United Nations. Like most of the world's people today, I was not alive during the convulsive world war that convinced humankind of the need for this organization, nor during the San Francisco conference that led to its birth. Yet I have followed the work of the United Nations throughout my life – with admiration for its accomplishments, with sadness for its failures, and conviction that through common effort, our generation can take the bold steps needed to redeem the mission entrusted to the United Nations 48 years ago.

I pledge to you that my nation remains committed to helping make the UN's vision a reality. The start of this General Assembly offers us an opportunity to take stock of where we are as common shareholders in the progress of humankind and in the preservation of our planet.

It is clear that we live at a turning point in human history. Immense and promising changes seem to wash over us daily. The Cold War is over. The world is no longer divided into two armed and angry camps. Dozens of new democracies have been born.

It is a moment of miracles. We see Nelson Mandela stand side by side with President de Klerk, proclaiming a date for South Africa's first non-racial election. We see Russia's first popularly-elected president, Boris Yeltsin, leading his nation on its bold democratic journey. We have seen decades of deadlock shattered in the Middle East as the prime minister of Israel and the chairman of the Palestine Liberation Organization reached past enmity and suspicion to shake each other's hands and exhilarate the entire world with the hope of peace.

We have begun to see the doomsday weapons of nuclear annihilation dismantled and destroyed. Thirty-two years ago President Kennedy warned this chamber that humanity lived under a nuclear sword of Damocles that hung by the slenderest of threads. Now the United States is working with Russia, Ukraine, Belarus and others to take that sword of annihilation down to lock it away in a secure vault. Let us pray it ever remains there.

It is a new era in this hall as well. The superpower standoff that stymied this body's work, almost from its first day, has yielded to a new promise of practical cooperation. Yet today we must all admit that there are two powerful tendencies working from opposite directions, to challenge the authority of nation states everywhere and to undermine the authority of nation states to work together.

From beyond nations, economic and technological forces all over the globe are compelling the world toward integration. These forces are fueling a welcome explosion of entrepreneurship and political liberalization. But they also threaten to destroy the insularity and independence of national economies, quickening the pace of change and making many of our people feel more insecure.

At the same time, from within nations, the resurgent aspirations of ethnic and religious groups challenge governments on terms that traditional nation states cannot easily accommodate. These twin forces lie at the heart of the challenges not only to our national government, but also to all our international institutions. They require all of us in this room to find new ways to work together more effectively in pursuit of our national interests and to think anew about whether our institutions of international cooperation are adequate to this moment.

Thus, as we marvel at this era's promise of new peace, we must also recognize that serious threats remain. Bloody ethnic, religious and civil wars rage from Angola to the Caucasus to Kashmir. As weapons of mass destruction fall into more hands, even small conflicts can threaten to take on murderous proportions. Hunger and disease continue to take a tragic toll, especially among the world's children. The malignant neglect of our global environment threatens our children's health and their very security.

The repression of conscience continues in too many nations, and terrorism, which has taken so many innocent lives, assumes a horrifying immediacy for us here, when militant fanatics bombed the World Trade Center and planned to attack even this very hall of peace.

Let me assure you: whether the fathers of those crimes or the mass murderers who bombed Pan Am Flight 103, my government is determined to see that such terrorists are brought to justice.

At this moment of panoramic change, of vast opportunities and troubling threats, we must all ask ourselves what we can do and what we should do as a community of nations. We must once again dare to dream of what might be, so our dreams may be within our reach. For that to happen, we must all be willing to honestly confront the challenges of the broader world. That has never been easy.

When this organization was founded 48 years ago, the world's nations stood devastated by war or exhausted by its expense. There was little appetite for cooperative efforts among nations. Most people simply wanted to get on with their lives. But the far-sighted generation of leaders from the United States and elsewhere rallied the world. Their efforts built the institutions of post-war security and prosperity.

We are at a similar moment today. The momentum of the Cold War no longer propels us in our daily actions. And with daunting economic and political pressures upon almost every nation represented in this room, many of us are turning to focus greater attention and energy on our domestic needs and problems. And we must. But putting each of our economic houses in order cannot mean that we shut our windows to the world. The pursuit of self-renewal, in many of the world's largest and most powerful economies – in Europe, in Japan, in North America – is absolutely crucial because, unless the great industrial nations can recapture their robust economic growth, the global economy will languish.

Yet, the industrial nations also need growth elsewhere in order to lift their own. Indeed, prosperity in each of our nations and regions also depends upon active and responsible engagement in a host of shared concerns.

For example, a thriving and democratic Russia not only makes the world safer, it also can help to expand the world's economy. A strong GATT agreement will create millions of jobs worldwide. Peace in the Middle East, buttressed as it should be by the repeal of outdated UN resolutions, can help to unleash that region's great economic potential and calm a perpetual source of tension in global affairs. And the growing economic power of China, coupled with greater political openness, could bring enormous benefits to all of Asia and to the rest of the world.

We must help our publics to understand this distinction: Domestic renewal is an overdue tonic. But isolationism and protectionism are still poison. We must inspire our people to look beyond their immediate fears toward a broader horizon.

Let me start by being clear about where the United States stands. The United States occupies a unique position in world affairs today. We recognize that, and we welcome it. Yet, with the Cold War over, I know many people ask whether the United States plans to retreat or remain active in the world; and if active, to what end. Many people are asking that in our own country as well. Let me answer that question as clearly and plainly as I can.

The United States intends to remain engaged and to lead. We cannot solve every problem, but we must and will serve as a fulcrum for change and a pivot point for peace.

In a new era of peril and opportunity, our overriding purpose must be to expand and strengthen the world's community of market-based democracies. During the Cold War, we sought to contain a threat to the survival of free institutions. Now we seek to enlarge the circle of nations that live under those free institutions.

So our dream is of a day when the opinions and energies of every person in the world will be given full expression, in a world of thriving democracies that cooperate with each other and live in peace.

With this statement, I do not mean to announce some crusade to force our way of life and doing things on others or to replicate our institutions. But we now know clearly that, throughout the world, from Poland to Eritrea, from Guatemala to South Korea, there is an enormous yearning among people who wish to be the masters of their own economic and political lives. Where it matters most and where we can make the greatest difference, we will, therefore, patiently and firmly align ourselves with that yearning.

Today, there are still those that claim that democracy is simply not applicable to many cultures, and that its recent expansion is an aberration, an accident, in history that will soon fade away. But I agree with President Roosevelt, who once said, 'The democratic aspiration is no mere recent phase of human history. It is human history.'

We will work to strengthen the free-market democracies, by revitalizing our economy here at home, by opening world trade through the GATT, the North American Free Trade Agreement and other accords, and by updating our shared institutions, asking with you and answering the hard questions about whether they are adequate to the present challenges.

We will support the consolidation of market democracy where it is taking new root, as in the states of the former Soviet Union and all over Latin America. And we seek to foster the practices of good government that distribute the benefits of democracy and economic growth fairly to all people.

We will work to reduce the threat from regimes that are hostile to democracies and to support liberalization of non-democratic states when they are willing to live in peace with the rest of us.

As a country that has over 150 different racial, ethnic and religious groups within our borders, our policy is and must be rooted in a profound respect for all the world's religions and cultures. But we must oppose everywhere extremism that produces terrorism and hate.

And we must pursue our humanitarian goal of reducing suffering, fostering sustainable development, and improving the health and living conditions, particularly for our world's children.

On efforts from export controls to trade agreements to peacekeeping, we will often work in partnership with others and through multilateral institutions such as the United Nations. It is in our national interest to do so. But we must not hesitate to act unilaterally when there is a threat to our core interests or to those of our allies.

The United States believes that an expanding community of market democracies not only serves our own security interests, it also advances the goals enshrined in this body's charter and its universal declaration of human rights. For broadly-based prosperity is clearly the strongest form of preventive diplomacy, and the habits of democracy are the habits of peace.

Democracy is rooted in compromise, not conquest. It rewards tolerance, not hatred. Democracies rarely wage war on one another. They make more reliable partners in trade, in diplomacy, and in the stewardship of our global environment. And democracies, with the rule of law and respect for political, religious and cultural minorities are more responsive to their own people and to the protection of human rights.

But as we work toward this vision, we must confront the storm clouds that may overwhelm our work and darken the march toward freedom. If we do not stem the proliferation of the world's deadliest weapons, no democracy can feel secure. If we do not strengthen the capacity to resolve conflicts among and within nations, those conflicts will smother the birth of free institutions, threaten the development of entire regions, and continue to take innocent lives.

If we do not nurture our people and our planet through sustainable development, we will deepen conflict and waste the very wonders that make our efforts worth doing.

Let me talk more about what I believe we must do in each of these three categories: non-proliferation, conflict resolution, and sustainable development. One of our most urgent priorities must be attacking the proliferation of weapons of mass destruction, whether they are nuclear, chemical or biological; and the ballistic missiles that can rain them down on populations hundreds of miles away.

We know this is not an idle problem. All of us are still haunted by the pictures of Kurdish women and children cut down by poison gas. We saw Scud missiles dropped during the Gulf war that would have been far graver in their consequences if they had carried nuclear weapons. And we know that many nations still believe it is in their interests to develop weapons of mass destruction or to sell them or the necessary technologies to others for financial gain. More than a score of nations likely possess such weapons, and their number threatens to grow.

These weapons destabilize entire regions. They could turn a local conflict into a global human and environmental catastrophe. We simply have got to find ways to control these weapons and to reduce the number of states that possess them by supporting and strengthening the IAEA and by taking other necessary measures.

I have made non-proliferation one of our nation's highest priorities. We intend to weave it more deeply into the fabric of all of our relationships with the world's nations and institutions.

We seek to build a world of increasing pressure for non-proliferation, but increasingly open trade and technology for those states that live by accepted international rules. Today, let me describe several new policies that our government will pursue to stem proliferation.

We will pursue new steps to control the materials for nuclear weapons. Growing global stockpiles of plutonium and highly enriched uranium are raising the danger of nuclear terrorism for all nations. We will press for an international agreement that would ban production of these materials for weapons forever.

As we reduce our nuclear stockpiles, the United States has also begun negotiations toward a comprehensive ban on nuclear testing. This summer I declared that to facilitate these negotiations our nation would suspend our testing if all other nuclear states would do the same. Today in the face of disturbing signs, I renew my call on the nuclear states to abide by that moratorium as we negotiate to stop nuclear testing for all time.

I am also proposing new efforts to fight the proliferation of biological and chemical weapons. Today only a handful of nations has ratified the Chemical Weapons Convention. I call on all nations, including my own, to ratify this accord quickly so that it may enter into force by January 13th 1995.

We will also seek to strength the Biological Weapons Convention by making every nation's biological activities and facilities open to more international scrutiny. I am proposing as well new steps to thwart the proliferation of ballistic missiles. Recently, working with Russia, Argentina, Hungary and South Africa, we have made significant progress toward that goal. Now, we will seek to strengthen the principles of the Missile Technology Control Regime by transforming it from an agreement on technology transfer among just 23 nations to a set of rules that can command universal adherence.

We will also reform our own system of export controls in the United States to reflect the realities of the post-Cold War world. Where we seek to enlist the support of our former adversaries in the battle against proliferation at the same time that we stop deadly technologies from falling into the wrong hands, we will work with our partners to remove outdated controls that unfairly burden legitimate commerce and unduly restrain growth and opportunity all over the world.

As we work to keep the world's most destructive weapons out of conflict, we must also strengthen the international community's ability to address those conflicts themselves. For, as we all now know so painfully, the end of the Cold War did not bring us to the millennium of peace. Indeed, it simply removed the lid from many cauldrons of ethnic, religious and territorial animosity.

The philosopher, Isaiah Berlin, has said that a wounded nationalism is like a bent twig, forced down so severely that, when released, it lashes back with fury. The world today is thick with both bent and recoiling twigs of wounded communal identities.

This scourge of bitter conflict has placed high demands on the UN peace-keeping forces. Frequently, the blue helmets have worked wonders. In Namibia, El Salvador, the Golan Heights and elsewhere, UN peacekeepers have helped to stop the fighting, restore civil authority and enable free elections.

In Bosnia, UN peacekeepers, against the danger and frustration of that continuing tragedy, have maintained a valiant humanitarian effort. And if the parties of that conflict take the hard steps needed to make a real peace, the international community, including the United States, must be ready to help in its effective implementation.

In Somalia, the United States and the United Nations have worked together to achieve a stunning humanitarian rescue, saving literally hundreds of thousands of lives and restoring the conditions of security for almost the entire country. UN peacekeepers from over two dozen nations remain in Somalia today, and some, including brave Americans, have lost their lives to ensure that we complete our mission and to ensure that anarchy and starvation do not return just as quickly as they were abolished. Many still criticize UN peacekeeping, but those who do should talk to the people of Cambodia, where the UN's operations have helped to turn the killing fields into fertile soil for reconciliation. Last May's elections in Cambodia marked a proud accomplishment for that war-weary nation and for the United Nations, and I am pleased to announce that the United States has recognized Cambodia's new government.

UN peacekeeping holds the promise to resolve many of this era's conflicts. The reason we have supported such missions is not, as some critics in the United States have charged, to subcontract American foreign policy, but to strengthen our security, protect our interests, and to share among nations the cost and effort of pursuing peace. Peacekeeping cannot be a substitute for our own national defense efforts, but it can strongly supplement them.

Today, there is wide recognition that the UN peacekeeping ability has not kept pace with the rising responsibilities and challenges. Just six years ago, about 10,000 UN peacekeepers were stationed around the world. Today the UN has some 80,000 deployed in 17 operations on 4 continents. Yet, until recently, if a peacekeeping commander called in from across the globe when it was nighttime here in New York, there was no one in the peacekeeping office even to answer the call. When lives are on the line, we cannot let the reach of the UN exceed its grasp.

As the secretary-general and others have argued, if UN peacekeeping is to be a sound, security investment for our nation and for other UN members, it must adapt to new times. Together we must prepare UN peacekeeping for the 21st century. We need to begin by bringing the rigors of military and political analysis to every UN peace mission.

In recent weeks, in the Security Council, our nation has begun asking harder questions about proposals for new peacekeeping missions: Is there a real threat to international peace? Does the proposed mission have clear objectives? Can an end point be identified for those who will be asked to participate? How much will the mission cost? From now on, the United Nations should address these and other hard questions for every proposed mission before we vote and before the mission begins.

The United Nations simply cannot become engaged in every one of the world's conflicts. If the American people are to say yes to UN peacekeeping, the United Nations must know where to say no. The United Nations must also have the technical means to run a modern world class peacekeeping operation.

We support the creation of a genuine UN peacekeeping headquarters with a planning staff, with access to timely intelligence, with a logistics unit that can be deployed on a moment's notice, and a modern operations center with global communications.

And the UN's operations must not only be adequately funded but also fairly funded. Within the next few weeks, the United States will be current in our peacekeeping bills. I have worked hard with the Congress to get this done. I believe the United States should lead the way in being timely in its payments and I will work to continue to see that we pay our bills in full. But I am also committed to work with the United Nations to reduce our nation's assessment for these missions.

The assessment system has not been changed since 1973, and everyone in our country knows that our percentage of the world's economic pie is not as great as it was then. Therefore, I believe our rates should be reduced to reflect the rise of other nations that can now bear more of the financial burden. That will make it easier for me as president to make sure we pay in a timely and full fashion.

Changes in the UN's peacekeeping operations must be part of an even broader program of United Nations reform. I say that, again, not to criticize the United Nations but to help to improve it. As our Ambassador, Madeleine Albright, has suggested, the United States has always played a twin role to the UN, first friend and first critic.

Today, corporations all around the world are finding ways to move from the industrial age to the information age, improving service, reducing bureaucracy, and cutting costs. Here in the United States, our Vice President, Al Gore, and I have launched an effort to literally reinvent how our government operates. We see this going on in other governments around the world. Now the time has come to reinvent the way the United Nations operates as well.

I applaud the initial steps the secretary-general has taken to reduce and to reform the United Nations bureaucracy. Now we must all do even more to root out waste. Before this General Assembly is over, let us establish a strong mandate for an office of inspector general so that it can attain a reputation for toughness, for integrity, for effectiveness. Let us build new confidence among our people that the United Nations is changing with the needs of our times.

Ultimately, the key for reforming the United Nations, as in reforming our own government, is to remember why we are here and whom we serve. It is wise to recall that the first words of the UN Charter are not 'We, the governments,' but 'We, the peoples of the United Nations.' That means in every country the teachers, the workers, the farmers, the professionals, the fathers, the mothers, the children, from the most remote village in the world to the largest metropolis, they are why we gather in this great hall. It is their futures that are at risk when we act or fail to act. And it is they who ultimately pay our bills.

As we dream new dreams in this age when miracles now seem possible, let us focus on the lives of those people, and especially on the children who will inherit this world. Let us work with a new urgency, and imagine what kind of world we could create for them in the coming generation.

Let us work with new energy to protect the world's people from torture and repression. As Secretary of State Christopher stressed at the recent Vienna conference, human rights are not something conditional, founded by culture, but rather something universal granted by God. This General Assembly should create at long last, a high commissioner for human rights. I hope you will do it soon and with vigor and energy and conviction.

Let us also work far more ambitiously to fulfill our obligations as custodians of this planet, not only to improve the quality of life for our citizens and the quality of our air and water and the earth itself, but also because the roots of conflict are so often entangled with the roots of environmental neglect and the calamity of famine and disease.

During the course of our campaign in the United States last year, Vice President Gore and I promised the American people major changes in our nation's policy toward the global environment. Those were promises to keep, and today the United States is doing so.

Today we are working with other nations to build on the promising work of the UN's Commission on Sustainable Development. We are working to make sure that all nations meet their commitments under the Global Climate Convention. We are seeking to complete negotiations on an accord to prevent the world's deserts from further expansion. And we seek to strengthen the World's Health Organization's efforts to combat the plague of AIDS, which is not only killing millions, but also exhausting the resources of nations that can least afford it.

Let us make a new commitment to the world's children. It is tragic enough that one and a half million children died as a result of wars over the past decade. But it is far more unforgivable that in that same period, 40 million children died from diseases completely preventable with simple vaccines or medicines. Every day – this day, as we meet here – over 30,000 of the world's children will die of malnutrition and disease.

Our UNICEF director, Jim Grant, has reminded me that each of those children had a name and a nationality, a family, a personality, and a potential. We are compelled to do better by the world's children. Just as our own nation has launched new reforms to ensure that every child has adequate health care, we must do more to get basic vaccines and other treatments for curable diseases to children all over the world. It's the best investment we'll ever make.

We can find new ways to ensure that every child grows up with clean, drinkable water, that most precious commodity of life itself. And the United Nations can work even harder to ensure that each child has at least a full primary education, and I mean that opportunity for girls as well as boys.

And to ensure a healthier and more abundant world, we simply must slow the world's explosive growth in population. We cannot afford to see the human race double by the middle of the next century. Our nation has, at last, renewed its commitment to work with the United Nations to expand the availability of the world's family planning education and services. We must ensure that there is a place at the table for every one of our world's children. And we can do it.

At the birth of this organization 48 years ago, another time of both victory and danger, a generation of gifted leaders from many nations stepped forward to organize the world's efforts on behalf of security and prosperity. One American leader during that period said this: 'It is time we steered by the stars rather than by the light of each passing ship.' His generation picked peace, human dignity and freedom. Those are good stars, they should remain the highest in our own firmament.

Now history has granted to us a moment of even greater opportunity, when old dangers and old walls are crumbling, future generations will judge us, every one of us, above all, by what we make of this magic moment. Let us resolve that we will dream larger, that we will work harder so that they can conclude that we did not merely turn walls to rubble, but instead laid the foundations for great things to come.

Let us ensure that the tide of freedom and democracy is not pushed back by the fierce winds of ethnic hatred. Let us ensure that the world's most dangerous weapons are safely reduced and denied to dangerous hands. Let us ensure that the world we pass to our children is healthier, safer and more abundant than the one we inhabit today.

I believe – I know – that together we can extend this moment of miracles into an age of great work and new wonders.

Bibliography

UNITED STATES GOVERNMENT DOCUMENTS, LEGISLATION
AND OFFICIAL SPEECHES

Albright, Ambassador Madeleine K. (United States Permanent Representative to the United Nations-Designate), Confirmation Hearing Statement before the Senate Foreign Relations Committee, 21 Jan. 1993, reprinted in the *US Department of State Dispatch*, Vol.4, No.15, 12 April 1993, pp.229–31

Albright, Ambassador Madeleine K. (United States Permanent Representative to the United Nations), 'Current Status of US Policy on Bosnia, Somalia, and UN Reform', Statement before the Subcommittee on Foreign Operations, Export Financing, and Related Programs of the House Appropriations Committee, 12 March 1993, reprinted in *US Department of State Dispatch*, Vol.4, No.4, 5 April 1993, pp.207–11

——, 'A Strong United Nations Serves US Security Interests', Address to the Council on Foreign Relations Conference on Cooperative Security and the United Nations, New York City, 11 June 1993

——, 'Myths of Peacekeeping', Statement before the Subcommittee on International Security, International Organizations, and Human Rights of the House Committee on Foreign Affairs, 24 June 1993, reprinted in *US Department of State Dispatch*, Vol.4, No.26, 28 June 1993, pp.464–7

——, 'Use of Force in a Post-Cold War World', Address at the National War College, National Defense University, Fort McNair, Washington DC, 23 Sept. 1993, reprinted in *US Department of State Dispatch*, Vol.4, No.39, 27 Sept. 1993, pp.665–8

——, 'Building a Consensus on International Peacekeeping', Statement before the Senate Foreign Relations Committee, 20 Oct. 1993, Federal Document Clearing House, Inc. 1993, Lexis/Nexis; also reprinted in *US Department of State Dispatch*, Vol.4, No.46, 15 Nov. 1993, pp.789–92

——, 'The Clinton Administration's Policy on Reforming Multilateral Peace Operations', Statement before the Subcommittee on Foreign Operations,

Export Financing and Related Programs, 5 May 1994, reprinted in *US Department of State Dispatch*, Vol.5, No.20, 16 May 1994, pp.315–18

——, Testimony before the Senate Armed Services Committee/Coalition Defense and Reinforcing Forces FY95 Defense Authorization, 12 May 1994, Federal Document Clearing House, Inc. 1994, Lexis/Nexis

——, Testimony before the Subcommittee on International Security, International Organizations and Human Rights, of the House Foreign Affairs Committee, 17 May 1994, Federal Document Clearing House, Inc. 1994, Lexis/Nexis

——, 'Principle, Power and Purpose in the New Era' at the US Department of State, Washington DC, 28 Oct. 1994, *USUN Press Release* 160-(94)

——, 'The United States and the United Nations: Confrontation or Consensus?', Address to the Council on Foreign Relations, Washington DC., 26 Jan. 1995, *US Department of State Dispatch*, Vol.6, No.6, pp.79–83

——, 'Advancing American Interests Through the United Nations', Statement before the Subcommittee on International Operations and Human Rights of the House International Relations Committee, Washington DC, 8 Feb. 1995, *US Department of State Dispatch*, 20 Feb. 1995, Vol.6, No.8, pp.125–30

——, 'Contract With America's Defense Policy Provisions: The Administration's Response to S.5 and H.R.7 Senate Foreign Relations Committee, 21 March 1995, Federal Document Clearing House, Inc. 1995, Lexis/Nexis

——, 'The United States and the United Nations: What's In It For Us', address to the Chicago Mid-America Committee, Chicago, 23 June 1995, *USUN Press Release*, #98-(95)

Aspin, Les, 'The Use and Usefulness of Military Forces in the Post-Cold War, Post-Soviet World', address by Congressman Aspin (Chairman of the House Armed Services Committee) to the Jewish Institute for National Security Affairs, Washington DC, 21 Sept. 1992

Aspin, Les (Secretary of Defense) and General Colin Powell (Chairman of the Joint Chiefs of Staff), 'Defense Department Briefing: DoD Bottom-Up Review', *Federal News Service*, 1 Sept. 1993, Lexis/Nexis

Bacon, Kenneth, Pentagon Spokesman, 'Defense Department Briefing', *Federal News Service*, 21 Nov. 1996, Lexis/Nexis

Bennet, Douglas J. Jr (Assistant Secretary for International Organization Affairs), 'Peacekeeping and Multilateral Relations in US Foreign Policy', Address before the UN Association, Princeton University, Trenton NJ, 29 Nov. 1994, reprinted in *US Department of State Dispatch*, Vol.5, No.49, 5 Dec. 1994, pp.808–10

——, 'Leveraging US Resources Through the United Nations', Statement before the Subcommittee on International Operations and Human Rights of the House International Relations Committee, Washington DC, 8 Feb. 1995, *US Department of State Dispatch*, 20 Feb. 1995, Vol.6, No.8, pp.131–3

Bolton, John R. (Assistant Secretary for International Organization Affairs), 'FY 1992 Budget Requests For International Organizations', Statement before the Subcommittees on International Operations and on Human Rights and International Organizations of the House Foreign Affairs Committee, 5 March 1991, reprinted in *US Department of State Dispatch*, 11 March 1991, pp.172–4

——, 'UN Peace-keeping Efforts to Promote Security and Stability', Excerpts from a statement before the Subcommittee on International Operations, Human Rights and International Organizations of the House Foreign Affairs Committee, 25 March 1992, reprinted in *US Department of State Dispatch*, 30 March pp.244–6

——, Testimony before the Subcommittee on Airland Forces of the Senate Armed Services Committee, 3 May 1995, Federal Document Clearing House, Inc. 1995, Lexis/Nexis

Browne, Marjorie Ann, *United Nations Peacekeeping: Issues for Congress*, Washington DC: Foreign Affairs and National Defense Division, 12 Sept. 1994

Bruner, Edward F., *US Forces and Multinational Commands: PDD 25 and Precedents*, CRS 94–887 F, Washington DC: Congressional Research Service, Updated 29 Aug. 1996

Bush, President George, 'The World After the Persian Gulf War', Address before a joint session of Congress, 6 March 1991, reprinted in *US Department of State Dispatch*, 11 March 1991, pp.161–3

——, 'The United Nations in a New Era', Address before the UN General Assembly, 23 Sept. 1991, reprinted in *US Department of State Dispatch*, 30 Sept. 1991, pp.718–21

——, 'The United Nations: Power to Act For Peace and Freedom', Address to the Summit Session of the Security Council, 31 Jan. 1992, reprinted in *US Department of State Dispatch*, Vol.3, No.2, 3 Feb. 1992, pp.76–7

——, 'Humanitarian Mission to Somalia', Address to the Nation, Washington DC, 4 March1992, reprinted in *US Department of State Dispatch*, Vol.3, No.49, 7 Dec. 1992, pp.865–6

——, 'The Need for an Active Foreign Policy', Excerpts of address given at the Nixon Library, Washington DC 11 March 1992, reprinted in *US Department of State Dispatch*, 16 March 1992, p.211

——, 'Address by the President of the United States of America to the 47th Session of the United Nations General Assembly', 21 Sept. 1992, *USUN Press Release* 84-(92)

——, Letter from President Bush to the Speaker of the House and the President Pro Tempore of the Senate, 10 Dec. 1992, reprinted in *US Department of State Dispatch*, Vol.3, No.50, 14 Dec. 1992, p.877

——, 'America's Role in the World', Address to the West Point Military Academy,

West Point, NY, 5 Jan. 1993, reprinted in *US Department of State Dispatch*: Vol.4, No.2, 11 Jan. 1993, pp.13–15

Christopher, Secretary-Designate Warren, 'Statement at Senate Confirmation Hearing', Statement before the Senate Foreign Relations Committee, 13 Jan. 1993, reprinted in *US Department of State Dispatch*, Vol.4, No.4, 25 Jan. 1993, pp.45–9

Christopher, Secretary of State Warren, 'Foreign Policy Review', Testimony before the Senate Foreign Relations Committee, 4 Nov. 1993, Federal Document Clearing House, Inc. 1993, Lexis/Nexis; also reprinted in *US Department of State Dispatch*, Vol.4, No.47, 23 Nov. 1993, pp.797–802

——, 'Foreign Policy Overview', Testimony before the Senate Foreign Relations Committee, 23 Feb. 1994, Federal Document Clearing House, Inc. 1994, Lexis/Nexis

——, 'Foreign Policy: Year-End Review and Goals for 1995', News Conference Statement, Washington DC, 20 Dec. 1994, *US Department of State Dispatch*, 2 Jan. 1995, Vol.6, No.1, pp.1–2

——, 'Principles and Opportunities For American Foreign Policy', Address before the John F. Kennedy School of Government, Harvard University, 20 Jan. 1995, *US Department of State Dispatch*, 23 Jan. 1995, Vol.6, No.4, pp.41–5

Secretary Christopher, Secretary Aspin and Admiral Jeremiah, 'Remarks at White House Press Briefing', 7 Oct. 1993, reprinted in *US Department of State Dispatch*, Vol.4, No.42, 18 Oct. 1993, pp.715–16

Clinton, President William J., 'Address by the President of the United States of America to the 48th Session of the United Nations General Assembly', 27 Sept. 1993, *USUN Press Release* 141-(93)

——, 'US Military Involvement in Somalia', Address to the Nation, 7 Oct. 1993, reprinted in *US Department of State Dispatch*, Vol.4, No.42, 18 Oct. 1993, pp.713–14

——, 'Report of Military Operations in Somalia Transmitted to Congress', 13 Oct. 1993, reprinted in *US Department of State Dispatch*, Vol.4, No.43, 25 Oct. 1993, p.747

——, 'Strengthening American Security Through World Leadership', Excerpt on foreign policy from State of the Union address, Washington DC, 24 Jan. 1995, *US Department of State Dispatch*, 30 Jan. 1995, Vol.6, No.5, p.53

——, *A Time For Peace, Promoting Peace: The Policy of The United States*, Annual Report to Congress on Peacekeeping, Volumes I and II, Feb. 1995

——, 'The Vital Tradition of American Leadership in the World', Speech to the Nixon Center for Peace and Freedom Policy Conference, Washington DC, 1 March 1995, *US Department of State Dispatch*, 6 March 1995, Vol.6, No.10, pp.157–60

Collier, Ellen C., *War Powers and UN Military Actions: A Brief Background of the Legislative Framework*, CRS 93-1058 F, Washington DC: Congressional Research Service, 21 Dec. 1993

Crigler, T. Frank (former US Ambassador to Somalia), 'Turning Triumph Into Tragedy', Statement before the Subcommittee on Africa of the House Foreign Affairs Committee, 29 July 1993, Federal Document Clearing House, Inc. 1993, Lexis/Nexis

Department of the Army, *Peace Operations FM 100-23*, Washington DC: Department of the Army, Headquarters, Dec. 1994

Dole, Senator Robert (Senate Majority Leader), 'Contract With America's Defense Policy Provisions: S 5, The Peace Powers Act of 1995', Testimony before the Senate Foreign Relations Committee, 21 March 1995, Federal Document Clearing House, Inc. 1995, Lexis/Nexis

Eagleburger, Lawrence (Acting Secretary of State), 'Charting the Course: US Foreign Policy in a Time of Transition', Address before the Council on Foreign Relations, Washington DC, 7 Jan. 1993, reprinted in *US Department of State Dispatch*, Vol.4, No.2, 11 Jan. 1993, pp.16–19

Friedman, Townsend (Special Coordinator For Rwanda), Statement to the Joint Hearing of the Senate Foreign Relations Subcommittee on Africa and the House International Relations Subcommittee on Africa on Rwanda and Burundi, 5 April 1995, Federal Document Clearing House, Inc. 1995, Lexis/Nexis

Grimmett, Richard F., *War Powers Resolution: Presidential Compliance*, CRS IB 81050, Washington DC: Congressional Research Service, 23 July 1996

Harper, Conrad K. (Legal Advisor, Dept. of State), 'On Legal Authority for UN Peace Operations', Statement before the Legislation and National Security Subcommittee of the House Government Operations Committee, 3 March 1994, reprinted in *International Legal Materials*, 33 I.L.M., 821, May 1994, pp.822–9

Houdek, Robert (Deputy Assistant Secretary of African Affairs), 'Update on Progress in Somalia', Statement before the Subcommittee on Africa of the House Foreign Affairs Committee, 17 Feb. 1993, reprinted in *US Department of State Dispatch*, Vol.4, No.8, 22 Feb. 1993, pp.99–101

Joint Chiefs of Staff, *National Military Strategy of the United States of America: A Strategy of Flexible and Selective Engagement*, Washington DC: JCS, Feb. 1995

——, *Joint Doctrine for Military Operations Other Than War*, Washington DC: JCS, 16 June 1995, Joint Publication 3-07

Joint Warfighting Center, *Joint Task Force Commander's Handbook for Peace Operations*, Fort Monroe VA: JWC, 28 Feb. 1995

Lake, Anthony (National Security Advisor) 'From Containment to Enlargement', Address to the School of Advanced International Studies, Johns Hopkins University, Washington DC, 21 Sept. 1993, reprinted in *US Department of State Dispatch*, Vol.4, No.39, 27 Sept. 1993, pp.658–64

——, 'A Strategy of Enlargement and the Developing World', Address to the Overseas Development Council, 13 Oct. 1993, reprinted in *US Department of State Dispatch*, Vol.4, No.43, 25 Oct. 1993, pp.748–51

——, 'Peacekeeping Directive Designed to Impose More Discipline', Transcript of remarks by Mr Lake and Lt General Weseley Clark, White House, EUR511, 6 May 1994, 5870

Lowenthal, Mark M., *Peacekeeping in Future US Foreign Policy*, CRS 94–260 S, Washington DC: Congressional Research Service, Update 10 May 1994

McCain, Senator John (Arizona), 'US Participation in UN Peacekeeping Operations', Statement to the Subcommittee on Legislation and National Security of the House Government Operations Committee, 3 March 1994, Federal Document Clearing House, Inc. 1994, Lexis/Nexis

McCandless, Representative Al (California), Statement to the Subcommittee on Legislation and National Security of the House Government Operations Committee, 3 March 1994, Federal Document Clearing House, Inc. 1994, Lexis/Nexis

Moose, George E. (Assistant Secretary of State for African Affairs), 'Crisis in Rwanda', Statement before the Subcommittee on Africa of the House Foreign Affairs Committee, 4 May 1994, reprinted in *US Department of State Dispatch*, Vol.5, No.21, 23 May 1994, pp., 341–2

——, 'The Crisis in Rwanda: US Response', Statement before the Subcommittee on Africa of the Senate Foreign Relations Committee, 26 July 1994, reprinted in *US Department of Dispatch*, Vol.5, No.32, 8 Aug. 1994, pp.540–1

National Security Revitalization Act, United States' Congress, 104th Congress, 1st Session, 25 Jan. 1995

Nixon, President Richard M., 'Message from the President, Vetoing the House Joint Resolution 542, A. Joint Resolution Concerning the War Powers of Congress and the President', 24 Oct. 1973

Peace Powers Act of 1995, United States' Senate, 104th Congress, 1st Session, 4 Jan. 1995

Powell, General Colin L. (Chairman of the Joint Chiefs of Staff), 'Defense Writers' Group: Breakfast Meeting', *Federal News Service*, 23 Sept. 1993, Lexis/Nexis

Scheffer, David J. (Senior Advisor and Counsel to the US Permanent Representative to the United Nations), 'Introductory Note, United States: Administration Policy on Reforming Multilateral Peace Operations', in *International Legal Materials*, 33 I.L.M., 705, May 1994, pp.795–6

Sewall, Sarah B. (Deputy Assistant Secretary of Defense for Peacekeeping and Peace Enforcement Policy), 'Remarks to International Peacekeeping '95', Ottawa, Ontario, 15 Nov. 1995, no further information

Shalikashvili, General John, 'Hearing of the Senate Armed Services Committee: Nomination Hearing', *Federal News Service*, 22 Sept. 1993, Lexis/Nexis

Sloan, Stanley R., *The United States and the Use of Force in the Post-Cold War World: Toward Self-Restraint?*, CRS 94-581 S, Washington DC: Congressional Research Service, 20 July 1994

Smith, James M., Testimony before the Senate Armed Services Committee, 12 May 1994, Federal Document Clearing House, Inc. 1994, Lexis/Nexis

Tarnoff, Peter (Under-Secretary of State for Political Affairs), 'US Policy in Somalia', Statement before the Senate Foreign Relations Committee, 29 July 1993, reprinted in *US Department of State Dispatch*, Vol.4, No.32, 9 Aug. 1993, pp.567–8

Tutwiler, Margaret (State Department Spokesperson), 'US Arrearage Payments to UN Organizations', Press Release, 12 July 1991, reprinted in *US Department of State Dispatch*, 22 July 1991, p.538

United States General Accounting Office, *National Security: The Use of Presidential Directive to Make and Implement US Policy*, Washington DC: GAO, Jan. 1992, GAO/NSIAD-92-72

——, *United Nations: US Participating in Peacekeeping Operations*, Washington DC: GAO, Sept. 1992, GAO/NSIAD-92-247

——, *UN Peacekeeping: Observations on Mandates and Operational Capability*, Statement of Frank C. Conahan, Assistant Comptroller General, National Security and International Affairs Division before the Subcommittee on Terrorism, Narcotics and International Operations, Senate Committee on Foreign Relations, Washington DC: GAO, 9 June 1993, GAO/T/NSIAD-93-15

——, *UN Peacekeeping: Lessons Learned in Managing Recent Missions*, Washington DC: GAO, Dec. 1993, GAO/NSIAD-94-9

——, *Peace Operations: Cost of DoD Operations in Somalia*, Washington DC: GAO, March 1994, GAO/NSIAD-94-88

——, *Humanitarian Intervention: Effectiveness of UN Operations in Bosnia*, *Briefing Report to the Honorable Robert S. Dole, US Senate*, Washington DC: GAO, April 1994, GAO/NSIAD-94-156BR

——, *Peace Operations: Withdrawal of US Troops from Somalia*, Washington DC: GAO, June 1994, GAO/NSIAD-94-175

——, *United Nations: How Assessed Contributions for Peacekeeping Operations Are Calculated*, Washington DC: GAO, Aug. 1994, GAO/NSIAD-94-206

——, *Peace Operations: Heavy Use of Key Capabilities May Affect Response to Regional Conflicts*, Washington DC: GAO, March 1995, GAO/NSIAD-95-51

Walker, Ambassador Edward S. (United States Deputy Permanent Representative to the United Nations), 'Explanation of Vote on the Situation in Haiti', 23 Sept. 1993, *USUN Press Release* 140-(93)

War Powers Resolution, Public Law 93-148, 7 Nov. 1973

Warner III, Edward L. (Assistant Secretary of Defense for Strategy and

Requirements), 'Statement before the Senate Armed Services Subcommittee on Coalition Defense and Reinforcing Forces', 13 April 1994, reprinted in *International Legal Materials*, 33 I.L.M. 814, May 1994, pp.815–20

——, 'Statement to the Senate Armed Services Committee, Subcommittee on Airland Forces', 3 May 1995

Weinberger, Casper W. (Secretary of Defense), 'The Uses of Military Force', address to the National Press Club, Washington DC, 28 Nov. 1984

White House, *The Clinton Administration's Policy on Reforming Multilateral Peace Operations (PDD 25)*, *USUN Press Release* 74-(94)

United Nations Participation Act, 20 Dec. 1945

UNITED NATIONS' DOCUMENTS

Annan, Secretary-General Kofi, UN Press Release SG/SM/6393, 14 Nov. 1997

Boutros-Ghali, Secretary-General Boutros, *Report on the Work of the Organization from the Forty-seventh to the Forty-eighth Session of the General Assembly*, New York: United Nations, Sept. 1993

——, *Report of the Secretary-General on the Work of the Organization, Advanced Copy*, New York: United Nations, Sept. 1994

——, *An Agenda for Peace*, Second Edition, New York: United Nations DPI, 1995

General Assembly Resolution 3101, *Financing of the United Nations Emergency Force*, adopted at the 2196th plenary meeting, 11 Dec. 1973

General Guidelines for Peace-keeping Operations, New York: United Nations DPKO, Oct. 1995, 95-38147

Letter dated 8 Dec. 1992 from Secretary-General Boutros-Ghali to United States President Bush, in *United Nations and Somalia, 1992–1995*, United Nations Blue Book Series, Vol. VIII, New York: United Nations, DPI, 1996, Document 39, pp.216–17

Letter dated 18 Sept. 1995 from Secretary-General Boutros Ghali to the President of the Security Council

Pérez de Cuéllar, Secretary-General Javier, *Anarchy or Order: Annual Reports 1982–1991*, New York: United Nations, 1991

Provisional Verbatim, S/PV.3060, United States Representative Watson's statement to the Security Council, 17 March 1992

Provisional Verbatim, S/PV.3188, United States Ambassador Albright's statement to the Security Council, 26 March 1993

Provisional Verbatim, S/PV.3288, United States Representative Walker's statement to the Security Council, 5 Oct. 1993

Provisional Verbatim, S/PV.3358, United States Representative Inderfurth's statement to the Security Council, 5 April 1994

Provisional Verbatim, S/PV.3377, United States Representative Inderfurth's statement to the Security Council, 16 May 1994

Provisional Verbatim, S/PV.3385, United States Representative Gnehm's statement to the Security Council, 31 May 1994

Provisional Verbatim, S/PV.3388, United States Representative Inderfurth's statement to the Security Council, 8 June 1994

Provisional Verbatim, S/PV.3392, United States Ambassador Albright's statement to the Security Council, 22 June 1994

Provisional Verbatim, S/PV.3400, United States Representative Gnehm's statement to the Security Council, 1 July 1994

Provisional Verbatim, S/PV.3432, United States Ambassador Albright's statement to the Security Council, 30 Sept. 1994

Provisional Verbatim, S/PV.3447, United States Ambassador Albright's statement to the Security Council, 4 Nov. 1994

Provisional Verbatim, S/PV.3473, United States Ambassador Albright's statement to the Security Council, 30 Nov. 1994

Security Council Resolution 794, adopted 3 Dec. 1992

Security Council Resolution 814, adopted 26 March 1993

Security Council Resolution 837, adopted 6 June 1993

Security Council Resolution 865, adopted 22 Sept. 1993

The Blue Helmets: A Review of United Nations Peace-keeping, Third Edition, New York: United Nations, DPI, 1996

BOOKS AND REPORTS

Adibe, Clement, *Managing Arms in Peace Processes: Somalia*, Geneva: UN, UNIDIR Disarmament and Conflict Resolution Project, 1995

Annan, Kofi, 'Peace Operations and the United Nations: Preparing for the Next Century', New York: International Peace Academy, 1997

Bennis, Phyllis, *Calling the Shots: How Washington Dominates Today's UN*, New York: Olive Branch Press, 1996

Blechman, Barry M. and J. Matthew Vaccaro, *Training for Peacekeeping: The United Nations' Role*, Washington DC: The Henry L. Stimson Center, Report No.12, July 1994

Boutros-Ghali, Boutros, *Unvanquished: A US–UN Saga*, New York: Random House, 1999.

Clark, Dick (ed.), *The United Nations, Peacekeeping, and US Policy in the Post-Cold War World, A Conference Report*, Queenstown MD: The Aspen Institute, 1994

Clarke, Walter S., *Humanitarian Intervention in Somalia: Bibliography*, Carlisle PA: Center for Strategic Leadership, Peacekeeping Institute, US Army War College, March 1995

Clarke, Walter and Jeffrey Herbst (eds), *Learning From Somalia: The Lessons of Armed Humanitarian Intervention*, Boulder CO: Westview Press, 1997

Coate, Roger A. (ed.), *US Policy and the Future of the United Nations*, New York: Twentieth Century Fund Press, 1994

Cook, Thomas D. and Donald T. Campbell, *Quasi-Experimentation: Design and Analysis Issues for Field Settings*, Chicago IL: Rand McNally Publishing Company, 1979

Daniel, Donald C.F. and Bradd C. Hayes (eds), *Beyond Traditional Peacekeeping*, New York: St Martin's Press, 1996

Durch, William J. (ed.), *The Evolution of UN Peacekeeping: Case Studies and Comparative Analysis*, London: The Macmillan Press Limited, 1993

—— (ed.), *UN Peacekeeping, American Policy and the Uncivil Wars of the 1990s*, New York: St Martin's Press, 1996

Durch, William J. and Barry Blechman, *Keeping the Peace: The United Nations in the Emerging World Order*, Washington DC: The Henry L. Stimson Center, Report No.2, March 1992

Gregg, Robert W., *About Face? The United States and the United Nations*, Boulder CO: Lynne Rienner Publishers, 1993

Haass, Richard N., *Intervention: The Use of American Military Force in the Post-Cold War World*, Washington DC: The Carnegie Endowment for International Peace, 1994

Halperin, Morton H., *Bureaucratic Politics and Foreign Policy*, Washington DC: The Brookings Institution, 1974

Hamilton, Heather, *Briefing Book on United Nations Preventive Diplomacy*, Washington DC: World Federalist Association, 1996

Hilsman, Roger with Laura Gaughran and Patricia A. Weitsman, *The Politics of Policy Making in Defense and Foreign Affairs: Conceptual Models and Bureaucratic Politics*, Third Edition, Englewood Cliffs NJ: Prentice Hall, 1993

Hirsch, John L. and Robert B. Oakley, *Somalia and Operation Restore Hope: Reflections on Peacemaking and Peacekeeping*, Washington DC: United States Institute of Peace Press, 1995

Hoffmann, Walter (ed.), *Rethinking Basic Assumptions About The United Nations*, Washington DC: World Federalist Association, February 1993

Holt, Victoria K., *Briefing Book on Peacekeeping: The US Role in United Nations Peace Operations*, Washington DC: Council for a Livable World Education Fund, Dec. 1994

Ikenberry, G. John (ed.), *American Foreign Policy: Theoretical Essays*, New York: HarperCollins Publishers, 1989

Karns, Margaret P. and Karen A. Mingst (eds), *The United States and Multilateral Institutions: Patterns of changing instrumentality and influence*, New York: Routledge, 1992

Kull, Steven and Clay Ramsay, *US Public Attitudes on US Involvement in Somalia*,

Program on International Policy Attitudes, University of Maryland, 26 Oct. 1993

——, *US Public Attitudes on UN Peacekeeping*, Program on International Policy Attitudes, University of Maryland, 7 March 1994

——, *US Public Attitudes on US Involvement in Bosnia*, Program on International Policy Attitudes, University of Maryland, 4 May 1994

——, *US Public Attitudes on US Involvement in Haiti*, Program on International Policy Attitudes, University of Maryland, 22 Aug. 1994

Kull, Steven, *Americans on UN Peacekeeping: A Study of US Public Attitudes, Summary of Findings*, Program on International Policy Attitudes, University of Maryland, 27 April 1995

Kull, Steven, I.M. Destler and Clay Ramsay, *The Foreign Policy Gap: How Policymakers Misread the Public*, Program of International Policy Attitudes, University of Maryland, Oct. 1997

LaRose-Edwards, Paul, *The Rwandan Crisis of April 1994: The Lessons Learned*, Ottawa: Department of Foreign Affairs and International Trade, 30 Nov. 1994

van Leeuwen, Marianne and Auke Venema (eds), *Selective Engagement: American Foreign Policy at the Turn of the Century*, The Hague: Netherlands Atlantic Commission and the Netherlands Institute of International Relations, 1996

Lewis, William H. (ed.), *Military Implications of United Nations Peacekeeping Operations*, McNair Paper 17, Institute For National Strategic Studies, Washington DC: National Defense University, June 1993

——(ed.), *Peacekeeping: The Way Ahead? Report of a Special Conference*, McNair Paper 25, Institute For National Strategic Studies, Washington DC: National Defense University, Nov. 1993

Liu, F.T., *United Nations Peacekeeping and the Non-Use of Force*, Boulder CO: Lynne Rienner Publishers/International Peace Academy, Occasional Paper Series, 1992

McDermott, Anthony, *United Nations Financing Problems and the New Generation of Peacekeeping and Peace Enforcement*, Providence RI: The Thomas J. Watson Jr Institute for International Studies, 1994, Occasional Paper #16

Makinda, Samuel M., *Seeking Peace from Chaos: Humanitarian Intervention in Somalia*, New York: International Peace Institute, Occasional Paper Series, 1993

Maynes, Charles William and Richard S. Williams (eds), *US Foreign Policy and the United Nations System*, New York: W.W. Norton and Company, 1996

Minear, Larry and Philippe Guillot, *Soldiers to the Rescue: Humanitarian Lessons From Rwanda*, Paris: OECD, 1996

Powell, Colin L. with Joseph E. Persico, *My American Journey*, New York: Random House, 1995

Reed, Pamela, J. Matthew Vaccaro and William J. Durch, *Handbook on United Nations Peace Operations*, Washington DC: The Henry L. Stimson Center, Handbook No.3, April 1995

Renner, Michael, *Remaking UN Peacekeeping: US Policy and Real Reform*, Washington DC: National Commission for Economic Conversion and Disarmament, Briefing Paper 17, Nov. 1995

Report of the Working Group on Peacekeeping and the US National Interest, *Peacekeeping and the US National Interest*, Washington DC: The Henry L. Stimson Center, Report 11, Feb. 1994

Righter, Rosemary, *Utopia Lost: The United Nations and World Order*, New York: The Twentieth Century Fund Press, 1995

Rivlin, Benjamin, *UN Reform from the Standpoint of the United States*, Tokyo: The United Nations University, 1996

Rosner, Jeremy D., *The New Tug-of-War: Congress, the Executive Branch and National Security*, Washington DC: The Carnegie Endowment For International Peace, 1995

Sahnoun, Mohamed, *Somalia: The Missed Opportunities*, Washington DC: The United States Institute of Peace, 1994

Seiple, Chris, *The US Military/NGO Relationship in Humanitarian Interventions*, Carlisle PA: Center for Strategic Leadership, Peacekeeping Institute, US Army War College, 1996

Steering Committee of the Joint Evaluation of Emergency Assistance to Rwanda, *The International Response to Conflict and Genocide: Lessons from the Rwanda Experience*, Copenhagen, 1996

Thakur, Ramesh and Carlyle A. Thayer (eds), *A Crisis of Expectations: UN Peacekeeping in the 1990s*, Boulder CO: Westview Press, 1995

Ward, Thomas J., Frederick A. Swarts and Alan Thibideau (eds), *The 104th Congress & The United Nations: Understanding the Issues*, New York: American Leadership Conference, Washington Times Foundation and the World Leadership Conference, 1996

Warner, Daniel (ed.), *New Dimensions of Peacekeeping*, Dordrecht: Martinus Nijhoff Publishers, 1995

CHAPTERS AND ARTICLES

Artaud, Denise, 'La notion de puissance dans la politique étrangère des Etats-Unis: le difficile mariage du moralisme et de la géostratégie', *Le trimestre du monde*, 3e trimestre 1995, pp.145–52

Aspin, Les, 'Challenges to Value-Based Military Intervention', address to the Managing Chaos Conferences, reprinted in *Peaceworks* No.3, Feb. 1995, United States Institute of Peace

Augelli, Enrico and Craig Murphy, 'Lessons of Somalia for Future Multilateral Humanitarian Operations', *Global Governance*, Vol.1, No.3 (Sept.–Dec. 1995), pp.339–65

Barnett, Michael, 'The United Nations Politics of Peace: From Juridical Sovereignty to Empirical Sovereignty', *Global Governance*, Vol.1, No.1 (Winter 1995), pp.79–97

——, 'The UN Security Council, Indifference, and Genocide in Rwanda', *Cultural Anthropology*, Vol.12, No.4, pp.551–78

Berdal, Mats R., 'Fateful Encounter: The United States and UN Peacekeeping', *Survival*, Vol.36, No.1 (Spring 1994), pp.30–50

Blechman, Barry M., 'The Intervention Dilemma', *The Washington Quarterly*, Vol.18, No.3, pp.63–73

Bloomfield, Lincoln P., 'Collective Security and US Interests', in Thomas G. Weiss (ed.), *Collective Security in a Changing World*, Boulder CO: Lynne Rienner Publishers, 1993, pp.189–205

Bolton, John R., 'Wrong Turn in Somalia', *Foreign Affairs*, Vol.73, No.1, Jan./Feb. 1994, pp.56–66

Boutros-Ghali, Boutros, '*An Agenda for Peace*: One Year Later', *Orbis*, Vol.37, No.3 (Summer 1993), pp.323–32

——, 'Global Leadership After the Cold War', *Foreign Affairs*, Vol.75, No.2 (March/April 1996), pp.86–98

Cerjan, Lieutenant General Paul E. (US Army, President, National Defense University), 'The United States and Multilateral Peacekeeping: The Challenge of Peace', in Fariborz L. Mokhtari (ed.), *Peacemaking, Peacekeeping and Coalition Warfare: The Future Role of the United Nations, Proceedings of a Conference*, Washington DC: National Defense University Press, 1994, pp.3–7

Clarke, Walter and Jeffery Herbst, 'Somalia and the Future of Humanitarian Intervention', *Foreign Affairs*, Vol.75, No.2 (March/April 1996), pp.70–85

Coicaud, Jean-Marc, 'Les Nations Unies en Somalie: entre maintien et imposition de la paix', *Le trimestre du monde*, 1er trimestre 1994, pp.97–134

——, 'L'ONU peut-elle assurer la paix?', *Le trimestre du monde*, 4^e trimestre 1995, pp.29–54

Cowin, Andrew J., 'Expanding United Nations Peacekeeping Role Poses Risk for America', *The Heritage Foundation Backgrounder*, No.917, 13 Oct. 1992

Daalder, Ivo H., 'The United States and Military Intervention in Internal Conflict', in Michael E. Brown (ed.), *The International Dimensions of Internal Conflict*, Cambridge MA: The MIT Press, 1996, pp.461–88

Daniel, Donald C.F., 'The United States', in Trevor Findley (ed.), *Challenges for the New Peacekeepers*, SIPRI Research Report #12, Oxford: Oxford University Press, 1996, pp.85–98

Destler, I.M., 'Foreign Policy and the Public: Will Leaders Catch the *Full* Message?', *The Brown Journal of World Affairs*, Vol.3, No.1 (Winter/Spring 1996), pp.265–9

Dimoff, Steven A., 'Congress's Budget-cutting Fervor Threatens US Standing at UN', *The Interdependent*, Vol.19, No.3, Fall 1993, p.6

Dunlap Jr, Colonel Charles J., 'The Last American Warrior: Non-Traditional Missions and the Decline of the US Armed Forces', *The Fletcher Forum of World Affairs*, Vol.18, No.1, Winter/Spring 1994, pp.65–82

Eagleburger, Lawrence S., 'Making Foreign Policy: A View From the Executive Branch', an interview by J. Peter Scoblic, *The Brown Journal of World Affairs*, Vol.3, No.1 (Winter/Spring 1996), pp.243–57

Farrell, Theo, 'Sliding into War: The Somalia Imbroglio and US Army Peace Operations Doctrine', *International Peacekeeping*, Vol.2, No.2 (Summer 1995), pp.194–214

Feingold, Russ, 'The Role of Congress in Deploying US Troops Abroad', *The Brown Journal of World Affairs*, Vol.3, No.1 (Winter/Spring 1996), pp.305–9

Friedman, Will, and John Immerwahr, 'Discussing Foreign Policy with the Post-Cold War Public', *The Brown Journal of World Affairs*, Vol.3, No.1 (Winter/Spring 1996), pp.259–64

Goulding, Marrack, 'The Evolution of United Nations Peacekeeping', *International Affairs*, Vol.69, No.3, pp.451–64

Haass, Richard N., 'Foreign Policy by Posse', *The National Interest*, No.41, Fall 1995, pp.58–64

Hamilton, Lee, 'Congress and Foreign Policy: The Case of Bosnia', *The Brown Journal of World Affairs*, Vol.3, No.1 (Winter/Spring 1996), pp.299–304

Harper, Captain Gregory, 'Creating a UN Peace Enforcement Force: A Case for US Leadership', *The Fletcher Forum of World Affairs*, Vol.18, No.1, Winter/Spring 1994, pp.49–63

Helman, Gerald B. and Steven R. Ratner, 'Saving Failed States', *Foreign Policy*, No.89 (Winter 1992/92), pp.3–20

Helms, Jesse (Chairman of Senate foreign Relations Committee), 'Saving the UN: A Challenge to the Next Secretary-General', *Foreign Affairs*, Vol.75, No.5, Sept./Oct. 1996, pp.2–7

Hindrickson, David C., 'The Recovery of Internationalism', *Foreign Affairs*, Vol.73, No.5, Sept./Oct. 1994, pp.26–43

Holl, Jane E., 'We the People Here Don't Want No War: Executive Branch Perspectives on the Use of Force', in Aspen Strategy Group Report, *The United States and the Use of Force in the Post-Cold War Era*, Queenstown MA: The Aspen Institute, 1995, pp.111–32

Holmes, Kim R., 'Clinton's Red Herring: The Accusations of Congressional Isolationism', *The Heritage Foundation Backgrounder*, No.1037, 9 June 1995

Holt, Victoria K., 'Reforming UN Peacekeeping: The US Role and the UN Financial Crisis', *The Brown Journal of World Affairs*, Vol.3, No.1 (Winter/Spring 1996), pp.125–34

Howe, Jonathan T., 'The United States and United Nations in Somalia: The Limits of Involvement', *The Washington Quarterly*, Vol.18, No.3, pp.49–62

——, 'Will the United States Lead a New World Order', *The Fletcher Forum of World Affairs*, Vol.18, No.1, Winter/Spring 1994, pp.23–9

Kohut, Andrew and Robert C. Toth, 'Arms and the People', *Foreign Affairs*, Vol.73, No.6, Nov./Dec. 1994, pp.47–61

——, 'The People, the Press and the Use of Force', in Aspen Strategy Group Report, *The United States and the Use of Force in the Post-Cold War Era*, Queenstown MD: The Aspen Institute, 1995, pp.133–70

Kull, Steven, 'Misreading the Public Mood', *The Bulletin of the Atomic Scientists*, March/April 1995, pp.55–9

——, 'What the Public Knows that Washington Doesn't', *Foreign Policy*, No.101, Winter 1995–96, pp.102–15

Lake, Anthony, 'American Power and American Diplomacy', Speech delivered at Harvard University on 21 Oct. 1994, reprinted in *The Fletcher Forum of World Affairs*, Vol.19, No.2 (Summer/Fall 1995), pp.87–94

Larrabee, F. Stephen, 'La politique américaine et la crise yougoslave', *Politique étrangère*, Vol.59, No.4 (hiver 94/95), pp.1041–55

Lavin, Franklin L., 'Isolationism and US Foreign Policy', *The Brown Journal of World Affairs*, Vol.3, No.1 (Winter/Spring 1996), pp.271–8

Lian, Bradley and John R. O'Neal, 'Presidents, the Use of Force, and Public Opinion', *Journal of Conflict Resolution*, Vol.37, No.2, June 1993, pp.277–300

Lehmann, Ingrid A., 'Public Perceptions of UN Peacekeeping: A Factor in the Resolution of International Conflicts', *The Fletcher Forum of World Affairs*, Vol.19, No.1 (Winter/Spring 1995), pp.109–19

Lindsay, James M., 'Congress and the Use of Force in the Post-Cold War Era', in Aspen Strategy Group Report, *The United States and the Use of Force in the Post-Cold war Era*, Queenstown MD: The Aspen Institute, 1995, pp.71–110

Logan, Carolyn J., 'US Public Opinion and the Intervention in Somalia: Lessons for the Future of Military-Humanitarian Interventions', *The Fletcher Forum of World Affairs*, Vol.20, No.2, Summer/Fall 1996, pp.155–80

Mandelbaum, Michael, 'Foreign Policy as Social Work', *Foreign Affairs*, Vol.75, No.1, Jan./Feb. 1996, pp.16–32

Maynes, Charles William, 'A Workable Clinton Doctrine', *Foreign Policy*, No.93, Winter 93/94, pp.3–20

Mermin, Jonathan, 'Television News and American Intervention in Somalia: The Myth of a Media-Driven Foreign Policy', *Political Science Quarterly*, Vol.112, No.3, pp.385–403

Miller, Linda B., 'The Clinton Years: Reinventing US Foreign Policy', *International Affairs*, Vol.70, No.4 (1994), pp.621–34

Miller, Admiral Paul David, 'In the Absence of War: Employing America's Military Capabilities in the 1990s', *The Fletcher Forum of World Affairs*, Vol.18, No.1, Winter/Spring 1994, pp.5–21

Morales, Waltraud Queiser, 'US Intervention and the New World Order: Lessons from Cold War and post-Cold War Cases', *Third World Quarterly*, Vol.15, No.1, 1994, pp.77–101

Morris, Justin, 'Force and Democracy: UN/US Intervention in Haiti', *International Peacekeeping*, Vol.2, No.3 (Autumn 1995), pp.391–412

Muravchik, Joshua, 'Affording Foreign Policy: The Problem Is Not Wallet, But Will', *Foreign Affairs*, Vol.75, No.2 (March/April 1996), pp.8–13

Norton, Augustus R. and Thomas G. Weiss, 'Superpowers and Peace-keepers', *Survival*, Vol.32, No.3 (May/June 1990), pp.212–20

Ornstein, Norman, 'Foreign Policy and the 1992 Election', *Foreign Affairs*, Vol.71, No.2 (March/April 1992), pp.1–16

Parsons, Anthony, 'The UN and the National Interests of States' in, Adam Roberts and Benedict Kingsbury (eds), *United Nations, Divided World: The UN's Role in International Relations*, Second Edition, Oxford: Clarendon Press, 1993, pp.104–24

Perry, William J., 'Military Action: When to Use It and How to Ensure Its Effectiveness', in Janne E. Nolan (ed.), *Global Engagement: Cooperation and Security in the 21st Century*, Washington DC: Brookings Institution, 1994, pp.235–41

Powell, General Colin L., 'US Forces: The Challenges Ahead', *Foreign Affairs*, Vol.72, No.5, Winter 1992/93, pp.32–45

Puchala, Donald J., 'Outsiders, Insiders, and UN Reform', *The Washington Quarterly*, Vol.17, No.4, pp.161–73

Rieff, David, 'The Illusions of Peacekeeping', *World Policy Journal*, Vol.11, No.3 (Fall 1994), pp.1–18

Rivlin, Benjamin, 'The Crisis Over UN Peacekeeping: Reflections on American and Japanese Attitudes', in *The US and Japan in the Changing Environment for Multilateral Organizations: Final Report and Recommendations*, New York: The Ralph Bunche Institute on the United Nations, 1994, pp.87–103

Roberts, Adam, 'The Crisis in UN Peacekeeping', *Survival*, Vol.36, No.3 (Autumn 1994), pp.93–120

Rosenau, William, 'Non-Traditional Missions and the Future of the US Military', *The Fletcher Forum of World Affairs*, Vol.18, No.1 (Winter/Spring 1994), pp.31–48

Rosner, Jeremy D., 'The Know-Nothings Know Something', *Foreign Policy*, No.101, Winter 1995–96, pp.116–29

Rubner, Michael, 'The Reagan Administration, the 1973 War Powers Resolution, and the Invasion of Grenada', *Political Science Quarterly*, Vol.100, No.4, Winter 1985–86, pp.627–47

Ruggie, John Gerard, 'The UN: Wandering in the Void', *Foreign Affairs*, Vol.72, No.5, pp.26–31

——, 'Peacekeeping and US Interests', *The Washington Quarterly*, Vol.17, No.4, pp.175–84

Seitz, Colonel Richard, 'The US Military and UN Peacekeeping', in *Peace-making and Peacekeeping: Implications for the United States Military*, Panel Report of the United States Institute of Peace, Washington DC: USIP Press, May 1993, pp.25–32

Sigal, Leon V., 'The Last Cold War Election', *Foreign Affairs*, Vol.72, No.5, Winter 1992/93, pp.1–15

Sokolsky, Joel J., 'Great Ideas and Uneasy Compromises: the United States Approach to Peacekeeping', *International Journal*, Vol.L, No.2 (Spring 1995), pp.266–93

Spence, Floyd D., 'What to Fight For? American Interests and the Use of Force', *The Brown Journal of World Affairs*, Vol.3, No.1 (Winter/Spring 1996), pp.279–84

Stedman, Stephen John, 'The New Interventionists', *Foreign Affairs*, Vol.72, No.1, Winter 1993/94, pp.1–16

Summers Jr, Colonel Harry G., 'US Participation in UN Peacekeeping Operations', *Strategic Review*, Fall 1993, pp.69–72

Terry, James P. (US Department of the Interior), 'UN Peacekeeping and Military Reality', *The Brown Journal of World Affairs*, Vol.3, No.1 (Winter/Spring 1996), pp.135–43

Urquhart, Sir Brian, 'Beyond the 'Sheriff's Posse', *Survival*, Vol.32, No.3 (May/June 1990), pp.196–205

——, 'Who Can Police the World', *The New York Review of Books*, 12 May 1994, pp.29–33

'US Pullback from UN Peace-keeping Role Puts Post-Cold War Agenda in Question', *International Documents Review, The Weekly Newsletter on the United Nations*, Vol.4, No.37, 25 Oct. 1993, pp.1–2

Washburn, John L., 'United Nations Relations with the United States: The UN Must Look out for Itself', *Global Governance*, Vol.2, No.1 (Jan.–April 1996), pp.81–96

Weiss, Thomas G., 'Overcoming the Somalia Syndrome – "Operation Rekindle Hope?", *Global Governance*, Vol.1, No.2 (May–Aug. 1995), pp.171–87

Welch, David A., 'The Organizational Process and Bureaucratic Politics Paradigms: Retrospect and Prospect', *International Security*, Vol.17, No.2, pp.112–46

Wolfowitz, Paul D., 'Clinton's First Year', *Foreign Affairs*, Vol.73, No.1, Jan./Feb. 1994, pp.28–43

UNPUBLISHED WORKS

Adams, Martin P. *The US Role in UN Sanctioned Peace Enforcement Operations*, Paper prepared for the Advance Research Project Certification at the Naval War College, Newport RI, June 1994

Finklestein, Lawrence S., 'PDD-25: A Failure of Nerve?', Paper presented at the workshop: 'The T.I.E.S. that Bind: Technology, Intervention, Ethnicity and Conflict Management in the Post-Cold War Era', 19 Nov. 1994, University of Illinois at Urbana-Champaign

Poor, Robert W., *The United States in United Nations Military Operations*, Paper prepared for the Naval Post-graduate School at the Naval War College, Rhode Island, Sept. 1992

Summary of Proceedings of the Law, Ethics and National Security Conference at the University of Virginia School of Law, 'The United Nations, Regional Organizations and Military Operations', 12–13 April 1996

NEWS MEDIA

Adams, Jim, 'Clinton Acts Head Off Peacekeeping Curbs', *Reuters North American Wire*, 29 Sept. 1993, Lexis/Nexis

'Albright Upbraids UN For Attacks on US Policy', *Washington Post*, 18 Aug. 1993, p.A25

Associated Press, 'UN Chief Lauds US Plans on Peace Role', *Boston Globe*, 29 May 1994, p.2

Baker, Peter, 'US Near Approval of Mission To Aid Central Africa Refugees', *Washington Post*, 28 Nov. 1996, p.A44

'Behind the Zairean Shambles', *The Economist*, Vol.341, No.7990, 2 Nov. 1996, p.47

Bennet, James, 'Size of US Force Bound for Africa is Cut Below 1,000', *New York Times*, 20 Nov. 1996, pp.A1 and A11

Blitzer, Wolf, 'US Policy to Shift on Somalia', *CNN*, transcript #537-2, 28 Sept. 1993

Bogart, Carroll, 'Most Likely to Succeed', *Newsweek*, Vol.128, No.26, 23 Dec. 1996, pp.10–12

de Borchgrave, Arnaud, 'The Change in the Administration's Position is a Mystery', *Washington Times*, 11 Nov. 1996, Lexis/Nexis

Byrd, Senator Robert C. (D, W-Virginia), 'The Perils of Peacekeeping', *New York Times*, 19 Aug. 1993, p.A26

'Can It Keep the Peace?: The United Nations at 50', *The Economist*, Vol.337, No.7937, 21 Oct. 1995, p.18

Clayton Jr, William E., 'Placing US Troops under Foreign Commanders not New: Precedents Date as farBack as World War I', *Houston Chronicle*, 20 Sept. 1993, p.A16

Cohen, Andrew 'Albright Accuses Congress of Blackmail', *Globe and Mail* (Toronto), 14 Jan. 1998, p.A8

'Crisis in Zaire: A Primer', *Toronto Sun*, 17 Nov. 1996, p.13

Crossette, Barbara, 'Christopher Scours Africa and the UN is Watching', *International Herald Tribune*, 11 Oct. 1996, pp.1 and 8

——, 'US Sets Conditions for Using Troops to Aid Refugees in Zaire', *New York Times*, 15 Nov. 1996, p.A7

——, 'UN Chief Assails US Congress for Killing Plan to Pay Dues', *International Herald Tribune*, 15 Nov. 1997, IHT Website

'Death Shadows Africa's Great Lakes', *The Economist*, Vol.341, No.7988, 19 Oct. 1996, pp.51–3

Devroy, Ann, 'Clinton Signs New Guidelines for UN Peacekeeping Operations', *Washington Post*, 6 May 1994, p.A30

Dewar, Helen, 'Senate Debates US Role in Somalia: Lawmakers Seek Clarification of Administration's Objectives', *Washington Post*, 9 Sept. 1993, p.A35

——, 'Senators Approve Troop Compromise: Clinton Authority Is Left Unrestricted', *Washington Post*, 21 Oct. 1993, p.A1

Dewar, Helen and Kevin Merida, 'From Congress, More Questions: Byrd Assails "Misplaced Policy", Dole Cites "Confusion Over Objectives"', *Washington Post*, 5 Oct. 1993, p.A25

Dole, Bob, 'Peacekeepers and Politics', *New York Times*, 24 Jan. 1994, p.A15

Duke, Lynne, 'Zaire Rebels Allow Search For Refugees', *Washington Post*, 21 Nov. 1996, pp.A27 and A32

Erlanger, Steven, 'Waiting for Clinton: Allies Still Hope for US Leadership in Crisis', *New York Times*, 18 Nov. 1996, p.A6

Evans, David, 'Gen. Shalikashvili Supports Use of GIs under Foreign Commanders', *Chicago Tribune*, 23 Sept. 1993, p.7

Farah, Douglas and Michael Tarr, 'Haitians Block US Troop Arrival', *Washington Post*, 12 Oct. 1993, p.A1

Friedman, Thomas L., 'Clinton, at UN, Lists Stiff Terms For Sending US Forces to Bosnia', *New York Times*, 28 Sept. 1993, p.A1

——, 'Theory vs. Practice: Clinton's Stated Foreign Policy Turns Into More Modest "Self-Containment"', *New York Times*, 1 Oct. 1993, p.A3

——, 'Clinton's Foreign Policy: Top Adviser Speaks Up', *New York Times*, 31 Oct. 1993, p.A2

Gellman, Barton, 'Wider UN Police Role Supported', *Washington Post*, 5 Aug. 1993, p.A1

——, 'Defense Program Exceeds Budget Target, Aspin Says', *Washington Post*, 15 Sept. 1993, p.A6

——, 'US Reconsiders Putting GIs Under UN: Concern over Somalia and Bosnia Prompts Backlash in Congress', *Washington Post*, 22 Sept. 1993, p.A1

——, 'US Rhetoric Changed, but Hunt for Aideed Persisted', *Washington Post*, 7 Oct. 1993, p.A37

———, 'The Words Behind A Deadly Decision: Secret Cables Reveal Maneuvering Over Request for Armor in Somalia', *Washington Post*, 31 Oct. 1993, p.A1

Gellman, Barton and Daniel Williams, 'A Grand Bargain: Administration Would Rather Switch Than Fight', *Washington Post*, 20 Oct. 1993, p.A36

Gordon, Michael R., 'New Strength for UN Peacekeepers: US Might', *New York Times*, 13 June 1993, p.A2

———, 'US Officers Were Divided on Somalia Raid', *New York Times*, 13 May 1994, p.A8

Goshko, John M., 'Clinton Seen Calming Hill on Peacekeeping: Caution in Committing US Forces Said to Defuse Confrontation on Presidential Prerogatives', *Washington Post*, 2 Oct. 1993, p.A16

———, 'America 1996: Looking Inward: Among Conservatives, a Deep Suspicion of United Nations', *International Herald Tribune*, 24 Sept. 1996, pp.1 and 8

Graham, Bradley and Stephen Buckley, 'US Sharply Cuts Back Africa Force', *Washington Post*, 20 Nov. 1996, pp.A1 and A24

Green, Robert, 'Dole Urges Clinton to Reconsider Foreign Policy', *Reuters North American Wire*, 1 Sept. 1993, Lexis/Nexis

Grier, Peter, 'As Violence in Somalia Escalates, Senate Steps Up Troop Oversight', *Christian Science Monitor*, 14 Sept. 1993, p.6

Hoagland, Jim, 'Less Appetite for Military Involvement Abroad', *International Herald Tribune*, 13 March 1997, p.8

'House Rejects Clinton Peacekeeping Funds', *Reuters*, 30 Sept. 1993, Lexis/Nexis

Jehl, Douglas, 'US Showing New Caution On UN Peacekeeping Missions', *New York Times*, 18 May 1994, p.A1

———, 'Officials Told to Avoid Calling Rwanda Killings "Genocide"', *New York Times*, 10 June 1994, p.A8

———, 'The Rwanda Disaster; Did US Err on Rwanda?', *New York Times*, 23 July 1994, p.A1

Kenworthy, Tom and John Lancaster, 'At Least 5 Americans Killed in Somali Attack', *Washington Post*, 4 Oct. 1993, p.A1

Knox, Paul, 'UN States Blamed', *Globe and Mail* (Toronto), 5 Dec. 1997, p.A16

Kreisher, Otto, 'US troops for Bosnia and Africa OK'd', *Copley News Service*, 16 Nov. 1996, Lexis/Nexis

Lake, Anthony (National Security Advisor), 'The Limits of Peacekeeping', *New York Times*, 6 Feb. 1994, Opinion-Editorial Section

Lancaster, John, 'Aspin Lists US Goals in Somalia: Troop Pullout Hinges on Three Conditions: No Timetable is Set', *Washington Post*, 28 Aug. 1993, p.A1

———, 'US Prepares Peace Offer', *Washington Post*, 9 Oct. 1993, p.A1

Lewis, Paul, 'US Plans Policy on Peacekeeping', *New York Times*, 18 Nov. 1993, p.A7

——, 'United Nations Journal: The Peacekeeper in Chief Needs More Soldiers', *New York Times*, 4 March 1994, p.A4

Lippman, Thomas W., 'US, UN Aides Defend Somalia "Police Action"', *Washington Post*, 30 July 1993, p.A15

——, 'Articulation of Policy Draws Mixed Reviews: Clinton Team's Speechmaking Blitz Offered Little More Than Generalities, Critics Say', *Washington Post*, 29 Sept. 1993, p.A10

——, 'Administration Sidesteps Genocide Label in Rwanda', *Washington Post*, 11 June 1994, p.A1

——, 'US Ground Troops May Not Go To Zaire', *Washington Post*, 19 Nov. 1996, pp.A1 and A17

——, 'US Remains Uncertain on Response in Zaire', *Washington Post*, 8 Dec. 1996, p.A34

Lippman, Thomas W. and Barton Gellman, 'Humanitarian Gesture Turns Deadly', *Washington Post*, 10 Oct. 1993, p.A1

Lippman, Thomas W. and Peter Baker, 'US May Send Up to 5,000 Troops to Africa', *Washington Post*, 14 Nov. 1996, pp.A1 and A25

Lippman, Thomas W. and Dana Priest, 'Pentagon Wants Cease-Fire Pledge in Zaire', *Washington Post*, 15 Nov. 1996, pp.A1 and A28

Luck, Edward (guest), on 'World Chronicle', Programme No.566, recorded 14 Oct. 1994, Media Division, Department of Public Information, United Nations, New York

MacNeil/Lehrer Newshour (Transcript), 'Department of Defense', guest: Secretary Les Aspin, transcript #4764, 28 Sept. 1993, Lexis/Nexis

——, 'Peacekeeping Fight', guests: Rep. William Goodling (R-Penn) and Rep. Lee Hamilton (D-Ind.), transcript #5150, 26 Jan. 1995

——, 'Rescue Mission', guest: Dr Susan Rice (National Security Council), transcript #5698, 13 Nov. 1996

Mannion, Jim, 'US Suspends Reconnaissance Flights over Zaire', *Agence France Presse*, 22 Nov. 1996, Lexis/Nexis

Marcus, Ruth and John Lancaster, 'US Pulls Rangers Out of Somalia', *Washington Post*, 20 Oct. 1993

McIlroy, Anne, 'Proof Surfaces of Long Trek to Death in Congo', *Globe and Mail* (Toronto), 17 Nov. 1997, p.A8

'Midlife Crisis', *Newsweek*, 30 Oct. 1995, pp.14–21

Mitchell, Alison, 'Clinton Offers US Troops to Help Refugees in Zaire', *New York Times*, 14 Nov. 1996, pp.A1 and A14

Molotsky, Irvin, 'Administration Is Divided On Role for US in Peacekeeping Efforts', *New York Times*, 22 Sept. 1993, p.A8

Muravchik, Joshua, 'New Isolationism, Same Old Mistakes', *New York Times*, 28 Aug. 1996, p.A6

'New Poll Finds Rightward Shift in Public Backing For UN', United Nations

Association of the USA, *Press Release*, 11 May 1992

'New Poll Shows US Voters Prefer Pro-UN Candidates', United Nations Association of the USA, *Press Release*, 11 April 1996

Nordwall, Eric, 'US Needs 'de Facto' Zaire Cease-fire', *United Press International*, 14 Nov. 1996, Lexis/Nexis

Perlmutter, Amos, 'Peacekeeping Guidelines are Full of Pitfalls; Bill Clinton's Policy on UN Peacekeeping Missions' Column, *Insight on the News*, Vol.10, No.1, 3 Jan. 1994, p.29

Pfaff, William 'An Active French Role in the 1994 Genocide in Rwanda', *International Herald Tribune*, 17 Jan. 1998 Editorial-Opinion page, IHT Website

Pianin, Eric and Thomas W. Lippman, 'Republicans Withhold funds for UN and IMF', *International Herald Tribune*, 14 Nov. 1997, IHT Website

Pick, Hella and Mark Huband, 'US Shifts Focus From Manhunt for Aideed: Clinton Seeks New Strategy in Face of Congressional Ire', *Guardian*, 29 Sept. 1993, p.9

Preston, Julia, 'UN to Stay in Somalia Until 1995: Resolution Adopted on Building Nation', *Washington Post*, 23 Sept. 1993, p.A27

'Remarks by President On Bosnia and Africa', *New York Times*, 16 Nov. 1996, p.A7

Reuters, 'UN Force Nears Collapse in Chaotic Rwanda', *Washington Post*, 21 April 1994, p.A26

Richburg, Keith B., '4 US Soldiers Killed in Somalia: UN Blames Land-mine on Warlord', *Washington Post*, 9 Aug. 1993, p.A1

Ross, Michael, 'Nunn Criticizes UN Hunt For Somali Warlord Aidid', *Los Angeles Times*, 27 Sept. 1993, p.A12

Rupert, James, 'Ivory Coast Chief Criticizes UN Wrangle', *International Herald Tribune*, 16 Dec. 1996, p.6

Sallot, Jeff, 'Dallaire Stands by Actions in Rwanda', *Globe and Mail* (Toronto), 13 Dec. 1997, p.A6

——, 'Stint in Rwanda Seared General's Soul', *Globe and Mail* (Toronto), 26 Feb. 1998, p.A9

Scally, William, 'Defense Panel Sets Limits on US Peacekeeping', *Reuters*, 22 Sept. 1993, Lexis/Nexis

Schmitt, Eric, 'US Set to Limit Role of Military In Peacekeeping', *New York Times*, 29 Jan. 1994, p.A2

Sciolino, Elaine, 'US Narrows Terms for Its Peacekeepers', *New York Times*, 23 Sept. 1993, p.A8

——, 'Pentagon Changes Its Somalia Goals as Effort Falters', *New York Times*, 28 Sept. 1993, p.A1

——, 'New US Peacekeeping Policy De-emphasizes Role of the UN', *New York Times*, 6 May 1994, p.A2

'Security Council, Reflecting US Policy, Sets Firmer Guidelines for UN Peacekeeping', *International Documents Review: The Weekly Newsletter on the United Nations*, 9 May 1994, Vol.5, No.16, pp.1–2

Smith, R. Jeffrey and Julia Preston, 'US Evolves a New Peacekeeping Role', *Japan Times*, 21 June 1993, p.45, originally published in *Washington Post*, 18 June 1993

Smith, R. Jeffery, 'US Military Role May be Scaled Back', *Washington Post*, 18 Nov. 1996, p.A16

'Somalia Pullout Would Hurt US Credibility Warns Powell', *Agence France Presse*, 9 Sept. 1993, Lexis/Nexis

'Someone Else's Doing, Someone Else's Problem', *The Economist*, Vol.341, No.7991, 9 Nov. 1996, p.57

Sonenshine, Tara, 'Looking Inward Hurts US Policy', *Newsday*, 22 Nov. 1996, p.A59

Straus, Scott, 'UN Ignored my Pleas: Dallaire', *Globe and Mail* (Toronto), 26 Feb. 1998, pp.A1 and A9

Summers, Harry G., 'Should US Troops Be Sent to Africa to Provide Humanitarian Relief?', *Washington Times*, 23 Dec. 1996, p.27

Talbott, Strobe, 'America Abroad: Peacekeeping Loves Company', *Time* (US Edition), 18 May 1992, p.54

'The Great Escape', *The Economist*, Vol.341, No.7993, 23 Nov. 1996, p.53

'The UN at 50: Who Needs It?', *Time*, Vol.146, No.17, 23 Oct. 1995, pp.22–42 and 67–71

'The World Makes up its Mind(s) About Zaire', *The Economist*, Vol.341, No.7992, 16 Nov. 1996, p.55

Turner, Craig and Stanley Meisler, 'UN Chief Must Step Down, Clinton Insists: Diplomacy: Boutros-Ghali's Supporters Say he Will Fight for Second Term As Secretary-General Despite Opposition', *Los Angeles Times*, 25 Sept. 1996, Lexis/Nexis

'United Nations: To Bury or to Praise', *The Economist*, Vol.337, No.7937, 21 Oct. 1995, pp.18 and 25–9

Urquhart, Brian, 'Momentous Humiliation for the United Nations', *International Herald Tribune*, 11 Dec. 1996, p.10

Washington Post editorial, 'Holding up foreign aid', *International Herald Tribune*, 28 Feb. 1998, IHT Website

Williams, Daniel, 'US Troops To Remain in Somalia: Force Assisting UN in 'Re-creating' Nation', *Washington Post*, 11 Aug. 1993, p.A1

Williams, Daniel and Ann Devroy, 'Defining Clinton's Foreign Policy: Spate of Speeches Will Seek to Kill Suspicions of US Retreat', *Washington Post*, 20 Sept. 1993, p.A16

Index

DATE DUE

JAN 2 2 2005			